T0341119

Making It in IT

Making It in IT

Terry Critchley

CRC Press
Taylor & Francis Group
Boca Raton London New York

CRC Press is an imprint of the
Taylor & Francis Group, an **informa** business

AN AUERBACH BOOK

CRC Press
Taylor & Francis Group
6000 Broken Sound Parkway NW, Suite 300
Boca Raton, FL 33487-2742

First issued in hardback 2019

First issued in paperback 2022

© 2017 by Taylor & Francis Group, LLC
CRC Press is an imprint of Taylor & Francis Group, an Informa business

No claim to original U.S. Government works

ISBN 13: 978-1-03-247713-8 (pbk)
ISBN 13: 978-1-4987-8276-0 (hbk)

DOI: 10.1201/9781315366784

Library of Congress Cataloging-in-Publication Data

Names: Critchley, Terry. author.
Title: Making it in IT / Terry Critchley.
Other titles: Making it in information technology
Description: Boca Raton : Taylor & Francis, a CRC title, part of the Taylor &
Francis imprint, a member of the Taylor & Francis Group, the academic
division of T&F Informa, plc, [2017] | Includes bibliographical references
and index.
Identifiers: LCCN 2016021824 | ISBN 9781498782760 (alk. paper)
Subjects: LCSH: Information technology--Vocational guidance.
Classification: LCC T58.5 .C744 2017 | DDC 004.023--dc23
LC record available at https://lccn.loc.gov/2016021824

Visit the Taylor & Francis Web site at
http://www.taylorandfrancis.com

and the CRC Press Web site at
http://www.crcpress.com

Contents

Foreword

My background until about 12 years ago was enterprise IT, forming the Enterprise Computing Institute in 1993, then moving onto lifestyle coaching and, as a result, I feel well qualified to write the Foreword to this book, which covers both my areas of interest.

It is in essence a *road map* to getting into IT and succeeding by avoiding the negative situations that the author has encountered in his long career. He freely admits that your success can depend on his failures, but only if you work on the principle of learning from others' mistakes. It covers IT in a technical but comprehensible way from the IT scene when he joined IBM many years ago to the fluid, often mind-blowing scene today.

The world of virtualization, abstraction in its many forms, including the software-defined entities such as software-defined networks, data centers, and other physical infrastructures are skillfully explained, patently abiding by the maxim of scientist Lord Rutherford: *Everything should be explained in such a way as to inform a barmaid.*

An important part of the book is a fascinating look at the people skills you will need to make your way in this fast-moving world of technology. Author Terry Critchley takes you through all these areas in such a way that his vast experience is amply evident in his observations, anecdotes, and subtle career-enhancing conclusions.

An example is a thought-provoking section "Evolve or Die" (Chapter 2), which is the key message in developing your career and yourself in the helter-skelter world of technology. He does, however, show how it can be done, covering novel ways of learning, understanding other people's body language, developing writing and presentation skills, plus a host of other tricks of the information technology trade.

Who Is the Book For?

This book is for everyone in IT. It is especially useful for people considering a career in IT, who can learn a great deal from the book, and who are already working in their IT harness, especially those whose careers seem to have stalled. Reading it can give a boost to morale and point a way of moving forward once more. Even experts in IT can learn from this book, the content of which has been 40 years in the making.

The book is suitable for IT managers, IT staff, system operators, programmers, and administrators to provide them a fresh perspective of the world they inhabit and encourage them not to hide from technical advances but embrace them.

All in all, Critchley's book is a complete discussion of IT life in all its tragicomic nature: informative, funny, thought-provoking, and original in its thinking. This book could be the best investment you ever make.

Harris Kern
Founder of the Enterprise Computing Institute
Frisco, Texas

Preface

This book is about me: not in a self-aggrandizing or autobiographical way, instead, it is a map of a long IT (information technology) career with its ups, downs, and mistakes—plenty of them—plus the elation of getting it (and IT) right. This IT journey provides personal experience, the experience and wisdom of others, and a knowledge of customers, along with their hopes and dreams. These are not the same as yours and if you recognize this, you are halfway to being the complete IT professional.

> Your motto in IT service should be "Who cares, wins," a slightly modified motto of the British SAS (Special Air Service) elite force.

There are people who know more than I do about technology and its management; and for these people I have no message—my message is not about technology but is for people who know less than I do about the management of technology and of personal development. Less than I know is not enough, hence this book, which draws on the successes and failures of my own career, to draw conclusions and present messages metaphorically marked "do this" and "avoid like the plague," respectively. Someone once said "those who fail to learn from history are doomed to repeat its mistakes," or words to that effect.

> Mistakes are inevitable, though they can be minimized via correct skills and risk management techniques. The cardinal sin about making mistakes is not learning from them and thus repeating them.

I also include triumphs and failures from friends and colleagues, who I have worked with and met, both within the organizations where I worked, and the many customers I served. However, I will not name them since litigation, particularly in the United States, can be an expensive business for the slanderer or libeler, leading to penury and shame, neither of which are on my bucket list.

One thing that readers or potential readers may say is "This guy must be way out of date with technology, so why is he preaching to me about IT?" The first phrase of this sentence is partly true, but its essence is my strength since I can look outside technology for solutions to business and scientific issues, which is *IT's sole purpose*. There is an apt expression, "A fool with a tool is still a fool," and this applies to information technology as well as elsewhere.*

You can give me the world's most modern carpentry tools but I still couldn't make a cabinet or a wardrobe, even though I can *use* those tools. I lack the skills to *employ* them correctly and therein lies the difference between *using* and *employing* technology in IT. The position of technology in the development and use of IT for business and other applications will become clear later in the book.

You might come across a man who knows everything about cars, their components, and has a working knowledge of the Carnot cycle but who can't drive. I hope I've made my point now.

There is an implication in what I say about history that it has a habit of repeating itself but that does not mean *exactly* the same incidents will occur; just as certain situations will recur or that certain assumptions will be made. One of these is that things will progress exactly as they are now and in the way they reached that point. This has proved erroneous since the world at the time of the data center paper I wrote about a migration (1987), it was thought that the future was BAU (business as usual) IT plus data warehouses, relational databases, and offices. The only fixed thing in IT is change.

Clouds, virtualization, Java, the Internet, and other modern entities were not even dreamed of, at least in mainstream IT. The point here is don't assume that what you see today is what you will see in the future or even a simple evolution of it. You will need to watch what is happening, learn about it, and adapt it to IT usage in the support of business or science.

I have added some history to my writing about IT success for at least three reasons:

1. It is interesting in its own right and, I feel, provides a broad perspective that allows the IT person to assess the value and permanence of technology and, sometimes, techniques. There is still a lot of hot air and blue sky technology around—what DEC cofounder Ken Olsen called *snake oil*.

   The way I recommend assessing innovation is to define to yourself what the problem is to which it is the solution. In addition, when deciding on its

---

* "Foolproof systems do not take account of the ingenuity of fools."—Gene Brown

applicability in situations where there are conflicting views, seek the *consensus* of people who should know about these things.

2. Much of this book tracks my own experience, especially embarrassing and amusing incidents—from which you will get a feel for the "correct way" to make *It in IT* and avoid time-consuming detours.

3. To use an analogy, I'm not trying to teach you the breaststroke or crawl in swimming; rather, my goal is to make you feel comfortable in and around water by splashing about in it. Learning specific swimming styles then becomes much, much easier.

Audience

Who might benefit from reading this book? My view is anyone connected with IT from coalface technical personnel through to management, including business managers who have a vested interest in IT supporting their business. Much of this book will benefit people who are starting out in a career (IT or non-IT) or moving within it to another role. You can take the messages with you across the great skills divide!

Warning

As they say on television when showing dangerous stunts: Don't try this at home. The whole point of describing mistakes and humorous incidents in this book is so that you learn from them and don't repeat them. In particular, don't try to engineer amusing incidents since you may cause damage or, in extreme cases, injury to yourself, others, and possibly your career.

Terminology

There are some terms I use in this book that may confuse people, so I'll clarify them here:

Customer—In this book, a customer is any person or organization that receives products, services, or support from you and your IT department. Thus, a customer may be internal (your finance department or the research laboratories if you work for ACME Widgets company), or it may be a buyer of IT equipment, services, and so on; from a company that sells to others, for example, Dell, IBM, or HP.

If you work for the latter type of company, you may work with internal customers or external customers but not both, unless you are a very small company. In the latter case, you may also be chief exec, finance officer, company lawyer, and head chef.

Generalist—Often defined as a person who knows a little about a lot of things and eventually knows less and less about more and more so that he or she eventually knows nothing about everything. In reality, this person is a general all-rounder who may specialize in some areas.

Specialist—A fairly obvious term applied to a person who knows more and more about less and less as he or she becomes more specialized until eventually this person knows everything about nothing. The specialist almost always comes via a generalist role.

Job rotation—This practice is common in large companies where staff members are encouraged to rotate jobs within a discipline, not just IT. In IT, it's a good thing to do as it prevents the mover from getting into a rut and provides a different experience that can stimulate their personal and technical development. I was in and out of these two areas three or four times in my career and sometimes resided in one but had a small role in the other. The thing to watch is the timescale—you don't want to be swapping around every couple of weeks, especially if you are to form a relationship with a customer. The rotation period should be about 2 to 3 years to prevent staleness or apathy setting in.

Company/Organization—I use these interchangeably to describe a "body": business, scientific, consultancy, software house, web designers, and so on, whenever it is used.

Management—I use this almost exclusively in the sense of IT management of things not people. Pay and rations managers do not come into my use of the term, although there may be the odd implicit reference to a business manager involved in the IT usage context. They will come under the umbrella term of *user*.

Language—I have used U.S. English, the common IT language, but any humor is strictly British or even North West England where I am from.

Summary

Many years ago, I watched a comedy program called *Days of Thrills and Laughter*, which featured Laurel and Hardy, the Keystone Cops, and many other rib-ticklers. It was a random selection of funny sketches that lifted the soul. Information technology* should be like that except in the inevitable disasters that befall the inhabitants of that comedy program: custard pies in the face, banana skins, wrecked Model T Fords, drenchings, and so on. They have their parallels in IT and hopefully this book will teach you enough to avoid those pies and misfortunes but retain the laughter.

---

* I would prefer the term *information management* but that's the way it is.

As a parting shot, I'll share two ideas floated by a senior IT person and a well-known research outfit in recent papers and reports. The essence of what they are saying is that IT and all its accoutrements are irrelevant and the thrust in 2016 and onward is on doing things for the business. Wonderful insight. I say this in the book and have been saying it to anyone who will listen for the past 40 years: Concentrate on business processes and applications and the hardware and software will come along with it.

Acknowledgments

The World of IT

My first acknowledgment must go to all the people I've worked with, for, and in some cases against, during my long IT career. They have provided the ingredients for all my triumphs, mistakes, and near misses. The sum total of these ingredients, when mixed, is called *experience*, which hopefully can be passed on to others.

Winston Churchill promised the people of Britain blood, sweat, and tears during World War II. Your job will offer some of those things but also a lot of fun and satisfaction if you learn how to handle situations correctly. You can have the fun without the blood, sweat, and tears but you won't achieve anything.

People

My thanks also go to the following people who have contributed to this (I hope) groundbreaking publication in the IT universe.

- Everyone I have worked with; this book is based on those experiences
- The erudite writers of various articles and books on IT, who have given me knowledge and inspiration
- Dr. Bill Highleyman of *Availability Digest* for his constructive reviews and comments
- Harris Kern, long-time IT guru and author on personal development, for his comments
- People who I have corresponded with over technical and other points while composing this book
- Colleagues at IBM, Oracle, and Sun Microsystems for persevering with me despite my errors

What you will get from this book, therefore, is not just my experience and knowledge but also that of dozens of others.

Passport to the IT World

Making It in IT

PASSPORT

To the IT World

A guide to making your way into or through the jungle of modern IT and making it look easy. This book is your passport, whether you are thinking about IT as a career or are already in it. I was in IT for 40 years and I'm still learning.

This is a true story, based on my own and others' experiences and we all have the scars on our backs to prove that they were *real* experiences. The book won't win the Booker Prize or become a movie but I believe that absorbing it will make you a better IT person and more in demand. Most of the book applies to non-IT jobs since its disciplines, other than technical ones, are in the main, common across industries and, indeed, life in general. Fasten your seatbelts and let's reach for the sky.

Both passports have words to the effect that others must let the bearer of the passport move "without let or hindrance." If you achieve the status in IT that this book can give you, together with your own efforts, it should be sufficient to allow you to go almost anywhere in IT land, unhindered by an ever-increasing burden of ignorance or technical "passport control" hurdles.

Dr. Terry Critchley
Manchester, United Kingdom

Author

I have been in and out of the IT arena since 1969, with 24 years in IBM, 3 years with Oracle, 6 years working for Sun Microsystems, and 1 year for a major UK bank. I have been involved with more areas of IT than you could shake a stick at: Y2K, IMS, CICS, storage, laser printing, OCR, OMR, UNIX, MVS, MUMPS, Pick, training, platform migrations, data center migration, customer planning, architecture, support, and much more. I have done some great things and also fallen flat on my face.

In addition, I have presented at conferences numerous times, and written numerous papers and a book *High Availability IT Services*, published by CRC Press (2015). I have been involved with customers almost *ad nauseam* and most of my experience and scars come from those engagements.

I am also a minor authority on the Anglo-Zulu War of 1879, should any queries relating to that topic be raised by the content of this book. Incidentally, the Defence of Rorke's Drift* in that war was used by a U.S. professor in a lecture on operations research. He pointed out that it was a classic example of maximizing the use of available resources and not simply bemoaning the lack of others. This type of behavior is an object lesson for all IT people.

I have also had a great deal of fun in IT as well as outside it, and the balance of work and fun, together with the right skills and personal accountability is an ideal mix for IT success.

In this book, I have made liberal use of diagrams and graphs as I believe in the old adage that a picture is worth a thousand words. In addition, I have tried to lead people to solutions rather than push them with severe action checklists since I am unaware of any readers' company business requirements, only where the pitfalls might lurk.

My message to the reader is to read this book, take mine and others' mistakes on board, and try to avoid them, either specific ones or generic, and try to adapt to the "rules of the roles" outlined near the end of the book. Try them and they will become part of your daily IT life, although it's taken me a long time to recognize

---

* The defense by 120 soldiers of a mission station in Natal, South Africa, against a 4000-strong Zulu impi on January 22–23, 1879.

these things. Don't try them all at once but do the equivalent of the author Hilaire Belloc's take on the Ten Commandments: "Candidates are advised to attempt only six of these at a time."

My Scribblings

I have written several articles for various websites that the reader may find interesting and, in some cases, controversial where I examine, and often challenge, conventional IT wisdom. They come under the headings of *availability* and *performance*, and they should be of use to IT people who want to make *It in IT* and, perhaps, give my scribbling credibility.

*Web Articles**

DatacenterDynamics
■ http://www.datacenterdynamics.com/it-networks/high-availability-more-than-meets-the-eye/94313.article (High availability)
■ http://www.datacenterdynamics.com/it-networks/performance-myths-and-legends-i/94881.blog (I/O performance)

Aberdeen TechPro Essentials
■ http://www.techproessentials.com/when-is-an-outage-not-an-outage/ (Availability)
■ http://www.techproessentials.com/optimizing-cache-memory-performance-and-the-math-behind-it-all/ (Memory cache usage)

APMdigest
■ http://apmdigest.com/performance-and-availability-author-joins-the-bsm-blog (Author)
■ http://apmdigest.com/availability-time-warp (Availability: Time warp)
■ http://www.apmdigest.com/ios-per-second-myths (I/Os per second myths)

Continuity Software
■ http://www.continuitysoftware.com/wp-content/uploads/2014/01/IT-SERVICES-AVAILABILITY-MGMT-Book-Preview.pdf (Book excerpt)

ITBusinessEdge
■ http://www.itbusinessedge.com/blogs/it-tools/how-your-enterprise-can-provide-high-availability-it-services.html (Book review)

Computer Weekly
■ http://www.computerweekly.com/opinion/IT-availability-the-whole-truth (Availability)

---

* The subjects are in parentheses.

Availability Digest
- http://www.availabilitydigest.com/public_articles/1001/critchley_book.pdf (Book review)
- http://www.availabilitydigest.com/public_articles/0808/software_reliability .pdf (Software reliability)

Data Center Knowledge
- http://www.datacenterknowledge.com/archives/2015/03/17/evolution-high -availability/ (High availability)

Books

High Availability IT Services (CRC Press, 2015)
- CRC: http://www.crcpress.com/product/isbn/9781482255904
- Amazon: http://www.amazon.com/High-Availability-Services-Terry-Critchley /dp/1482255901/ref=sr_1_1

High-Performance IT Services (CRC, in press)

Open Systems: The Reality with K.C. Batty (Prentice Hall, 1993)

What the IT World Owes Me

If I can help somebody
From doing wrong
My living shall not be in vain.

"If I Can Help Somebody"
Lyrics by Alma Bazel Androzzo

This book is partly founded* on my mistakes, supplemented by a few made by others, who shall remain anonymous. The value of my errors can be shown by the phrase, paraphrased from the words of the character Sherlock Holmes†: *If you eliminate the wrong way to do things, what remains, however bizarre, must be the right way.* This book then consists to a large extent of salutary tales and anecdotes, laced with some humor, intentional and unintentional. I am the equivalent of the wagon train scout, looking for water, finding paths through the wilderness, and taking Native American arrows in my hat for my pains. If you, the reader, become familiar with the wrong ways of doing things, the right way will become clearer and easier to follow.

This, my friends, is what the IT world, your world, potential or current, owes me as a latter day IT savior.

---

* About Dodge City, Kansas: "On the ashes of my camp fire, this city was built." For me, this might read: "On the ashes of my errors, your IT career is built."

† Sherlock Holmes said: "If you eliminate the impossible, what remains, however improbable, must be the truth."

Chapter 1

On Your Marks ...

Making What in IT?

We are talking in this book about "making it in IT," which, in simple terms, means being as good as you can be at the job and being a role model for it (Figure 1.1). But which job? Listed later are a variety of positions in IT. Am I going to cover them all? The answer is a resounding—no! What I am going to cover are the elements of disciplines and techniques that are common to all IT positions, including managers. Most of them are ageless and technology-independent but will need to be complemented by the technology knowledge pertaining to your chosen job.

Reasons for Your IT Career

There are many reasons for choosing, or perhaps falling, into IT and I am not privy to them all. Mine was of the "fall" variety after graduation. I chased two plum jobs: one with UK Atomic Energy and the other with IBM. I was offered a job at Windscale, northwest England and one at IBM, the latter offering an inferior salary. However, Windscale is about as accessible as Death Valley but enjoying about one third the temperature and 32,000 times the rainfall, and since I wasn't married then, it would have been a very lonely place. I plumped for IBM and never regretted it. Whatever your reasons for choosing the IT route, read the following tale:

> There's an old story about two men working on a railroad track many years back. As they are laying track in the heat of the day, a person drives by and rolls down the window (not enough to let the air conditioning out, but enough to be heard). He yells, "Tom, is that you?" Tom, one of the men working on the track, replies, "Chris, it's great to see you! It must have been 20 years ... how are you?" They continue the conversation

Figure 1.1 Master of all he surveys in IT!

and eventually Chris drives off. When he leaves, another worker turns to Tom and says, "I know that was the owner of the railroad and he's worth nearly a billion dollars. How do you know him?" Tom replies, "Chris and I started working on the railroad, laying track, on the same day 20 years ago. The only difference between Chris and me is that I came to work for $1.25/hour and he came to work for the railroad."*

Pick Your Spot

1. Manager
2. Database architects
3. Technical (general) architects
4. Web administrators
5. Computer systems engineers/architects
6. Computer user support specialists
7. Network and computer systems administrators
8. Software developers, applications
9. Computer programmers
10. Information security analysts
11. Computer systems analysts
12. Data scientists

---

* "Understanding Big Data," https://www.ibm.com/developerworks/vn/library/contest/dw-free books/Tim_Hieu_Big_Data/Understanding_BigData.PDF.

13. Data stewards
14. Business intelligence
15. Information management
16. Business analytics
17. Data analysts
18. Computer and information systems managers
19. Computer hardware engineers
20. Computer network support specialists
21. Computer network architects
22. Database administrators
23. Web developers*
24. Computer and information research scientists
25. Computer science teachers (various levels)
26. Multimedia artists and animators
27. Desktop publishers
28. Computer operators
29. Scientific/high-performance computing (HPC)
30. University computer science (CS) teaching positions
31. All other computer occupations, including self-employment and sales
32. A hybrid job that encompasses multiple skills under one heading
33. A job chosen by your preference to work for a specific vendor, for example, Microsoft, Cisco, IBM, Google, Facebook

An example of a hybrid job is a data and information specialist, which might encompass big data, databases, storage access methods like RAID, and so on.[†]

The following link explores careers in computer science and links to job descriptions, which include information such as daily activities, skill requirements, salary, and training required. It also provides links to a host of other IT-related topics, such as IT history and operating systems.

"Computer Career Descriptions:" http://www.khake.com/page17.html

The next link condenses the IT jobs world to three broad areas; consultants, project managers and developers and expands on these roles.

---

* This area is vital in sites where public access is involved, particularly sales sites. The number of websites I have tried to access without success are legion because they are so badly designed in the area of human interface. I now believe 100% that your company or other organization will live or die by a website if it constitutes a large part of your business simply because an unusable, badly performing website augurs death or, at the very least, mediocrity.

† See "The Downward Spiral of IT Job Descriptions," https://dzone.com/articles/the-downward -spiral-of-it-job-descriptions.

"The Future of IT Jobs? Its in Three Types of Roles:" http://www.zdnet.com /article/the-future-of-it-jobs-its-in-three-types-of-roles/

The following is a link to another list but covering broad areas rather than specific jobs within those areas. However, it does go on to outline what the areas cover, which should be useful instead of choosing a very specific post upfront.

"What Jobs Are Available in the Computer Industry?:" http://www.computer hope.com/issues/ch000764.htm

Some not-so-good news in this link but forewarned is forearmed.

"7 Tech Jobs Hardest Hit By Layoffs in 2015:" http://www.informationweek .com/strategic-cio/7-tech-jobs-hardest-hit-by-layoffs-in-2015-/d/d-id/1 324526

Finally, there is a useful glossary of IT jobs at the following link:

"Glossary of Job Descriptions for IT:" http://www.itbusinessedge.com/itdown loads/glossary-of-job-descriptions-for-it/88859

Computer Science World

Computer science (CS) is a more esoteric subject than general IT and has its place in the IT universe. However, a CS graduate entering the normal IT world will probably need to adapt to some of the topics and disciplines outlined throughout this book. IT people making the reverse trip may be interested in a typical syllabus for a CS course, as outlined below:

- Fundamentals of computing
- Fundamentals of computer engineering
- Fundamentals of artificial intelligence (AI)
- Fundamentals of computer architecture
- Fundamentals of distributed systems
- Fundamentals of databases
- Object-oriented programming
- Cognitive topics
- Logic and modeling
- Processor microarchitecture
- Microcontrollers

- Software engineering
- Machine learning
- Symbolic AI
- Operating systems
- System architecture
- Algorithms and imperative programming
- Computer graphics and image processing
- Distributed computing
- Computer networks
- Mobile systems
- Cognitive neuroscience
- Cognitive computing in other areas
- Concurrency and process architecture
- Natural language systems
- Other subjects

Note that this is a typical syllabus and will vary widely across universities and countries. What is does do is give the IT generalist an idea what the CS landscape looks like. Likewise, the CS person can also see from later discussions in this book what the general IT world looks like.

Computer science graduates entering the world of commercial IT may feel a little uncomfortable as the environment is different from that they are used to. Many soft skills need to be taken on board, such as understanding body language, influencing people, reading upside down, suffering bores, and other vital skills.

Worry not though; you have the brains and they just need to turn a few degrees from forward to thrive in the great world of information technology.

Note: In my long experience, IT and CS are not the same, or even similar, so don't expect to cross the divide from one to the other with ease. There is often an urgency in commercial IT, which is not generally present in the CS environment.

2016 Hot Topics

An article hazards a guess at the five things in IT that will shape the year 2016 and possibly thereafter. These things may shape your thinking about IT skills and which direction appeals to you:

1. Application owners will own IT.
2. The data center will assume characteristics of the public cloud.
3. Web-scale IT architectures will become available to most enterprises.

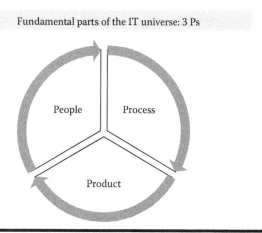

Figure 1.2 The IT universe and its components.

4. Chief information officers (CIOs) will face increased pressure to shift spend-ing to operating expenses.
5. Cyberattacks and data breaches in the cloud go from perception to reality.*

Note: One thing that seems certain as 2017 looms, based on what I am read-ing in the newsletters I subscribe to, is that spending on data centers/clouds is mushrooming.

Job Scope

If you consider the application of these 33 roles (under "Pick Your Spot" section) to different technologies (N) and the levels of job within them (n), then you have a large set of roles and variations, that is, $33 \times N \times n$. This is the reason I have not attempted to partition what I am preaching into each of this myriad of categories. I would probably have gone to that great data center in the sky by then.

Let's go, or as Ward Bond† would say in his Westerns, "wagons roll!"

Figure 1.2 shows the standard way of describing IT in its entirety. These are the equivalent of the protons, neutrons, and electrons which make up the atom; these

---

* See the article itself for an expansion of these points: "5 Reasons 2016 Will Be the Year of the 'New IT,'" http://www.cio.com/article/3014674/innovation/5-reasons-2016-will-be-the-year -of-the-new-it.html. Best bet is to search for the article title, perhaps including the author Thor Olavsrud.
† For the young whippersnappers among you, Ward Bond played Seth Adams, the wagon master in the 1950s TV series *Wagon Train*. Such a person saw the train through uncharted territory and handled perilous situations, which you can by using this book.

components make up the IT universe. Whatever IT activity you undertake, there will be elements of all three in it. If there are not, you shouldn't be in IT.

- *People* refer to human aspects: skills, level of competence, initiative, etc.
- *Process* means the flow of activity around business activity using IT, which includes systems management and management methods.
- *Products* encompass the technology aspects of IT projects (hardware and software) and is part of the trinity of factors in any IT tasks, except perhaps emergency system repairs and the like. People who speak only of technology when tackling IT jobs are deluding themselves and possibly others.

IT wannabes and IT combatants should always bear these three elements in mind until it becomes second nature. Those who don't are doomed to more failures than successes.

New Jobs

I've already implied that this book is an introduction to a career in IT, but it will also be a valuable resource to people already in that field who want to improve their nontechnical skills. The reasons for the latter will vary:

- I want to better myself and become more professional.
- I want to move up in my company, perhaps into a different discipline.
- I want to move to a job outside my company.

Whatever the reason, your chances will improve if you take on board the nontechnical discussions in this book and be aware of the technical topics, even if you only know what the acronyms mean, that I have outlined in Chapter 4.

Imagine the post or outside company you covet is very geared to subject X to run its business. If in the job interview you imply that you know subject X well, you may well find yourself asked about it, humiliated, and passed over. The correct way is to show passing knowledge* and indicate your keenness to learn more within that position or company.

The IT Life

InformationWeek has a useful section titled "IT Life" that covers topics just outside hardware, software, and IT techniques but are a very useful adjunct in

---

* This will only come by reading and taking part in courses, discussions, and other learning activities. Anyone who thinks he knows it all, or even knows sufficient has no place in IT. In other words, learning should be a constant companion during your career.

learning about IT (http://www.informationweek.com/whitepaper/topic/it-life). For example, there are articles entitled

- "The Role of DevOps in the Digital Transformation"
- "Outsourcing vs. Insourcing"
- "Tackling the Top 3 IT Service Management Challenges"
- "5 Steps to Make IT a Blue Chip Brand" (*Proving it is more than a cost center**)

Upside: If anything shows that you are a true IT pro, it is being able to talk sensibly outside your chosen specialty or job type. If, as a result, a senior customer person asks your opinion on some nontechnical issue, you've probably proved it.

Preamble

The advancement of IT hardware, software, and techniques over the past 25 or so years had been staggering.[†] Remember, I started my career in September 1969 and a short time afterward I knew about 40% of what there was to know about IT. Today, I know much more than I did then and now I know about 5% (or less) of what there is to know about IT.

This is good news but the progress has left me with a few regrets about things past:

- The glowing CPU light on the front panel of IBM (and other) systems whose brightness and flashing rate gave as good an indication of CPU utilization as most software tools today. An experienced IBMer could assess the CPU load within about 15%, a skill that today would save megabucks on performance monitors.
- Other multicolored lights, measuring who knows what and flashing gently in the corner of the machine room. The best one I came across was an English Electric KDF9, which had a large console face at an angle of about 45° with scores of lights all over it informing the cognoscenti of that era what was going on. Incidentally, a good KDF9 sported 192K of memory![‡]
- Peripatetic[§] disk units. In these bygone days, small disk units were housed in a metal cabinet which one could almost pick up. The IBM 2311 drives, holding

---

* My italicized comment on the content.
† http://www.computerconservationsociety.org/museums.htm
‡ "KDF9 Manual: Very High Speed Data Processing System for Commerce, Industry, Science," 1961. http://archive.computerhistory.org/resources/text/English_Electric/EnglishElectric.KDF9 .1961.102641284.pdf.
§ Walking about. The Peripatetic school was a school of philosophy in Ancient Greece, run by Aristotle. The name came from the dubious notion that he walked around when teaching his followers.

7 or 11 MB of storage were typical of the era. The trick in maximizing the performance of these disks lay in the placement of data and the associated indexes. The operations people had control of where this index set should go (it was called a VTOC, volume table of contents), so placing the application data near the VTOC, the programmers or data specialist's job, paid dividends. It meant that the arm of the drive worked in a relatively small area of the disk platter and gave better I/O performance.

If, however, the data and indexes were all over the disk, the arm would be dashing to and fro across the disk platter, which would eventually cause the disk housing unit to move. I have seen units wobbling about and in a few cases, a unit attempting to walk across the floor since when it started to move, it carried on in the same direction. Eventually, it would end up in the street, and probably be prosecuted for jaywalking, if it wasn't halted, usually by stopping the program or putting weights on the disk housing cabinet.

■ The IBM engineers (customer engineers [CEs]) were a clever bunch, not only at their job but at fun and games with IT equipment. One day, on entering a customer's premises, I heard a rough sound and suddenly realized the sound was "She'll Be Comin' Round the Mountain," a popular song. I asked a CE what the noise was and he pointed to an IBM 1403 line printer that was printing total garbage but in such a manner that it was playing that tune! Another CE managed to write a program such, that if you held a radio receiver close to the CPU, you could hear music generated by the CPU electrical signal variations.

■ Bob (old style IBM branch manager) did an announcement presentation. He had obviously just been on a course teaching that interactive presentations were better than lectures, so he started: "Gentlemen, if I were to announce a new tape drive, what new features would you want?" There was a short silence then a voice from the back said, "Update in place!" Bob never recovered!

■ The same manager came back from an IBM announcement meeting with two sets of foils: one IBM internal, one for customers. He managed to mix up the speaker's scripts so that when an IBM salesman was giving the internal presentation, he had the notes for the customer version. You can imagine the chaos as he tried to keep them in sync, saying "and the next slide shows" and it didn't. It was hilarious until the speaker decided he had had enough.

IT in a Nutshell

IT is the use and management of its components—products, people, and processes—to achieve business* objectives (Figure 1.3). Period.

---

* The word *business* here and in most of this book covers not only commercial but medical, scientific, and other areas of endeavour where people work.

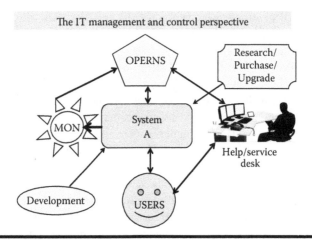

Figure 1.3 The IT world in operation. MON, monitor(s); OPERNS, operations.

IT Components

What follows is the whole of IT in a page or two, showing it is nothing to be afraid of. The outline covers the 3 Ps—products, process, and people—and from these diagrams and descriptions, nearly all the other things that are covered (and some not covered) in this book spring from them.

Products

The product world consists of hardware and the software or programs that fuel it, rather analogous to a car and the fuel that drives it (Figure 1.4).

With that out of the way, we can carry on. With me so far?

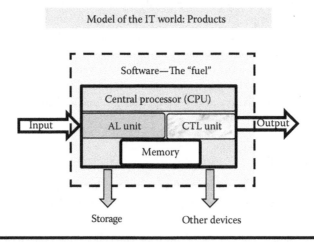

Figure 1.4 The whole IT product world in one diagram.

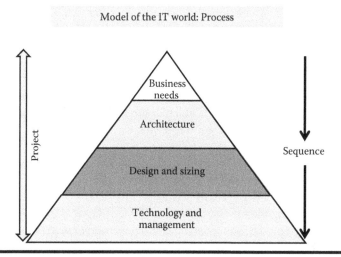

Figure 1.5   The whole IT process world in one diagram.

Processes

The use and management of the products is achieved by the processes devised to carry out the various tasks that are the responsibility of the two sets of people mentioned next (Figure 1.5). These tasks, particularly those involving design, are many and varied and are covered in this book, especially in the Appendices.

People

The people are in two basic classes: (1) those who design, provide, and manage the hardware and software, and (2) those who use those facilities. These two sets of people need to work in synergy to ensure success. Elementary.

Just as the understanding of matter comes from understanding that it is all composed of protons, neutrons and electrons, so understanding IT comes from knowing the base components of ITs.

Let's proceed.

IT End-to-End

There are some key factors that I have found are of most importance in designing, assessing, implementing, and operating IT systems, code name FUMPAS:

- *F*—Does it do what the end users want it to do (*functionality*)? If it doesn't, they will be reluctant to use it and certainly won't rely on it.
- *U*—Does it have an absolutely clear and logical *user interface*? Do you need a PhD in human–machine interaction to use the screens?

- ■ *M*—Can its host system(s) be *managed properly*? Manage means *measure (monitor)* the resources supporting the applications, *analyze*, and *act*.
- ■ *P*—Does it deliver the required (SLA) *performance*? Performance can be measured in different ways and expressed in many ways. Make sure you measure what the service level agreement wants delivered.
- ■ *A*—Is it designed and implemented to have the appropriate *availability* and *recovery* capabilities? This includes disaster recovery and other parameters such as recovery time and point to which recovery takes place. An hour ago, last week, etc.?
- ■ *S*—Does it/the system have appropriate *security*? This did not exist 15 years ago and is not a top priority. Neglect it at your peril (and job).

Other features are implied in the manageability (M) factor. If we spelled them all out, the acronym would be too long and slip the memory. These items must always be borne in mind at all stages of an IT project and if any of them is unsatisfactory, the whole project is jeopardized.

IT Project Cycle

Many people think that if you have superb project management skills and software, all will be well. Not so, Watson; observe the facts.

It is all very well getting to the top of the ladder but not if it is resting against the wrong wall.

Placard outside a church in Yorkshire, United Kingdom

If you are managing the wrong design, good project management simply gets you to disaster sooner. This escapes many people and then there is much head scratching, weeping, and gnashing of teeth, wondering what went wrong.

The following short discussion is a typical flow showing a project of some sort involving IT change and fits in with the philosophy of the project definition workshop (PDW) described in Appendix A. To summarize, the PDW works on a simple principle of a change in the IT environment from one state to another as follows in simple terms:

- ■ Define the current environment and the business it supports. This is called the A Point, which is where we start.
- ■ Define the new environment, including the new business it is to support as well as the current work. This is called the B Point.
- ■ We now need to work to define the activities that will take us from the A Point to the B Point, a sort of route map.

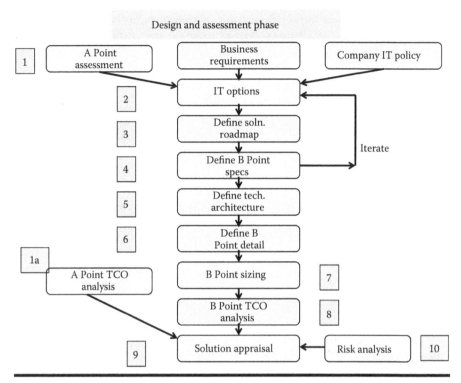

Design and assessment phase

Figure 1.6   Design and assessment: Getting it right the first time.

It looks simple and, in principle, it is if you stick to the definitions and the ethos of the transition from one state to another. Although it involves effort, working to the preceding three guidelines helps the flow.

Normally, the whole exercise is developed in a workshop run by a facilitator* who project manages this little project within a project. The initial output is a list of activities needed to make the transition from A to B, but in a random order as they arise. They are then sorted and assigned an IT area; operations, storage, database, Internet, and anything else that the brainstorm generates. Output includes a project initiation document (PID) and tasks as generated in the PDW, which are then assigned to people. The whole process and the resulting output is described in Appendix A.

The following list expands upon the design and assessment process flow diagram in Figure 1.6.

---

* Internal or external. The latter facilitator is likely to be more objective since he has no hidden agenda.

1. This features three boxes representing an assessment of the current IT setup, the business requirements (SLA) and company policy, for example, "Policy 12: z/OS or Linux over my dead body" or something similar.
2. This is the examination of the IT architecture options to suit 1.
3. Once an outline architecture is chosen, a more detailed sequence and other related requirements (skills, for example).
4. The specs for the end point (B Point), for example, volumes, availability, etc.
5. This allows a more detailed architecture to be defined, an expansion of 2.
6. A detailed specification of the B Point, suitable for preparing an ITT (Invitation to Tender).
7. The system is sized and technology assigned in rough detail.
8. This is the costing phase of the B Point; capital and ongoing, which can be compared with the ongoing costs of the original A Point (1a). The cost analyses are very organization-dependent so I haven't (and couldn't) elaborate on this step.
9. The gathering of the clans for a solution appraisal for cost, feasibility, timescale, and other factors. This is where a go/no-go decision may be made and we go back to activity item 2.
10. A risk assessment/analysis is carried out although it can be split across all the other phases as they progress.

This is not a fixed method, simply a disciplined outline that can be adapted to suit different A and B Points. It may also involve iterations, for example as in activity 4, but could be anywhere if a dead end* is reached.

The steps in this process are expanded upon in Appendix A under "IT Project Cycle Revisited."

IT Process Cycle

This is an alternative look at the flow of IT work and the first three steps were outlined in the "IT Project Cycle" of the previous section. This, along with the success factors mentioned earlier, represent the essence of information technology and which are changeless and eternal. Understand these concepts and follow them and you are nearly there as an IT professional. Figure 1.7 shows the cycle schematically and the description here puts some flesh on the bones of the pictorial representation. It should be noted here that reviews will be needed at the end of each step to check that what was envisaged has been delivered in that phase.

1. The *requirements* of the user(s) of the system(s) will dictate all the following steps. The uses might be the general public accessing a website to purchase something, a financial worker, a scientist, a manager, human resources, and anyone else you care to name. Their needs for access, information, and other forms of data

---

* A dead end might be cost, lack of skills, business upheavals, and other factors.

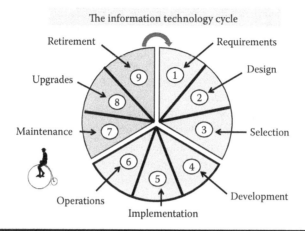

Figure 1.7   The process cycle of information technology.

processing are sacrosanct. The IT department is not an end in itself but a servant of the users. These requirements will include normal day-to-day processing with other quality requirements as outlined in a service level agreement (see Appendix A): performance, availability, security, disaster recovery, and others. These will be presented in business terms and not technical jargon.

2. The *design* stage is usually a team effort in anything but small projects and the outcome is usually some form of architecture(s) they will service the requirements in step 1. It will necessitate the translation of the business needs into an IT architecture or design and the gathering of volumetric information, timescales, response times, and so on. The design should then be subjected to a walkthrough, which is a process of explaining it to an impartial, mixed audience including a devil's advocate who will try to isolate any deficiencies.*

3. The *selection* phase is the first time we hit any technology. If you hit it any earlier you may well sink without a trace. This phase represents the choice of hardware, software, and any support needed. The choices are dictated by the business requirements that will generate network speeds, disk space, ballpark response times, and other volumetrics. Here, as in any other phases, there can be discussion, review, suggestions, and so on to satisfy the team and any business representation that everything is on track.†

4. The *development* phase consists of coding of various kinds, putting together tools and techniques for, say, system management and other things that need working on to ensure the system flies.

---

* Remember, the further you progress in such projects, the more expensive it is to correct and errors or omissions. The cost increases are not linear either and that is why getting each step right the first time is important.

† "Are we all agreed on things so far ... let us move on then" is the theme here and in other phases.

5. The *implementation* phase might involve a pilot scheme and then making any changes before going live with the system. Remember, the system may be phased so these actions listed here may need repeating for each phase.
6. The *operations* phase. This, to use a motoring analogy, is running the car, putting gas in, checking the tires and oil, washing the car, and the usual regime of keeping the car functional.
7. The *maintenance* phase can cover changes via change management, which arises as a result of checks during operations: tuning, adding virtual storage volumes, adjusting resources and priorities, and similar remedial activities.
8. The *upgrade* phase is the implementation of nontrivial changes, such as adding a bank of disks or clustering existing processors. This continues until, via capacity planning, the system can no longer be changed to meet growing functional and volume needs.
9. *Retirement.* A new system or significant partnering system will be required and this is going back to the drawing board. A plan for phasing to and transferring work and data to any new system is required here.
10. The cycle comes round again. The requirements phase may not be as onerous as the initial implementation but any changes or deficiencies will need to be catered for in the new system.

This list is proof, if proof were still needed, that technology, although important, is just one link in the chain of activities that make up any IT project, large or small. Moreover, it cannot be chosen upfront before other phases have dictated the needs to be fulfilled by a technical solution.

One thing not noted here is *project management* but that is taken as read as a necessity. However, project management needs something to manage and that is the outcome of the first phases of the preceding list. If the steps are not done properly, all that good project management achieves is to hit failure earlier than would otherwise be the case.*

IT Quantification

In the management of IT, the factors that assume importance are numeric and are related to the resources that define how well the system is running against expectations or established *baselines*, perhaps in a service level agreement. How well a system is running is very often termed quality of service (QoS). These numeric quantities are called *metrics* or key performance indicators (KPIs) by some people (Figure 1.8). The baseline might be a set of metrics that are the norm when the system is operating, and variations are acceptable within a certain range but should

---

* Another thing to be aware of is that the costs of correcting out-of-line situations increases dramatically the further you get into the project. Getting each step right is therefore key and corner-cutting militates against this.

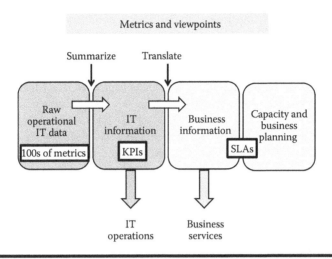

Figure 1.8   Data to information flow: IT operations to business.

one or more exceed this baseline and range, then some form of alert is generated. This will invoke the action part of the management equation:

$$Management = Design + Measurement + Analysis + Action$$

Examples of metrics are response time, network latency, and disk utilization.

The topic is too detailed to cover here but I'll give you a flavor of it. The metrics involved are different and their usefulness depends on who wants to see them to judge the QoS from his *viewpoint*. For example, the end user of a service is not interested in the disk utilization but is interested in how fast the output of a transaction, a query, or a web access comes back to him. A user manager might be interested in throughput, or number of pieces of work, or transactions processed in a unit time as a measure of how well business is going.

There are basically *five sets of system metrics* and applications that are usually of interest:

1. Internal metrics for operational people within an organization and these can be quite detailed and used for operational and also for capacity planning purposes.
2. Summary or *single sheet* metrics for IT management to assess QoS delivered internally to the "customers."
3. Metrics required by a service level agreement with internal users, often business users; a more detailed exposition of service details.
4. Metrics required by an organization from a cloud or other third-party SLA running IT on its behalf.
5. Application/middleware metrics that indicate performance in user terms.

Of course, they are not limited to performance management but that is what we are using as an example here. Different metrics will apply to different aspects of QoS for example:

■ *Availability*—Number of outages, average length, recovery time, etc.
■ *Security*—Number of attempted breaches, number successful, etc.

"The Handbook of Essential IT Service Desk Metrics" gives a description of eight key service (or help) desk metrics that are generated from base, lower-level metrics.*

IT in My Time

I have taken the liberty of going through the history of IT technology since I started with IBM in September 1969, shortly after the first men set foot on the moon, through to today. I am doing this for three main reasons; first, to show how technology changes immeasurably in that period, second to show how the use of that technology has mushroomed, and last lead you to develop IT-related skills that defy time and are as relevant today as they were then.

In fact, they are even more important today since the beast called modern technology can run all over you unless you acquire the skills to harness it and control it, rather like wind power being harnessed to produce electricity and not just blowing your hat off.

I will use IBM products as the demonstrations of power, capacity, and so forth, since I am more familiar with them than with other vendors' offerings. No superiority is implied and it is almost certain that those vendors' products will have followed along similar lines.

I will also try to document the comings and goings of newer players in the IT arena, some of whom died nobly in battle. Most of them, however, did play a role in shaping the future in many areas of information technology.

The Early Days

When I joined IBM, the main products were processors and storage, including tapes, and what was then known as unit record products (e.g., printers, card readers, card punches, paper tape readers, and communication controllers). If you see a photograph of an IBM installation from that era, you will see a large room with many different units on show. They were the items I have mentioned earlier, the biggest being the processor complex.

---

* "The Handbook of Essential IT Service Desk Metrics," https://www.manageengine.com/products /service-desk/servicedesk-metrics-kpi.html.

Products available at that time (1969) were

- System/360, announced in 1964, the 1130 scientific machine, and some other smaller items. Models were 360/30, /40, /50, /65, and specials /75 and /95. The top end of the range were prohibitively expensive. The standard workhorse for the average sizable business was the 360/50, with disks, the 2311* (7 or 11 Mbytes) and the 2314 (28 Mbytes). If you only had these models to cater for today's data volumes, you would fill Madison Square Garden, leaving no room for boxing, or even the Empire State Building with disk drives.
- 2420 tape drives, used for data files, backup files, and even a primitive operating system called Tape Operating System (TOS).

Operating systems and transaction processing software comprised (but not entirely):

- Multiprocessing with a Variable number of Tasks (MVT) and Multiprocessing with a Fixed number of Tasks (MFT), both of which could run comfortably in 128K (yes, K) of main storage. The disk operating system (DOS) was the workhorse for medium size accounts, MVT and MFT for larger ones.
- There were for a while tape operating systems and even a card based one (Card Basic Programming System). I could write a small paper on this topic of a totally card-based operating system, including a compiler and link editor. I am probably the only person alive who used this operating system.
- Online Transaction Processing (OLTP) with several contenders in the ring. Bread, Faster, Customer Information Control System (CICS), Information Management System (IMS), which had a TP part and a database part.

There were other pieces of software here and there but IBM rationalized† them all into what they called the Strategic Product Line (SPL).

These products comprised the data center of those days. Within a data center was an innovation called the *Information Center* (*IC*), which was a separate function to the day-to-day business functions carried out by the data center. Sometimes it resided on a separate computer.

The IC was a report and query system that fed, selectively, off the raw business data from the data center. Its uses were many and varied but summarized data, simple analytics, and projections were its main functions. We used to say that the

---

* The "2" at the start of these product numbers really signified an era of 2xxx products and that meant a strategic product. The "2" eventually became a "3" in the 1970s, for example, 3330 disks.

† A topic discussed in the Appendices.

Figure 1.9   Ye olde data center.

IC *played tunes* (information) with the basic *notes* (data) from the data center to support various business areas.

Figure 1.9 shows an old data center with a processor less powerful than the PC I am trying this manuscript on.

In 1970 IBM announced System/370, a S/360 follow-on along with 3330 disks, each having a gigantic 100 Mbytes of storage! A major part of this announcement as VM/370, a sort of hypervisor that could support interactive users, such as program developers and, more significantly, host other operating systems like DOS and MVS, a concept today familiar as virtualization, the basis of cloud computing and a precursor to the idea of software-defined everything, dealt with later.

In subsequent years, IBM announced upgrades and new versions of various software products and some new products. Virtual storage was announced in 1972, along with Virtual Storage Access Method (VSAM), a cleverer form of ISAM (Indexed Sequential Access Method).* New versions of S/370 were also unveiled and took advantage of virtual storage: a 379/145, /158 (turbo version of the/155), /168 (turbo/165), and later a /135, /125, and eventually, a /115. The 3033, 3032, and 3031 followed in the late 1970s. Systems Network Architecture (SNA) was unveiled in 1974 and became the benchmark for seven-layer architecture models, including the Open Systems Interconnection architecture (OSI).

---

* An indexed file, a step in function above flat and sequential files.

New disks were announced in 1975, the 3350s at 317.5 Mbytes and later the 3340 (Winchester disk, shaped like the USS Enterprise). The 3350s were the first nonremovable IBM disks.

The year 1981 saw the announcement of the 3081, a dual processor system, followed by the 3083 (1983) and 3084, a four-CPU system (1984), and 3380 disks boasting 1 GB per unit. New versions of most SPL software came along, sometimes with a slight change of name.

Another giant step for IBM was the announcement of an IBM PC in 1981 (UK 1983) and the love affair with the PC lasted until IBM offloaded it to Lenovo, where it still lives.

The 1990s saw the next generation of processors, the 3090 series, and the IBM Sysplex, a complex of processors aimed at high availability and presenting a single image view to the user and programmer; an early example of *abstraction*. Models rolled out over time, culminating in the Z series and z/OS in the 2000s, which can run thousands of Linux images on it.

The Future Systems Caper

This is neither a preannouncement nor a prediction but just a little true story* to tell your children or grandchildren and to round off this discussion about IBM hardware:

> Long, long ago (I will plump for 1975–1976) and far, far away (I would try Poughkeepsie, New York) there was much talk and wild rumors about a revolutionary new system coming out from IBM that would knock the pants off the competition and indeed IBM's own then current range (System/370). It would have a huge address space, brand new hardware and software, and a host of other wonderful things, including an exciting range of panel colors and pastel shades for lady CIOs and CFOs; the usual ones were red, blue, yellow, and pearl. It got customers asking IBMers, including me, what this was all about and should they delay IT purchases until nirvana arrived?
>
> This, of course, horrified IBM and for that and other reasons it eventually shelved the project. One "other" reason was that moving to the new system would entail a migration on a scale akin to that in migrating from, say, DEC to IBM or vice versa, and the customers would not like that at all. IBM didn't "unannounce" FS since in theory

---

* It was true from where I was sitting at the time. I had not signed a Letter 112, a famous piece of admin in IBM that customers had to sign if they were to be given access to information about future products. This would have been on a need-to-know basis or an "if you don't tell me what's coming, I'll stop buying your kit" basis. Needless to say, IBM didn't think much of the last sentence.

it didn't exist but let it ride away into the sunset (Who was that masked man?).

Knowing that people had suspected this new product, IBM reiterated, without acknowledging that FS ever existed, that it was in the game of *evolution* and not *revolution* in developing the product line and verily this prophecy came to pass. You can still run programs written for System 360 in, say, 1965 on today's servers and the FS "revolution" is but a distant memory.

Note: The FS concept in essence was a newly architected way of computing with three isolating interface layers to shield the programmer/user from lower level changes in hardware and software. One key factor was developing the idea of a single-level storage view of data storage from the programmer/user perspective so that memory, disks, and tape became unknown to these people. This would lead to systems managed storage (SMS) to make life easier for users. The architecture was in flux during the early 1970s; announcement timescale and estimated costs began to escalate. In the mid-1970s, the project was eventually abandoned.

To prove that it is an ill wind that blows nobody any good, IBM salvaged some of the FS concepts, like 64-bit addressing and some hardware abstraction, and embedded them in the System/38 and its follow-on product, the AS/400 (announced in 1988), now living happily as System i or IBM i.

FS, or course, would have had 100% availability until the end of time, just like most "vaporware" and everyone would live happily ever after. And that is the end of the story. Time for bed children.

Some years after this, Sun Microsystems joined the popular "nirvana tomorrow" movement with its Genesys program in the late 1990s. I saw it arrive and be touted everywhere but I didn't see it go—another mysterious masked man like the Lone Ranger, disappearing into the sunset.

The Future Systems/Series is discussed at length in a rather large book at 800-plus pages, titled *IBM's 360 and Early 370 Systems* by Pugh, Johnson, and Palmer, from IBM Research. It is a fascinating look at IBM in the 1960s–1970s and gives an insight into management thought processes as well as technical information.

Early Storage Device

The IBM 350 Disk Storage (capacity 5 Megabytes) was a major component of the IBM 305 RAMAC (Random Access Memory Accounting) system, introduced in September 1956 (Figure 1.10). The 305 was a flexible, electronic, general purpose data processing machine that enabled businesses to record transactions as they

A historical 5 megabyte disk drive

Figure 1.10   A compact storage unit: 5 Mbytes (1956).

occurred and concurrently reflect each entry in affected accounts. It maintained records on a real-time basis, provided random access to any record, eliminated peak loads, and could simultaneously produce output by either print or punched cards. The 305 system consisted of the IBM 305 Processing Unit and the IBM 350 Disk Storage Unit. The 305 also had other peripherals attached (printer, console, etc.).

Meanwhile, Back at the Ranch

In the background while all this was going on, UNIX came out as a viable operating system and morphed into Linux, both of which were supported by the major players of the day: IBM, HP, Sun, and DEC. Reduced instruction set computing (RISC) also emerged and was implemented in workstations and commercial systems.

Emerging players like Itel* with small systems at low prices, Data General, Prime, Sequent, and others with Intel-based multiprocessors, Cray, Ardent, Microsoft, and a host of scientific machine vendors, fought benchmark wars, open systems battles, juggled with POSIX, OpenGL, PHIGs, relational databases, communications architectures and products, standards for this, that, and the other plus a whole host of other things, many of which have gone the way of last year's snow.

The giants of the Internet and the World Wide Web (www) came on the scene with big hobnailed boots, along with Google, Amazon, eBay, big data, web

---

* Itel imploded when IBM announced the 43xx series of very affordable systems.

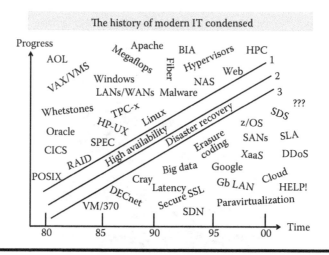

Figure 1.11   Simplified history of the IT world.

browsers, Internet service providers (ISPs), pay-as-you-go computing, virtualization, the cloud, software defined networks (SDNs), software defined storage (SDS), Y2000, high-performance computing (HPC), plus lots of other things I can't bring to mind at present.

Looking at all this and the valuable data in this morass of products were the baddies, waiting to relieve people of their cash, just like the baddies in the Westerns. The trouble with these latter day thieves is they aren't visible and don't wear black hats. This brings security into the equation where it didn't exist 20 years before when communications were private and on dedicated lines.

In addition, there are hackers who do it for fun or simple malice, including the DDoS (distributed denial of service) where multiple sources flood a site with fake transactions in the hope of bringing the site down or rendering it unusable.

In Figure 1.11, the lines show the progress in performance schematically for (1) processors, (2) storage, and (3) networks. No specific numbers or dates should be read into this figure. The picture presented is essentially a snowstorm of products, architectures, and techniques that are now your world.

The paper "IT Teams of The Future: Roles & Responsibilities" substantiates what I am saying about change and what 20 years ago was thought to be the future is totally different.* That is why I am saying "keep watching the skies" or rather the field of IT. The first two paragraphs of the article say it all for me, particularly the text that I italicized:

---

* "IT Teams of the Future: Roles & Responsibilities," Network Computing, November 10, 2015, http://www.networkcomputing.com/unified-communications/it-teams-of-the-future-roles-and -responsibilities/a/d-id/1323051. It is probably best to find the paper via a search on the title or go to www.networkcomputing.com to find it.

Few industries evolve at the rate of technology's seemingly breakneck pace. Whereas, one day it was wireless networking, today cloud computing is all the rage. As a result, the IT pros tasked with helping their organizations make the transitions to new technology must be able to learn and adapt on the fly.

With all this change comes new job roles and responsibilities. In fact, some IT positions are going way of the dodo bird. *It's paramount that IT pros always look ahead.* So, what does the IT team of the future look like?

Today

Today, the computing environment has morphed* into something very different from the early world I inhabited, it now involves concepts such as logical devices, virtual systems, and software-defined entities, often abbreviated as SDx, where "x" is that entity in question.

The different combinations of different atoms produce the bewildering array of substances we see around us but they are still made up of the basic particles of protons, neutrons, and electrons, plus other transient particles produced when attacked by other particles trying to break the speed of light.

Similarly, in modern IT, the same basic elements still exist but are often masked from the observer as views of those elements to simplify the use of them. I hope this makes sense and all will be explained further in Chapter 4 as this is the world you will, or perhaps already, inhabit.

The Future and You

The future in IT,[†] as it unfolds, may look to you nothing like the following predictions and guesstimates but that may be an illusion, based on admixtures of what already exists and sleight of hand. Anything obviously seminal will be immediately apparent. Personally, I take the future as it comes but with a weather eye of consensual opinions of respected IT people.

Did you know that there are only a limited number of unique two-dimensional patterns (17 if I remember from my extracurricular lectures at university)? So, the hundreds of wallpaper patterns you may see are really variations on these few base patterns. I feel the same applies to the proliferation of ideas presented as new discoveries in IT, whereas many are just increments on the old.

---

* Meaning it evolved and was not a "creationist" event, although it may have appeared so to people not watching things as they happened.
† If you are not already in IT, this section won't mean much to you so skip it, but keep it safe for the time you enter the hallowed halls of IT.

The Gurus Speak

Well, let's see what the gurus and crystal-ball gazers think about futures and trends and have made predictions. I have examined many of them, and take the essence of the opinion of the English conductor Sir Thomas Beecham who said of his extensive travels: "I've traveled all around the world and formed a very poor opinion of it." Nonetheless, I'll show you a selection of the predictions for you to make your own judgments. Table 1.1 is a list of three sets of predictions from three sources, and the following lists Gartner's studies on the same future topics.

First, is the Gartner group's Top 10 trends for 2013*:

1. Mobile device battles
2. Mobile applications and HTML5
3. Personal cloud
4. Enterprise app stores
5. The Internet of Things
6. Hybrid IT and cloud computing
7. Strategic big data
8. Actionable analytics
9. In-memory computing
10. Integrated ecosystems

But in Gartner's "Top 10 Strategic Technology Trends for 2016," we find the following:

1. The device mesh
2. Ambient user experience
3. 3D-printing materials
4. Information of Everything
5. Advanced machine learning
6. Autonomous agents and things
7. Adaptive security architecture
8. Advanced system architecture
9. Mesh app and service architecture
10. Internet of Things architecture and platforms

This is like predicting what will happen in a football or rugby match, pass by pass. The savvy player, especially one with experience, will watch the flow of the game and take appropriate action, be it strategic or tactical. That is my advice on handling the future.

---

* "Gartner Identifies the Top 10 Strategic Technology Trends for 2013," http://www.gartner .com/newsroom/id/2209615.

Table 1.1 IT Predictions from Three Sources

1. Web-based office software	1. Smart machines
2. Mobile business apps	2. Mobile device management
3. The touch kiosk	3. Mobile apps and applications
4. Office in a box	4. 3D printing
5. Business-class text messaging	5. Hybrid cloud services
6. The interactive sales pitch	6. The personal cloud
7. Bigger, faster office networks	7. Cloud/client architecture
8. The smarter ledger	8. Web-scale IT
9. The wall outlet that pays for itself	9. The Internet of Everything
10. Translation software goes mainstream	
11. The super-smart browser	1. No-touch interfaces
12. The appliance app	2. Native content
13. Talking to your computer	3. Massively online
14. PC-less desktop imaging	4. The Web of Things
15. The 3D peripheral	5. Consumer-driven supercomputing
16. The high-tech ceiling fan	
17. The ultraportable office	
18. Videoconferencing for everyone	
19. Everything goes automatic	
20. The projectable PC interface	
21. The flexible display	
22. The solar-powered office	
23. A smarter delivery van	
24. Making your inventory talk	
25. The virtual you	

Other Predictions

- "A Guide to the Technology Trends That Are Shaping Our Future:" http:// www.diygenius.com/a-guide-to-the-technology-trends-that-are-shaping-our -future/
- "The Future of ITSM: Service Management Platforms for Digital Transformation:" http://www.hp.azlan.com/Documents/IDC%20White%20 Paper_Service%20Management%20Platforms%20for%20Digital%20 Transformation.pdf. *This is an IDC paper on futures concentrating on service management but wraps the discussion around current and future topics in what it calls the "3rd Platform."*
- "4 Enterprise Technology Trends to Be Mindful of in 2016:" http://www .itbusinessedge.com/slideshows/four-enterprise-technology-trends-to-be -mindful-of-in-2016.html
- "Top 10 Strategic Technology Trends for 2016:" http://www.itbusinessedge .com/slideshows/top-10-strategic-technology-trends-for-2016.html

Future: Likely Contenders

The future is made up of the same stuff as the past.

Simone Weil
French philosopher

It looks as though you pay your money and you take your choice of futures, but here, for the record, are my thoughts based on experience and on consensus of all the predictions I have come across in the past few years. Like the horse racing pundits, I should put my money where my mouth is, as they say. Things that are slowly coming to the fore are, in no particular order:

- *The Internet of Things (IoT)*, a rather trendy term for the fact that 6 billion or more devices (nearly one for everyone on the planet) will be communicating via the Internet by about 2020. This total is not just a count of people on PCs or mobile devices but also refrigerators and all kinds of things once thought inanimate.
- *Mobile working*, where people can access anything from anywhere (subject to security and authorization) using bring your own device (BYOD).
- *Software-defined everything.* Software-defined networking (SDN), software-defined data center (SDDC), and so on.
- *Artificial intelligence (AI)*. I was somewhat involved 30-plus years ago in this topic when at IBM. It has moved on somewhat since then but not at such a rate as to be a threat to mankind as some otherwise intelligent people state. It is, however, here to stay but my money is on it being an academic subject for some time to come, whatever Stephen Hawking says.

- *Cognitive computing/inductive reasoning/data mining.** There are names for various techniques for analyzing vast amounts of data to extract information that would otherwise be impossible to do manually. This topic is too tricky for me to explain here, but in essence it tries to find correlations between factors that are not predicted or immediately obvious by the particular discipline they are related to.

  For example, if there was a mass of data collected about people with flat feet, normal medicine would look at established medical facts to analyze it. As a pseudoexample, imagine that the cognitive analysis of lots of data came up with the fact, among others, that 95% of the people with flat feet had dandruff.

  Medical knowledge would not predict this, but then a new avenue of research will have been uncovered, one that could not happen by manual scouring of the data. A rather trivial example I know, but illustrative I feel.

- *Big data*, data, and other digital media from many sources and undreamed of in my early days in IT. In fact, big data could not have happened because nobody could afford the disk storage to accommodate it all in those days. You would be talking millions of dollars for storage you can get today for $10.

- *Erasure coding*, a technique for storing data in a recoverable manner, superior to and faster than redundant arrays of independent disks (RAID) in recovery. This is necessary to reconstitute large swaths of data after a storage failure, a task becoming beyond the capabilities of RAID.[†]

- *Autonomic computing*, the semiautomation of computer operations where decisions on courses of action are taken by some form of AI on normal and error situations in running systems. According to *Wikipedia*,

  Autonomic computing refers to the self-managing characteristics of distributed computing resources, adapting to unpredictable changes while hiding intrinsic complexity to operators and users. Started by IBM in 2001, this initiative ultimately aims to develop computer systems capable of self-management, to overcome the rapidly growing complexity of computing systems management, and to reduce the barrier that complexity poses to further growth.[‡]

- *Security* is now an ever-present and future topic. Even if you aren't a security specialist you should have at least some inkling of what it is about and the consequences of security breaches.

- *Social media*, including movie and music downloads, global chatting, and all that stuff which you probably know better than I do.

---

[*] http://www.research.ibm.com/cognitive-computing/#fbid=pdbZn7a5h3l
[†] http://www.availabilitydigest.com/public_articles/1011/erasure_codes.pdf
[‡] https://en.wikipedia.org/wiki/Autonomic_computing

■ *Variations on current themes.* Clouds, virtualization, software-defined entities, and so on, plus relentless advances in speeds, capacity, and other physical properties of the underlying technologies. They may be grouped and given new names but, like all matter being protons, neutrons, and electrons, the base ingredients will probably be the same.

■ *Other techniques,* driven by the needs of medicine, DNA research, space physics, and dozens of other spheres of endeavor where technology is not the driver but the seeker of the optimum solution.*

There is a beautiful article in a DatacenterDynamics newsletter called "Slow and Steady" (November 19, 2015 by Chris Drake), which supports my thesis about the future happening slowly and not simply via whiz-bang technology conquering the IT world in an instant.†

However, for another view that is more on what to bank on for career purposes, the paper "The Shifting Technology Landscape: Reshaping Career Opportunities"‡ is interesting in what I am trying to say on two counts:

1. It is useful in looking at types of jobs and position you might aspire to, inside or outside your company.
2. It mentions some technologies that appear to be the current state of the art and implies they may last, that is, it is almost a prediction of futures in IT. I have italicized these topics in the following two extracts from the paper.

(I have not read every word and chart in the paper, but seen enough of it to know it is thorough and contains a lot of information that will be of use to you.)

> *Third platform technologies dominate activity.*
>
> Not surprisingly, when asked about the technology projects in which they were currently involved, those most frequently cited were related to the *Cloud, Software as a Service (SaaS),* and *Big Data.* Secondary to those were *Desktop Applications, Storage,* and *Security.*
>
> *Keeping up in a rapidly changing environment poses many challenges.*
>
> Refreshing technical skills, making strong networking connections, and hearing about job opportunities before the details are widely available are some of the prominent challenges IT professionals are grappling with in their job searches.

---

* Necessity is the mother of invention.

† "Slow and Steady," http://www.datacenterdynamics.com/design-strategy/slow-and-steady/95144 .article.

‡ "The Shifting Technology Landscape: Reshaping Career Opportunities," http://resources .idgenterprise.com/original/AST-0150317_Randstad_Recruitment_TabulatedPDF_AU-CA-US _English_FINAL.pdf.

Conclusion

The predictions made in the 1970s of what IT would look like in 10 or 15 years' time were essentially more of the same but using bigger and faster everything, with IBM owning half the world. This, as far as I know, did not happen. Similar predictions in the late 1980s and early 1990s were equally wayward.

"Keep watching the skies" (from *The Thing from Another World* [1951 movie]), especially watching out for the blue ones. If you take any serious notice of the latter and other "predictions," you believe in fairies. I'll probably get hate mail for my views but I've been at this game for so long I am willing to take on all comers, including Gates, Dell, Zuckerberg, Uncle Tom Cobley,* and any other prophets, bare-knuckle if necessary.

That's how confident I am that the future is whatever the future brings and that will be based mainly on requirements and cost, with technology progressing apace but sliding out of sight in the virtualized and software-defined world.

---

* Tom Cobley is a character in the English folk song *Widecombe Fair* and has come to be used as a humorous colloquialism meaning "anyone and everyone."

Chapter 2

Personal Skills and People Watching

Who Pays Your Salary?

The answer is your customer, be they internal parts or external contacts of your organization or customers of your organization, for example, if you are a vendor. You and the IT department are overheads *unless you provide the right quality of service (QoS) to those people*, in which case you are part of a productive process.

Dealing with Customers

Why Do People Buy Computers?

Easy; to run applications that support their work. Period.

Customer Assessment

This exercise is to gain a feel for the quality of management in various IT areas on some sort of scale (ranging from 1 = excellent to 5 = poor). It can be carried out in two main ways:

1. Informally without customer involvement or even knowledge. This will give you an indication of where support of the customer should focus.
2. As an exercise for and with the customer with a view to putting corrective actions in place where needed.

There is more detail in Appendix A under "Sample IT Assessment," which can be referred to later so as not to interrupt the flow of this chapter.

Customer Care

TLC was an acronym popular some years ago. I know it was used in IBM; whether they invented it or not I don't know. It stands for "tender loving care," which needs no explanation and led me to the parallel motto I devised many years ago, based on the UK Special Air Service's motto "Who dares wins": "Who cares wins."

The customer in 90%-plus of all situations and considerations comes first and it is often said the customer is always right.* Once you implant this idea in your psyche, many things in this book take on a more positive meaning than just discipline. Your job is not operating the Hokey Cokey 2000 billion squilliflop† computer but serving the people who pay your salary. A few thoughts about this before we progress:

- The telephone on your desk keeps ringing. Instead of groaning each time because it interrupts your IT plans to conquer the world, think "that is my job calling (and also my salary)."
- If you go on vacation, let the customer know. I used to spend a lot of time chasing trivial requests from customers, as well as important ones. Before I went on vacation I would ask someone to deputize for me and field important issues, then tell the customer.

    Dear X, I am on vacation from May 30 to June 13, inclusive. In my absence, Algernon Buckingham-Smythe will stand in for me on important issues. He can be reached at _____. If there are any things I can deal with prior to my departure, please give me a list of them soon. I can be reached at _____ as usual.

This was a magic calming move as nothing was ever communicated to me before my vacation and nothing of any importance occurred during it. My manager was pleased that my account was totally under control. Some other thoughts:

---

* The exception to this seems to be the pub in Manchester that IBM people frequented years ago. The landlord (Jack) was told by a customer over some minor issue, "The customer is always right Jack," to which Jack responded, "Not in this pub he isn't." In the pre-2007 days when you could smoke in UK pubs, Jack used to hand a brush over the bar to a random customer and tell him to sweep the cigarette ends off the floor. Some visiting senior IBM managers were involved sometimes, much to their amazement. The pub, in case you ever visit Manchester is The Railway and an instruction on the bar read, "When the floor is full, please use the ashtrays." This was in IBM's golden era.

† A squilliflop is a fictitious unit, derived from other xxxflops, and representing exaggerated super performance.

■ If you initiate or are involved in any changes where customer QoS is involved, ensure that, where necessary, the customer is aware and that his interests are prominent in any project plans. On other words, apply the so-what test as if you were the customer. Why? Well you may be asked to justify any expenditure on these changes by financially aware managers in your organization and if your reply is "It will improve our service to the customer's sales campaigns and enhance its success," it will be a brave manager who berates you for it.

■ Keep your customer posted on changes that affect him unless it is done for you. He will appreciate it. During the Y2000 events, I was deeply involved on behalf of Sun Microsystems and it was decided that over a 3-day period over that *doomsday date* and time, we would keep major customers informed about any problems reported as the new millennium dawned and spread from east to west. This was done by ringing them about every 2 hours (day and night) to say what the status was, based on information supplied by Sun personnel further east. They thought this was a fantastic service and even though we had next to nothing to tell them, they told Sun management after what was a nonevent that our service was the best they had received from any of their vendors.

Looking after customers sometimes has physical aspects to it, as these incidents I will now relate show:

■ On IBM Hundred Percent Clubs, a great trip to exotic places, some very senior customer executives would be invited along on this 3-day "bash." An IBM salesman would be assigned to look after them, show them around, buy them dinner, and so on. The salesman I worked alongside was given this task one year and his assignment was to chaperone Sir John Harvey Jones, chairman and chief executive of the chemical giant ICI. Sir John, ex-British intelligence, although not a James Bond, managed to escape the clutches of his minder. Panic ensued and the word went round the IBM community at the event to look out for him. After an afternoon rushing about Cannes (South of France), his chaperone met him casually strolling back to his hotel, telling his panicked host he had been out shopping for presents to take home.

■ IBM announced a Mass Storage Subsystem (MSS or 3850 in IBM-speak) in the 1970s and it boasted a capacity that today is supplied by a few disk units (I can't remember the exact figure). It worked by storing and retrieving data on tape-wrapped cylinders (mandrills) housed in a large honeycomb structure on both sides of a large storage unit. The storage and retrieval was done by a head mounted on a support that moved up and down the honeycomb at quite a speed. Operators were protected when it was operating by locked sliding doors. However, to demonstrate to customers how the MSS worked, the door was slid back and people could see the transport moving back and forth. One inquisitive customer decided to put his head inside to get a better view and was pulled back by the salesman just before the traversing unit removed the customer's head! I think such demos were continued but using a transparent door to watch though.

■ A second customer "loss" happened on a trip to IBM's plant at Montpellier in France. Myself, the salesman, and the customer spent half the night before the visit carousing in our hotel and got only about 1 hour's sleep before getting up for the visit. In a haze, the salesman and I dressed hurriedly and dashed off to the plant. It was only when we got there, and our heads began to clear, we realized we had forgotten the customer. Fortunately, he hadn't noticed he was alone and made his own way to the plant. We thought of telling him we did it as an initiative test for him but decided to come clean. He wasn't at all fazed and thought it was rather amusing. This an example of how not to treat a customer.

■ I was showing some customers around an IBM site on the UK south coast, having each traveled down in our own vehicles. I was unfamiliar with the territory and managed to get lost, the two customer personnel following me in their car. I was sailing along when I realized I was heading in the wrong direction and did a James Bond U-turn rather quickly. The customer followed faithfully with a screeching of tires but said afterwards he thought I was auditioning for a part in the *Starsky & Hutch* TV series.

Remembering Names

This is my Achilles heel I'm afraid and I have had to develop or learn techniques to try to master this failing. I am a member of a rugby club and often I used to be able to remember a person's telephone number but not his name, however odd that may seem. The best way I find is memory by association, which means attaching and remembering some phrase or word that helps you recall the actual name.

If the man you are dealing with is called Bill and is boring, Boring Bill is the ideal association to make. Similarly, a man called Robert who has red hair becomes Red Robert or Robert the Red, one called Basil with no hair is Baldy Basil, and so on. Some names you hit on may be cruel but as long as the target doesn't find out and it helps you remember, it's fair.*

A technique for remembering friends' wives' names, which may be unique to me, is to imagine that man saying their name if I've heard them say it often enough. It always amazes me when it works, which is on about one third of the occasions

---

* There is a tale, possibly apocryphal, about a draft letter intended for wealthy clients of a particular bank. The draft was designed to start "Dear X" where X would be replaced on a person-by-person basis during editing and printing. Unfortunately the drafter used something like "Dear Rich Swine" as the dummy greeting, assuming it was to change during printing by reference to a database of real names. Unfortunately, it wasn't and went out to some of the rich customers in this format.

I need to use it. Another way is to put the names alongside the entry in your diary and learn the names prior to the encounter.

Field Marshal Montgomery (of Alamein) had a morale-boosting way of pretending he knew all his soldiers' names. He would approach the man in a casual and friendly way and say, "And what is your name?" The soldier might reply, "Jenkins, sir." To which Montgomery would respond, "I know that Jenkins. Your first name, man." Very clever if you can use it in the right circumstances.

Humility

People who are perfect find it hard to be humble, and I understand this, but sometimes it pays dividends in enhancing your own reputation and that of your company/IT department. If there is something going on that is not exactly your responsibility but requires some "unskilled labor," volunteer and do whatever is asked of you even if your IT stature finds it demeaning. I'll illustrate this with an example. Years ago, my customer was having a major installation of IBM equipment one Sunday. It was engineers' work, but to show the customer I cared, I turned up in the machine room and went for coffee, tidied up cardboard equipment boxes after the kit was removed, and acted as a general "dogsbody" during the installation. The IBM engineers liked this help and the customer, who was also present in spectator mode, appreciated this. Simple but effective and part of TLC (tender loving care).*

Moral: Don't be afraid of performing menial tasks where they assist a greater task. Remember the Three Musketeers' motto: "One for all and all for one."

Assume Nothing: A Cautionary Tale

I was running a customer seminar in northeast England and just before starting, I counted of those who were present and saw that we were four or so short. There were some men in blue overalls milling about the room so I thought I'd ask them to leave and come back later to do whatever their tasks were. As I approached them, I noticed their lapel badges on them that read "Nissan." I realized just in time that they were key IT people from the Nissan car plant nearby and reacted accordingly, thus saving IBM and myself from embarrassment. It seems that everyone at the plant dressed this way.

---

* It was also a fraught exercise, as the computer room was on the second floor and the computer and some other large pieces of equipment had to be crane-lifted up through a window on that floor.

Other Hints

There are a few tips you need to take on board when dealing with customers (internal or external):

- Dress in a similar fashion to the person you are dealing with unless it is totally outrageous (rare); don't look as if you are from a different planet.
- Sometimes the customer does things a little out of the ordinary and normally you should go with it. IBM found this out once when a deal was struck with Harley-Davidson over a computer system sale. The H-D people invited IBM execs out to a celebratory lunch and picked them up on H-D motorbikes! The IBM execs, not famous for their senses of humor, went along with it.
- Look them in the eye (nonaggressively) when you meet and shake hands.
- You will often have to meet people you don't like; hide your disdain and treat them as you would someone you do like. Hard but it yields rewards.
- Ask if you can sit down when visiting someone's office.
- Ask if you might remove your coat and/or loosen your tie if it is hot.
- Remember to say thank you if you are meeting a new person or the person has gone out of their way to meet you.
- If they make a good suggestion, congratulate them in a restrained manner: "That is a good idea. I hadn't thought of that." Don't fawn* over them.
- If you make a commitment to do something, make a note of it and do it but don't give a silly timescale for its completion. If you make this miscalculation regularly, you will lose credibility and possibly business or promotion. There will, however, be differences in your ability to deliver so you should couch your commitment appropriately:
  - Things you know nothing about: "I'll talk to an expert and come back to you." Not "*get* back to you" as this sounds impersonal and less friendly.
  - Things you are slightly *au fait* with: "I understand the issue. I'll research that for you and come back with the results."
  - Things you are familiar with: "Yes, that is a good point and I think we ought to set some time aside to discuss the options."
  - Things you know quite well: "I have a few ideas about this. Perhaps we can go through them now."
  - Things you are well on top of: "What I think we should do is. ... I'll write that up and send it to you if you like and you can include it in your report."
- Don't criticize person A when talking to/e-mailing person B as these things have a habit of getting back to A, either via B or by C who overheard you. Always be conscious of your colleagues' views of you, as they are sometimes

---

* This is the prerogative of chat show hosts when talking to celebrities, especially movie stars.

consulted by your seniors who need to assess your capabilities for one reason or another.

- In general, treat them courteously, in a manner you would like to be treated but without overacting or laying it on too thick.

People will remember you for these things and forgive minor errors like forgetting to take a manual you promised to take. Finally, "Customer engagement is a more nuanced concept than many assume. Every interaction that a customer has with a company is consequential, as it contributes to that consumer's overall impression of, and engagement with, the business."*

For my own part, I totally agree with the phrase except I call this relationship TLC (tender loving care). It is the opposite of FUD (fear, uncertainty, and doubt), which is sometimes a useful technique for winning people over when logic doesn't seem to be working.

A Warning Preamble

There are hundreds of books and tracts on personal skills, lifestyle, and so forth, a lot of them plagiaristic or what IBM used to call *mouth music*; outpourings sounding deep and significant but content free. Phrases like "you must have a proper plan" and "have a definite purpose in life" ring pretty hollow when we know this already. I am not saying that you should distrust everything they say but take care in taking all their mantras as an axiom with the permanence of, say, Ohm's law (V = IR) or Einstein's E = mc². One of these lauded gurus says "Adopt the habits of successful people." Like the mafia? Like a J. R. Ewing, who trampled on people and feelings? Like Al Capone? No, some of these sentences sound pretty profound but are often common sense dressed up as key messages from on high. If you want to know about coal mining, ask a miner.

IBM managers often used to ask rookies in meetings what were IBM's major strengths. The answers ranged from various products to inane ramblings. The standard answer was "its people." Simple as that, but one implication is that if the people aren't first class, the organization won't be either and in a highly competitive environment this negative can be fatal.

---

* "The Significance of Customer Engagement: An Investigation into Customer Lifetime Value (CLV)," https://www.avaya.com/usa/registration/the-significance-of-customer-engagement-an-investigation/?PC=CE-FY16-CLV-ECON. The paper is quite useful in many areas, especially when it summarizes things with sentences like the one noted, but does contain some *motherhood*.

This is why I have put the "people" aspect as a separate section to emphasize its importance. It would be foolish to try to absorb all the tips and techniques and throw them into your repertoire at once; rather develop them over time, trying them one at a time until it becomes second nature. One every couple of days in not unrealistic if you believe that the techniques will work and benefit you.

Time Management

> All my possessions for a moment of time.
>
> **Last words of Elizabeth I, Queen of England**
> **(September 7, 1533–March 24, 1603)**

Time

Time, symbol, τ, t, or T, is that property of nature that ensures that everything in the universe doesn't happen at once and is therefore very useful. It is also the stuff of which your life is composed so wasting it means wasting your life, just as if you locked yourself in a cupboard for a period. It is a nonrenewable resource; once it's gone, it's gone. How much of it do you and I waste?

A quantitative way of estimating unused or wasted time is given in the book *Going from Undisciplined to Self-Mastery* by Harris Kern, where it can be seen that several days a month is not unusual:

12 Deadly Sins
   – Severe procrastination
   – No motivation
   – Disorganized
   – Not focused
   – Poor performance
   – Lack of energy
   – Failed goals
   – No sense of urgency
   – Lack of structure
   – Not managing sleep optimally
   – Poor time management
   – Inconsistency

This book could almost be seen as a follow-up to Kern's book and in a way it is. I read his book some months ago and afterward this book started to form in my mind as presenting an antidote to these deadly sins but in the context of information technology.

If in this exercise you compute a large number of days, imagine being told you must spend that time in prison (for no reason at all) or suddenly being told at age 40 that your life will be shortened by that period. You would not be too pleased would you?

There are any number of trees felled in the production in time management literature and I don't intend to cover them here. If I quote from them, I acknowledge and provide a reference to them, but many of the time users/savers come from my own bitter experience. Some things I've found I did and some I should have done in the interests of using that most valuable asset of time wisely and effectively.

In summary, here are some simple mantras to help you use your time effectively:

■ Set aside some time to do nothing but stare at the ceiling or out the window. This activity is a stress-buster and you'll get the time spent back in more effective working subsequently.
■ Set aside some time, say, after 4 p.m. on a Friday, to do things you do in haste in bits and pieces and often leave undone or in a mess.
  − Deal with your expenses and other administration.
  − Charge that cellphone/iPhone/iPad/ePod/xPad or whatever gizmo you use.
  − Make a to-do list of important items for next week with a more detailed one for Monday (or your next day at work). Each day add details for that day as necessary. It is difficult to practice time management without such a list or its equivalent.
■ At a slack time, ask yourself "What is the best use of my time right now?" If you don't get an answer, you may be superfluous to requirements.
■ Have I done this before and can I save time by reusing that experience?
■ Try to document (and file effectively*) notes from meetings, conversations, and so on. I used to do that in a large notebook; recorded everything but it wasn't indexed in any way to help me retrieve information quickly (if I could find it at all). I have seen a person use a card index to do this, writing on the cards under whatever letter was appropriate (Figure 2.1).
■ Improve your timekeeping. Being late for any appointment without a really genuine excuse says to the other person(s) "You aren't important enough for me to bother being prompt." Customers don't like that I'm afraid.
■ Use a larger diary to use as a notebook as well as an appointment recorder. I learned to do this, using the top dozen lines of a day-to-a-page A4 diary for any appointments and the rest for notes of that day and other items connected with whatever was the topic of that day.

---

* One of my great regrets in my IT education was not attending, for good reasons, an IBM internal 1-day course on "Organizing and Filing Your Information." My indexing and retrieval of information is improving but still suboptimal.

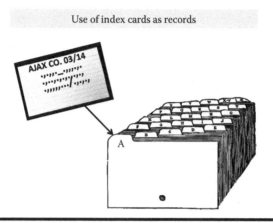

Figure 2.1 Index cards as a recording medium.

- It is a huge benefit in backward referencing events and notes. Previously I used a simple A4 notebook but later, looking back, all I had was a date (if I'd remembered to put it on the page) and some disconnected notes. Incidentally, you can also record other items such as mileage and incidental expenses for that day. It works and works well. You can use the usual 1-page year and month part of the diary (usually at the beginning of the diary with the previous year and the next year listed as well) as a place to mark off significant dates.
- Every so often, it is instructive to log your typical day to see how you have spent your time and how effective in your job each hour was. Your diary will help you with this.
- Don't hurry, don't worry, and (figuratively) stop and smell the flowers.
- Don't rush everything, even in urgent situations; you'll make errors that lose time. Make haste slowly. Wyatt Earp, buffalo hunter, gambler, and lawman, was asked about the fast draw. He said he made his fast draw slowly and deliberately and got it right the first time. Good, sound sense as he never got killed in a gunfight and died at home aged about 81.
- On a personal level, you can borrow time and composure by laying out your clothes the night before and doing the same with items you need to take with you the next day. I nearly always did the former but only much later did I do the clothes part.
- If you find you are always rushing out of the door in a morning you will (a) forget something you need and (b) become flustered. The solution is very easy: get up 10 minutes earlier.

If you cannot manage yourself, there is no way you can manage a project well. Getting up, getting ready and delivering on time is a project. Manage it.

Other People's Time

"He who wastes my time steals my life." What a saying!

We have talked about making best use of one's own time, but we ought not steal other people's time in the process. We should all be conscious of consuming the time of other people without an adequate reason, that is, mutual benefit. You should also thank people for their time if they are new to you or have made a special effort to give you that time but don't overdo it: "Thank you Mr. X for your extremely valuable and precious time. I will be eternally grateful for your gift of this valuable asset." Wrong, especially if you see the guy every day. Make your exit and say briefly "… and I appreciate your time today." Probably right.

Time Estimating

An important aspect of time management is the *estimation of time* in various activities: How long will it take to do X? We know that Einstein predicted that if you move very fast, then time slows down so, in theory, you can get more things done. Unfortunately this does not apply to IT since you would have to move very, very close to the speed of light (186,000 miles per second) to get more time to accomplish things.

The answer is to apply a simple method to timing projects and other activities and I will present an example. We all know that most projects, and in particular government projects, always apparently overrun in time and budget, giving newspaper declarations such as: "IT Project X: 3 Years Late, 150% over Budget Already."* You and I are not normally privy to the reasons for these situations, but personally I begin to suspect a time element is part of the problem as well as the selection of the wrong partners and, to be honest, gross incompetence. People point to first-class project management (PM) as the solution. Not so. If you aren't managing the right things then all that good PM does is get you to the disaster sooner. The ways of ensuring you are managing the correct activities is expanded upon in Chapter 3.

Breakdown Method

A fairly simple way of getting to a feasible number for the time it will take to do almost anything is to break it down into as many small steps as possible. This naturally assumes you understand the nature of the project in both business and IT

---

* In 2014, a study was published in *The Times* (London) that estimated that £30 billion ($45 billion) had been wasted on aborted and failed IT projects by the British government over about two decades. I am sure that the United States and some European countries are working very hard to beat that.

aspects. If you don't, or don't seek the correctly skilled help, you will probably get it wrong. This is illustrated by the phrases often used in IT:

Q: How do you eat an elephant?
A: One bite at a time.

If the project is big, then two divisions may be needed. Project and other literature suggest that you should break up anything you are dealing with into relatively small subdivisions, say, 5 to 9. The magic number often settled on is 7 for some reason. These relatively small numbers represent the best way of ensuring the human mind can cope with them and even remember them. This would not be the case if there were 67 subdivisions.

Where feasible, these subdivisions can be handed to different people to break into bite-sized portions for the purposes of time estimates. This is not rocket science but how many projects do it? The project failure record tells us not many. As an example, look at a software development project. This could be broken up in several ways but a typical one might be:

1. Collect requirements
2. Assess feasibility
3. Create a software map (parts of it and their flow, etc.)
4. Develop the software (including walkthroughs, etc.)
5. Test the software (pilot as well)
6. Implement the software (plus document it)
7. Manage and maintain it

This may not be a realistic breakdown to expert *DevOps* people but is illustrative of the principle. My experience tells me that skimping on steps 1, 2, 5, and the documentation part of 6 are the culprits in any gross miscalculations of how long things will take. Get step 1 wrong upfront and you might as well forget steps 2 through 7, and save aeons of time and pots of money.

Timing Example

Once you have done this breakdown, assign it to the right people, which may be just you, and break down each subdivision further and put a time estimate alongside each element. I was once asked to manage a mainly software conversion/migration project for a company, even though I was not a recognized project management person.* I knew enough about software to ask the company IT person responsible

---

* "Theirs not to reason why, / Theirs but to do and die," from "Charge of the Light Brigade" by Alfred Lord Tennyson.

on their side to make sure the coders did this breakdown, and document it, before starting work.

They did not like this but had to do it anyway. Managing the project was then simplified to a great extent. Although I did not (and could not) use sophisticated PM software, I managed to put the elements of the project on paper, along with the time estimates as the working document for the project. Armed with this information, it was easy to estimate where a portion of the software development was and whether anyone was not delivering the goods on time.

This method eliminated the flimflam often given by lazy coders. "It's 90% complete with just a few things to tidy up" since the coder in question had to point to the element he was up to in his/her part of the work and, if necessary, prove it. We were having a problem with the coder producing the screen maps (for IMS) as he didn't seem to be producing many. I suggested to my opposite number in the customer that he ought to have the secretary who keyed in these maps to visit the coder at the end of each day and ask for his day's maps.

It worked wonders and the maps started to flow and the rest of the project too. The whole thing was completed under the estimated time (a forgivable error) and as a result the teams got an award. I didn't. What this demonstrated was:

- I wasn't a genius so the simple PM method, suited to my ability, was employed and worked, an example of the KISS principle (keep it simple stupid).
- The time estimates developed by this decomposition method worked and worked better than I had hoped.
- Project tracking and progress estimation was made easier.

Of course larger projects may need software PM tools, but the decomposition method is still of immense value. Without it, it would be like trying to plait sawdust although some people try that.

In addition to this, there is the other gross timing error we all fall into sometimes: On a Monday, we say "I'll have that ready by Friday noon," when you haven't remembered that you have 13 other things to do on Tuesday to Thursday. We haven't thought it through and are firing from the hip. Your customers (internal or external) won't like this and, like the *Incredible Hulk* TV series, you won't like them when they are angry.

Another way is to try to find a similar project, if you are lucky, and draw some time estimates from that, but that can be dangerous if your project doesn't match the other project in most areas.

Multitasking versus Single Tasking

People often make a big thing out of the ability to multitask, that is, do several things in parallel. This is fine if you finish the top priority jobs on time but not if you don't. I know people who look outwardly impressive doing six jobs at the same time but at the end of the day say, "I worked my socks off but not finished anything." They have done some fraction of all six but probably not finished the key ones (a priority). You may not believe me but the article "Today's Multitasking Addiction Is Killing Productivity" shows another view of this situation.*

There is a case for single tasking in many instances and it takes strength to do what needs doing and not be sidetracked by low-hanging-fruit tasks or tasks you love to do. No rules here; just common sense and if you don't have any, IT is not the job for you.

Clean Desk

Two of the most talked about items in time management (in general) are

- *The clean desk policy.* This impacts personal effectiveness and a cluttered desk can be a security risk. Some outfits are not beyond bribing cleaners to scavenge offices looking for papers for them; the same ones that scour trash cans for pages thrown out by their competitors. Clearing your desk at the end of the day is 10 or 15 minutes well spent if you scan the stuff first for relevance and usefulness.
- *Deal with a piece of paper only once.* This is not always possible but thinking this way is a spur either to *act* on it or *trash* it. If neither is the case, it should be filed somewhere in your system so that it can be retrieved without effort when it is due for action.

There are also security issues related to untidy desks.† However, the great man had other ideas (Figure 2.2; *Einstein's Desk Hours after His Death*, http://www .talesmaze.com/wp-content/uploads/2015/01/Einsteins-desk-hours-after-his-death .jpg). But then we are not all Einsteins so let's go with the clean desk policy as a start.

Body Language

Here, I present some key body language gestures I have found most used in IT discussions. Rather than learning these and also spending days studying others in the references I give, I suggest you choose a few, observe your "prey," mentally note their mannerisms and then look them up in the references. This is a tailored solution to your needs. You may also come across other, possibly odd, undocumented

---

* "Today's Multitasking Addiction Is Killing Productivity," http://www.itbusinessedge.com /slideshows/todays-multitasking-addiction-is-killing-productivity.html.
† http://www.csoonline.com/article/2131082/data-protection/81971-Whats-wrong-with-this -picture-The-NEW-clean-desk-test.html?source=cso_top5

Einstein's desk shortly after his death

Figure 2.2   Einstein's "tidy" desk.

gestures that you will have to interpret but the ensuing analysis should give you the answer you need.

Body language and its interpretation is probably more important than many people think, equating it to posing as someone you aren't. This is far from the truth for three reasons:

1. It allows you to assess the mood and attitude of people you are dealing with and react accordingly. It includes the potentially dangerous technique of *pacing.*
2. It will help you to engender empathy in the person you are dealing with and convey friendliness and openness via this language. It is far more convincing than saying "I am the greatest, nicest, cleverest person you could ever meet!" It is also useful in dealing with your peers and even helpful on social occasions: "The name's Shufflebottom, James Shufflebottom," followed by the appropriate body language. You can't fail to impress.
3. It helps you to be more convincing and sincere when dealing with people, including those in your own organization. It can also help prevent gaffes when dealing with cultures that have different customs to Westerners, for whom some Western body language is insulting.

As an example of point 3, consider the Japanese. When you present your business card, the Japanese gentleman will probably read it and bow to a certain extent. The depth of the bow will reflect your perceived importance; a slight bow if you are a minion, a deep one if you are the chairman of a big company. You will be expected to do something similar to them, not necessarily via a bow, to show respect.

Warning: One thing you should be aware of is that with many non-Western cultures, prolonged eye contact is insulting and to some, it has other connotations.

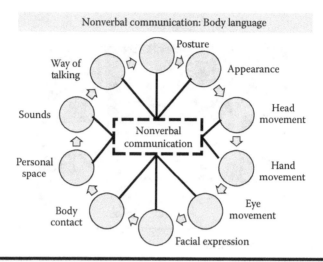

**Figure 2.3 Types of nonverbal communication. (Adapted from "Body Language,"
http://www.slideshare.net/PujaJha3/body-language-14197767.)**

For example, prolonged eye contact with a Zulu (should you ever deal with them) has sexual connotations and other cultures similarly. If unsure, avoid prolonged eye contact but don't give an impression of unfriendliness.

Body language is a valid communication vehicle that does not rely on speech or the written word and is often called *nonverbal communication* (Figure 2.3), a powerful adjunct to the latter two modes.

The interpretation of the body language of people you are talking to can be intuitive and complemented by looking at some of the references I give in this chapter. However, you must be proficient enough in it not to make mistakes in interpretation.

The difficult bit in using body language is to project your better side to someone. Again this is almost involuntary because, for example, if you feel friendly toward a person it will probably show. If you don't, but protocol and your bank balance mandate that you should, you may have to resort to appropriate body language. To do this you will have to make some effort to study it properly, otherwise you might imply "you are an idiot" when you meant "you are a nice chap and I'm glad to meet you." You will then look, in UK vernacular, a wally.*

---

* Wally—A silly or inept person, not unpleasant but not desirable company. A wally does things like putting outsize plastic gnomes in his garden, has a bright pink car, parks it in no parking areas without realizing, and dresses like a circus clown but thinks he is trendy and with it. It is not known what the female of the species is called, perhaps a wallyette or walliess. Origin, 1960s. Perhaps a shortened form of the given name Walter. There are many theories of the origin. One story tells of a Wally who became separated from companions at a 1960s pop festival; the name, announced many times over a loudspeaker, was taken up as a chant by the crowd. There is an excellent book called *How to Be a Wally* if you aspire to that exalted state. As such, you are unlikely to succeed in IT.

Initial Contact

"Well begun is half done" is the case in many activities, such as presentations. This saying also applies to person-to-person contact, as it puts both parties at ease with each other if done in a measured and (apparently) natural mode.

Facial Contact

Most of us are familiar at judging people's moods simply by looking at their faces*:

- ■ "He looks as if he's lost a dime but found a cent," indicating great despondency (American).
- ■ "He has a face like a gasman's mackintosh" (British), describing a face showing the depths of despair.

You may have a natural open and pleasant face, but if not, you may have to practice looking that way. This is your first contact as you walk through the door so make it count.

Tactile Contact

Innocuous body contact is a powerful way of gaining empathy with a person, particularly if you don't know them well or at all. A study some years ago showed that when a person touched a second person in, say, handing over an object or money, a slight contact with the hand or finger elicited empathy and friendliness in the receiver. This form of contact does not include wrapping your arms around a member of the opposite sex and giving then a big kiss, or variations on that theme. An interesting variation on this theme is the position of the knees of a person sitting next to you. Knees away from you means keep your distance, knees forward is neutral, knees toward you shows empathy toward you or even an indication of liking you a lot. Women do this a lot but seem unaware that their movements have these interpretations.

The Handshake

The handshake as form of greeting is covered well in the later references with some good diagrams of modes of handshaking. The basic tenet of this mode of contact is the correct distance between greeter and greeted; if you have to lean forward to shake the hand it shows coldness, too close the opposite. The correct stance is basically standing upright, standing about 2 feet apart and reaching out without stretching too far or too close, necessitating tucking your elbow under your armpit. Don't try to break the other person's metacarpals or have a very limp grip; make it

---

* "Well had the boding tremblers learned to trace / The day's disasters in his morning face," from "The Deserted Village" by Oliver Goldsmith, my favorite poem.

firm but natural. The former mode has connotations of superiority, the latter, total disinterest in that person and his/her interests.

The Greeting

Don't greet a stranger or partial stranger as if you have known them all your life; it's phony. "Hello, old chap, top o' the mornin' to ye," and so on. The astute recipient of your greeting will class you as a wally immediately. Also, don't feign complete familiarity with a person when you don't really know them that well: "Nice day for golf Jim ... and how's your lovely wife, Ann?" when his wife's name is Ermintrude, he doesn't a wife, or doesn't play golf. You will get off on the wrong foot and remain on the back foot throughout the subsequent meeting, especially if his name isn't Jim or he prefers the name James.

Eye Contact

The eyes are the window of the soul and can also indicate what a person is thinking or planning to do next. Steady eyes I have found mean interest and warm contact; moving, restless eyes mean possible attack in some form. Eyes have color, show movement, and the pupil size can often indicate emotion. For example, if the person opposite you is making body signals that imply he is interested in what you are saying but his eyes are wandering, beware. If his eyes are glazed, you've bored him silly so call it a day and retire gracefully.

Eyes Up, Down, Sideways

There are apparently specific intentions to be read into eye movements, depending on which direction they take when the person opposite is either speaking or listening:

- Eyes down suggests he is lying (speaking).
- Eyes upward suggests disbelief or "when is he [you] going to shut up?" (listening).
- Eyes movement to either side suggests he is getting restless and possibly wants the conversation to end or move on to another phase or topic (listening).
- If the eyes move in any other direction, suggest politely that he sees and optical surgeon.

Gunfighter Technique

The old Western gunfighters had the notion that you can tell an opposing gunman's intentions by his eyes; you can judge when he is about to draw on you by his eyes, not his hands. The eye movements, no particular direction, just twitching, presage hand movements; he's going to shoot you. In normal communications, and in the absence of other body movements, it indicates some significant shift in attitude.

True or not, it is a good indicator of the intentions of the person opposite you. Keep watching the eyes, but not too obviously. Remember though, that staring directly into someone's eyes is an affront to people of certain cultures, including the Japanese and Zulu people.

The Meeting Proper

The first thing to remember is that in meetings, body language is duplex, that is, it works two ways at once. You give body signals to the person opposite you and they give signals back, and it is both of these you need to understand and interpret. The following links provide a good indication of the messages given by configurations of different parts of the anatomy; arms, legs, head, eyes, and so on.

> "Body Language:" http://www.indiabix.com/body-language/basic-understanding/
> "Body Language—Meeting Seating:" https://www.youtube.com/watch?v=FTV hceRJuhw video
> "How a Speaker Impacts an Audience:" http://westsidetoastmasters.com/resources /talk_your_way/lib0009.html

I think it is pointless to learn all the body gestures upfront but study them as and when you come across them when meeting people, then enter the study, learn, and remember mode. The gestures that I remember best and encountered most frequently are those shown next, all involving a person sitting behind a desk and opposite you.

My Gesture List

There are basically two forms of body language in this book:

1. The well understood ones, which are described in the literature in consistent fashion.
2. Those that are peculiar to an individual, which you will need to observe and interpret if you wish to understand the person or persons you deal with.

The body language that sticks in my mind is that which occurs during a selling exercise, be it hardware, software or an idea. The gestures shown in Figure 2.4 indicate where you are in your efforts to bring the person opposite into your way of thinking. These can happen in any order depending on the target of your persuasion:

- Figure 2.4a shows a person who is about to come on board with your thinking, and with a bit of luck and skill, he may progress to state (d).
- Figure 2.4b shows a person who has heard your case but is not at all convinced of it. Don't dive in and try to close the deal/argument, as there is still some work to do.

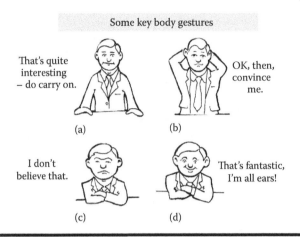

Figure 2.4 Four key body gestures.

- Figure 2.4c has heard it all and is still not on board, in fact you've lost him overboard. You have work to do, possibly in Six Thinking Hats mode, to get the person through b, a, and hopefully d.
- Figure 2.4d is hooked but don't overdo the elation; check if there is anything else he wants to know then strike with the sale or follow on from your idea.

The normal path to satisfactory conclusion is b, a, d, but if you are a star performer, you may skip b or even b and a to reach d. A person who gets to c very quickly isn't going to buy anything or agree to your idea so you may resort to plan X. Plan X for sales is to say "If we gave you this free, would you take it?" If he's honest and really doesn't want your offering, he'll hedge a bit but indicate no in some way or other. Thank him for his time and head for the hills. Plan X for dismissed ideas is to find some common ground and take it from there (Six Thinking Hats).

The other gesture you need to look for is the "I am lying" gesture, discussed in my environment a little later. This will vary from person to person, but unless they are a black belt fibber, there will be a consistent gesture that indicates economy with the truth.

Parting Contact

Finish as well as you started and hopefully behaved during the meeting; shake hands, thank him or her for their time, and indicate keenness to meet again should that be deemed necessary. Make the appointment there and then if at all possible. However, don't make this format a ritual if you meet regularly as it sounds phony, but vary it depending on the outcome of the meeting.

Some Basic Rules of Behavior

As well as being knowledgeable and physically smart, certain aspects should eventually permeate your business behavior and some of the rules or guidelines I have learned are necessary for success are outline next.

You should try to develop a friendly approach and not look like a geek, lauding your superiority over others, but do have a gravitas or appearance of being wise but approachable. It's difficult to say how one achieves this but look around and you will find some people who fit this verbally indefinable bill. Watch them and emulate them if possible.

I was never a technical giant during my career but in my more mature years I was often asked to meet senior IT people in customer accounts to discuss things with them. It's quite a thrill to be asked to advise a senior IT manager, but sometimes there is an ulterior motive. They may be seeking support for something they want to do or an item they want to buy and need their vendor's "expert" opinion to support them. Most of them are quite approachable and are vulnerable to the fear of failure in the eyes of their superiors. They may even pay to have a study/survey done to support some plan they wish to implement to show their superiors as proof of its necessity (assuming you play ball and support the notion).

Behavior List

1. Never denigrate your previous (or any other) employer or the competition. This applies doubly when seeking a job elsewhere or perhaps within the organization you work for. It shows rancor and does not count as a plus on your CV. Your previous employer(s) can be cited, however, as not providing enough challenges for you, which, of course, the employer you are currently wooing does. They'll like that.
2. Remember you have two ears and one mouth, so use them in that proportion:
   - The wise old owl lived in an oak,
   - The more he heard the less he spoke,
   - The less he spoke, the more he heard,
   - ITers should copy that wise old bird.
   (Slightly paraphrased old nursery rhyme. Does not apply when presenting.)
3. You may talk too fast. Slow your speech to match the speed of your brain and you'll make less gaffes (before engaging mouth, put brain in gear). Make allowances for the listener's hearing if it is obviously not perfect but don't make it obvious by shouting and waving your arms.
4. When you travel to and from work with lots to do and think about, switch your car radio off.* Despite what people say, it does not help concentration.

---

* If traveling by public transportation, tell everyone to shut up but make sure you either have a Black Belt in a Martial Arts or the address of the nearest medical center.

I found that silence helped my thought processes enormously when I was traveling on IBM business for 6 months without a radio. The company car did not have one and I was too mean and too underpaid to afford one. A letter I wrote on the subject was published in the *The Times* (London) in August 2013 during correspondence in the "Letters" column about the beneficial effects of music while driving a car.

Road Music

Sir, I do not agree about the beneficial effect of music on some drivers (report Aug 26; letter, Aug 28). In the 1980s I drove thousands of business miles without a car radio. The result of this enforced meditation was a calmer ride, sharper reactions and deeper analytical thinking in meetings and presentations. I recommend regular periods of "radio silence" for all, particularly young people.

I stand by this premise to this day.

5. Carry some sort of note facility (electronic or paper, the A4 diary notes pages) to record things to do, especially those you said you would do, perhaps off the cuff. Also note related things that other people said they would do so when someone says, "But you said you would do B, Terry," you can respond politely, "Yes, but you said you would do A first, without which B cannot be done." If you score such a triumph, let it rest ("park it up," as New Zealanders say) so you don't look like a big head. They will get the message that, in UK parlance, you know your onions.

6. Record other things in meetings as well, as it is always good to be able to say what happened when others have forgotten. I always carried a notebook and even though 80% was never looked at again, the other 20% proved invaluable. I was jeered and laughed at because I didn't have an electronic organizer and carried my materials in a supermarket shopping bag. However, I was always at meetings on time, knew what the agenda was and what happened at the previous meeting. The electronic devotees often missed the meeting or went to the wrong room.

7. Be a good timekeeper. If the meeting is at 2 p.m., get there at 1:50 p.m. If it's your meeting or presentation, get there even earlier to check things out. Nothing worse than setting up an important meeting/presentation to find the slide projector doesn't work or the marker pens are dry, just as everything else is geared up to go. Starting to write with a dry pen will make you look like a wally.

Many years ago, I was social secretary of a rugby club and responsible for, among other things, the annual dinner at which there would be distinguished guests. They sat at the top table and a microphone was provided for any speeches they were to make. As usual, I was fussing around the room to finally check things out well before people came into the room. I checked the things I had set up but I hadn't set up the microphone. That was done by the staff of the hotel we were in. I was wandering around the top table, checking name cards and so forth and picked up the microphone and spoke into it. Fine. I then moved, with the microphone to the end of the table where one of the main invited speakers was to sit. Aha! The microphone wouldn't reach as the flex was too short. Solution: Get the hotel staff to fix it ASAP, which they did. Embarrassment averted.

Moral: If you are using some type of setup (presentation or whatever), check everything out before the event, especially things that were set up by others. Essentially it is attention to detail.

8. Think about developing presentation skills. Others can help if necessary. (See the "Presentation Skills" section later.)

9. Don't be afraid of putting forward ideas as long as you have thought them through or think they are worth talking through with colleagues. Never present a solution to which there is no problem and never present a problem without suggesting a solution or, at least, a way forward.

    I once had a manager who used to rush out of his office in excitement five times a week with five or more ideas. In any five, one was complete rubbish, two were worthy of consideration but were shelved because of constraints like cost, effort, and so forth. The other two were usually good and excused the daft one. You have to crack eggs to make an omelet.

10. Dress code. Match the level (not the exact fashion) that the people/person you are dealing with favor. Don't dress for the beach when calling on a manager dressed in a tuxedo. If you don't know what they dress like, for example on a first visit, dress middle of the road and carry a tie in your pocket. In the United Kingdom, a regimental or public school tie will go down well with certain managers. Don't wear sneakers at any business meeting or other get together. If you wear leather shoes, make sure they are polished and add a quick shoe shine to your weekly expenses and other chores time.*

11. Think quality and improvement, both personal and work matters. IBM used to have an annual engineering quality award that was won regularly by IBM Japan. One year the award was won by the IBM Hursley Labs in the United Kingdom. Within a day or two, people from IBM Japan were on the plane to Hursley to quiz them about what they did to oust them from the top spot. It worked because IBM Japan got the award back soon afterward.

12. Don't interrupt people, even if they are talking nonsense. They will dig a big hole for themselves and fall into it or at the end you can destroy their argument since you will have had time to formulate your response.

---

* I always told my son that he could spot a con man, even if he was smartly dressed, by the fact that 90% of the time they would have dirty shoes.

13. Don't be afraid to make (considered) suggestions in areas that are outside your main sphere of knowledge. From years of sticking my oar in, and sometimes being successful, I know that an astute observer can see things that an expert cannot since many of them don't think outside the box. It would be tree-wasting and erosion of your time if I told you all the examples I have been involved in—me (observer) versus expert—so I'll illustrate this with an analogy:

Imagine a jungle expert, say a Vietnam veteran, in that environment but needing to escape. I (observer) can't help him in his travel in the jungle, as he is the expert. But I am flying a helicopter with a good view of that jungle and can see things he cannot. I see that the south, east, and west exits to that jungle are inhabited by cannibals, crocodiles, and greedy bankers. I can see that the north exit is the best way to go. Will he listen to me? It all depends on his ability to think laterally. He may think, I have been in this situation before and I know the jungle; the north exit is the best. Alternatively, he may ask why I think that and be open to advice, based on my skills as an observer. I have had discussions (not quite arguments) with economists and medical people about things that to me are glaringly obvious, but to them, because of their training, are not seen. Your argument may not be about the details of that subject but the process being followed.

I won a discussion with medics when all their medications were fine but the processes around them were faulty and error-prone, "But that is the way it is always done" was their response. I could go on about this but I'll desist. Suffice it to say, that if you have a reasoned point or argument about an unfamiliar topic, air it and say you are willing to be proved wrong.

14. Have a look/listen to the 3-minute London Marathon promo video (https://www.youtube.com/watch?v=2KOLxQEfmCI). It closely mirrors an IT career and is very inspirational. I feel it would be a great start to your new career or a revamping of your current one. Nothing in life stays the same and people need to adapt in line with that change.

Your Company

Your company—employed or self-employed—is part of your life so respect and nurture it. There are a few rules that will help you to do this without too much schmoozing. Read this piece of cracker-barrel philosophy, mentioned previously, that I think is pertinent to anyone's attitude to employment and work:

There's an old story about two men working on a railroad track many years back. As they are laying track in the heat of the day, a person drives by and rolls down the window (not enough to let the air conditioning out, but enough to be heard). He yells, "Tom, is that you?" Tom, one of the men working on the track, replies, "Chris, it's great to see you! It must have been 20 years … how are you?" They continue the conversation and eventually Chris drives off. When he leaves, another worker turns to Tom and says, "I know that was the owner of the railroad and he's worth nearly a billion dollars. How do you know him?" Tom replies, "Chris and I started working on the railroad, laying track, on the same day 20 years ago. The only difference between Chris and me is that I came to work for $1.25/hour and he came to work for the railroad.*

A Few Rules

Respect your company's ethos and reputation and treat its property as if it were your own; this includes its property in perks, like a car, and money, such as expenses. Here is a tale about an IBMer I knew, Jim Cotton (very nearly his real name) and his company car:

> Jim was driving home in his company car one summer day and decided to spend an hour of so on a beach just north of Liverpool, United Kingdom, and not far from where he lived. He parked his car on the beach, strolled off along it for while, then onto the sea front where he spent about an hour. When he returned to the beach, the tide was coming in and his car was standing in about a foot (30 cm) of water and was unmovable.
>
> With little choice, he made his way home, planning to retrieve the car the next day. When he returned, his car was sitting there trunk lid torn off, car looking battered, and a tire torn off, having been submerged by the rough incoming tide. Jim, being Jim, rang the office to get the OK to get a rental car as his would not start. The office asked him what he thought the problem was and his reply was "I think the engine has got damp."
>
> I visited that beach some ten years later with my children and there was rusty car chassis some 50 yards from the promenade. I am sure it was the skeleton of Jim's old car, claimed by the sea for its own!

Moral: Respect company property. Sorry Jim if you read this; I couldn't resist this one, particularly as it is true and I think the remnants of your car are still on that beach.

Plan your career as if you are going to leave your job in a year or so. What I mean by this is to put down some career markers that will serve you well in your current job and also if you do leave your job, because if you do so, for whatever reason, the

---

* "Foreword," in *Understanding Big Data*, https://www.ibm.com/developerworks/vn/library /contest/dw-freebooks/Tim_Hieu_Big_Data/Understanding_BigData.PDF.

other employer will ask you to tell him about your successes. Also, never look for a job just when you have lost yours; plan earlier in cementing your CV with impressive events. You are then prepared for any eventualities.

Careless talk costs business was a watchword posted in various places in Britain during World War II. There were enemy agents in Britain throughout the war and someone talking about "my job in the new munitions factory in Xville" would probably have seen Xville flattened within a week by enemy bombers. So, outside the office or other company premises, watch what you say about the company, its people, and its products. You never know who might be listening and the last thing you want is for someone to overhear you saying words to the effect "my company is rubbish, as are its people and products." It could well be overheard and give a competitor something to tell prospects about.

Double dealing. A London salesman I worked with was assigned to an account in Northern England because of his specialty knowledge in a particular industry sector. He would travel up the country on Monday morning and return home on Friday, staying in hotels in between. He sent his expenses claims to headquarters, who paid them, intending as usual to claim them back from the manager of the salesman at financial year end. However, this particular salesman was also claiming the same expenses from his manager, thus double claiming. It should have been obvious to this individual that at year end, headquarters and branch would do a reconciliation in such matters.

Come year's end, headquarters sent a bill to the branch manager asking for their money back as per normal. The branch manager protested that he had paid those same expenses himself and then, of course, the balloon went up. The company was entitled to fire the salesman immediately and prosecute him but chose instead to take a more subtle approach, perhaps on the grounds of possible adverse publicity: "Mr. X, would you like to resign and find work elsewhere?" The suggestion was gratefully accepted and the man moved on to find work elsewhere but I'm not sure that his new employer knew his history. The man was nicknamed "Tricky" by his colleagues in his first company and then after this event, we all knew why.

Now you see it, now you don't. A similar money scam occurred in the early days of one company's foray into the PC marketplace. In those days, third parties were assigned to market and sell PCs on behalf of the company, a normal practice for low margin items. However, the company salesmen still encouraged their customers to buy PCs to grow the account but initially they were not paid commissions on any sales of PCs into their account.

After a time, when PCs were selling like hot cakes, salesmen, spending quite some time "selling" PCs, asked to be paid some commission on these third-party sales. This was agreed by the company but mandated that clear evidence of such sales must be forthcoming from the third-party involved. This worked well for a time but then things went sour.

The company salesmen found out it was easy to persuade third parties to register sales that had not actually been made and this became, as we say in England, a nice little earner. Soon, the inevitable happened and the company found out what was going on and called the culprits to heel, any punishment depending on further enquiries into the matter.

While this inquiry was going on, the salespeople involved (and this included managers) sweated it out and waited—all except one person. This person, the calmest individual I have known, decided to drive to the top of a hill, a beauty spot, drink a bottle of champagne and inhale the fumes of his car exhaust. The result was inevitable. The company then toned down its anger and issued severe warnings to the others involved in the racket and little more was said.

Moral: It seems the old adage is true; honesty is the best policy. There are times, especially in selling, where being economical with the truth is the norm. There are other times where dishonesty might have serious consequences for you and your company.

There was an old chestnut of a joke circulating in the 1980s to the effect that IBM salesmen lie, and DEC salesmen do too. The difference is that the IBM salesman knows he is lying.

The Customer

The customer comes first in nearly all situations since he or she pays your salary. You probably know this but, like your umbrella, you often forget it. I won't labor the point but just give a trio of tales to illustrate this tenet.

Where's my software? A customer of mine heard of a new version of MVS (the main IBM operating system, Windows with muscles) and demanded an early copy.* There weren't copies in the United Kingdom at the time, only in the IBM software distribution center in Denmark. I had to chase my manager for permission to fly to Copenhagen to pick up the software ASAP. Having got that, I asked admin to do whatever was needed for me the clear customs with the tape(s), ordered the plane ticket, got up at 3:30 a.m., and caught the plane from Manchester to Copenhagen. I saw nothing of the city except from the inside of a taxi but managed to grab a beer in Tivoli Gardens with an old friend who worked there, then flew home in time for bed.

Where's the missing pages? A rather shirty customer ordered one of the first IBM 3081s in 1981. Its systems manager, who had a very bad temper, was in his element, especially when it took a long time to get hold of a photocopy of a manual he wanted ahead of the delivery. When he finally got it he counted the pages, compared the total to the last page number and then wrote to IBM in a huff to complain that four pages were missing. The long-suffering salesman showed remarkable restraint in his reply (in a formal letter of course) when he apologized for the error but said he now

---

* Meaning tomorrow.

only enclosed one of the missing pages, as they were all the same. Each page had on it "This page intentionally left blank," a common thing in IBM manuals.

Can I have it yellow? A well-known UK manufacturer of diggers and forklifts was in the market for an IBM system, and IBM was talking directly to the big boss of this outfit (called Joe X as it happened, where X was the company name). He patiently sat listening to all the talk about benefits, squilliflops, CPU registers, error correcting disks, and the like. At the end of all this, Joe, who had been on a visit to IBM in Poughkeepsie, said "I'd like to ask just two things: (a) Can I have the computer behind smoked glass like they have in Poughkeepsie? (b) Can I have it in X yellow, the company colors?" The salesman said of course, as all salesmen do even if asked the impossible. He then rushed around to find the detailed spec of X yellow as IBM only made the system in question in red, blue, and pearl gray versions. Joe's wishes were fulfilled, resulting in a happy customer.

Defusing Situations

You will, in your time in IT, come across explosive situations that need defusing, particularly if you caused them! Some defusing situations I am aware of are listed next.

Deflection. A sales manager in the branch I belonged to was obliged to send a report of something important to his manager (call him Charles) in London every month. Bob, ex-Army and the archetypal Englishman who we have met before, was very late doing this on one occasion despite his secretary telling him several times that Charles was regularly on the phone, hopping mad about the non appearance of this report. Eventually, Bob called Charles and before the latter could explode with anger said, "Splendid weather today Charles, isn't it. Is it nice where you are? Good weather for your golf." Charles slowly calmed down and had a perfectly normal conversation with Bob and was doubly pleased when Bob assured him the report would be with him the same day. Both thought they had won the day in the matter.

On another occasion, our friend Bob was in his office when a salesman charged in with an urgent customer problem to tell him about. Bob knew something was amiss but calmly said, "Look at these jumping beans Jim. Aren't they amazing things?" Jim looked at the beans jumping here and there, and by the time he was ready to tell Bob what the issue was, he realized he was much calmer than when he walked in the office. Bob was the master of pouring oil on troubled waters, an object lesson for us all.

Don't rush me. If you have ever read anything about the Zulu nation and their culture you will have come across their rules of conversation. Never approach the subject at hand directly but skirt around it with trivial chat about this and that before eventually getting to the point of the discussion.

Shadow boxing. At a time in my career when I was an optical character recognition (OCR) specialist, I was booked to give a presentation to a prospect about the IBM 1287 OCR. At the time, there were stories circulating that the toner used in the 1287 was carcinogenic (cancer inducing). I was told that there would be a trade union official at the presentation, obviously to check out these stories. Fortunately

I was forewarned about his planned presence and had to chase around in IBM for a story to tell him when he tackled me on the topic. I was able to get a reasonable answer to most fears about the toner and managed to satisfy the union man, although it did require a bit of sleight of hand; no lies though. I think the lesson here is, if possible, *know your audience* in advance and plan accordingly. I was lucky in that I was told upfront who was going to be at the talk; you may not be.

Stress Management

I am no expert in stress management but have picked up a few things that might help in stressful situations.*

Breaking off. This should be done if at all possible and a few minutes spent doing nothing in particular; stare out of the window or, if there isn't one, at the ceiling and concentrate hard on your breathing and nothing else. Think about the breath coming in and going out of your lungs for that period.

Sitting exercise. This is one we were taught in IBM and is very simple to do (and remember how to do it). Sit down in a relaxed, almost slouching position, and relax. Breathe in slowly and then breathe out, letting you abdomen flop in relaxation. It is the opposite of holding everything in when on the beach trying to impress the ladies around. If you do it slowly enough, again concentrating solely on your breaths in and out, you will feel less stressed.

Plastic bubble popping. This is one of my favorites. The plastic wrappers designed to protect the goods inside often have air bubbles in plastic covers. Popping them with your thumb and forefinger can be very relaxing especially in the sound it makes. You must, however, only pop bubbles of the correct IEEE size, which is about 1 cm to 2 cm diameter; anything bigger makes a loud noise and is harder to pop. I am popping a 1 cm sheet now, in between making typos in this script.

There are acres of books and articles on stress management if you find these simple remedies don't work. If you must choose one to trust, get a book by someone who has suffered from stress!

Too Much to Do

Yes, we've all had too much to do and most of us tackle it head-on, grinding through to the end. Is this the way to do things or is there better way? Perhaps:

■ Think "Is all this work necessary to achieve the objective?"
■ If it is, is this the best way of doing it? Is the process we're following right?
■ Doing it all without this thought will probably lead to everything being done, but in a half-baked fashion.
■ Think about prioritization and delegation, your two *get out of jail free* cards.

---

* Not chronic stress, as this needs medical expertise, not mine.

A Stress Generator

One stress generator I have experienced is looking too far ahead and worrying about everything on the horizon when in reality you should only live one day at a time. If you have your to-do list up to date, you can just concentrate on the next day or so since that comes before all the other days, believe it or not. If you have a concise list for the few days following, you can start concentrating on them in more detail after you have got the first day sorted out. To paraphrase Matthew 6:34, sufficient unto the day are the stresses thereof.*

If your worry list is not documented and your near-term activities are just an unordered list, tackled at random, you are going to get into trouble. Moreover, you will suffer additional stress because you have not achieved any of the tasks, despite working your socks off; 10 tasks, each only 85% finished with no priorities assigned signals to the observer (your manager?) that you haven't achieved anything.

Reducing Stress

You needn't become a Buddhist monk to learn to reduce stress,† that might take too long. There are trees felled to produce tomes on this topic, but I'll settle here for a consensus view, tempered by my own background. Here are the suggestions:

- Quiet meditation on nothing in particular
- Silence; no background noise like a radio you aren't really listening to
- Laughing, especially with friends (you laugh at your enemies)
- Deep breathing while concentrating on nothing but deep breathing
- Walking, more than likely alone or perhaps with a silent partner
- Gardening and other nonstressful outside activities (communing with nature I believe the tree-hugging gurus call it)
- Clearing up your working environment equals getting organized and reducing clutter (feng shui)
- Enjoyable exercise
- Possible use of supplements, for example, vitamin C and valerian, checking with a health professional first
- Don't hurry, don't worry, stop and smell the flowers every so often
- Reading this book and recommending it to all and sundry
- Washing dishes by hand (I find this a relaxing pastime and I'm sure I'm not alone)

---

* Matthew 6:34 (New American Standard Bible): "So do not worry about tomorrow; for tomorrow will care for itself. Each day has enough trouble of its own." I'm sure that other faiths dispense similar advice.
† Summarized by some as "fear of the unknown and of failure."

Well-Being at Work

Time magazine (March 14, 2016), had a small section on well-being at work which I summarize here, some of which are related to the hints I've already provided:

- Do someone a 5-minute favor; helping others helps one recover from stress if the techniques mentioned above either don't work or are impractical to attempt at the time
- Hide your phone (assuming you aren't using it); this allows you to focus on the tasks at hand
- Take a break before lunch; this is the "look out of the window every so often" technique
- Let yourself procrastinate; studies show people who played a mind-absorbing game for 5 minutes before settling down to a task were more creative (I'm not too sure about this one but it fits in with the Zulu habit of trivia before business)
- Disappear for a bit; take a 10-minute walk daily and forget work for that period
- Gossip with coworkers; must be a detached conversation and not work-related
- End the day like you mean it; essentially means that when you have finished, finish and don't grind on in extra hours (my feeling is that this should be at a good break point in work, finished or major block completed)

I've often wondered why laid-back people often seem to be strolling through the day, yet still seem to get more work done than I do. Now I know.

Learn to Say No

Saying no sometime is self-evident, but protocol often prevents us saying it. If you are overloaded and have prioritized your tasks, then the chances are someone is going to be upset. When they ask you to put their task up the list and it is not up there already, you should say "Sorry, no can do" and explain the logic of your prioritization.*

The Wrong Way

As mentioned before, if you eliminate the wrong ways to do things, then you will probably be doing the right things. This following action list provides a salutary lesson in doing things when you aren't sure what you are doing, especially when things go wrong. The tribal wisdom of the Dakota Indians, passed from generation

---

* If it is your boss asking, you may have to rework your priorities. Please read another book that deals with schmoozing.

to generation, warns: When you find that you are riding a dead horse, best strategy is to dismount. However, in some IT installations, this advice is translated into more advanced recovery strategies and ensuing tactics, such as:

■ Switching the system off and then on again (tell your boss this is the "global master reset" technique in case he asks; it is used by TV repairmen to fool the customer that they know what they are doing)
■ Kicking the system components harder, perhaps changing your boots first
■ Changing the system operators
■ Hiring outside contractors to operate the system
■ Appointing an IT committee to study the system and report back in 6 month's time
■ Arranging pleasant visits to other countries to see how other enterprises handle IT projects; countries with warm climates are preferred
■ Lowering the service-level agreement (SLA) standards so that dead or useless systems can be accepted as operational within its terms and rewriting the incriminating aspects of the SLA
■ Reclassifying the system as "availability impaired" instead of "dead"*
■ Doing a productivity study to see if fewer users would improve the management of the functionally impaired system
■ Clustering several dead or slow systems together to increase the speed and availability
■ Seeking additional funding and/or training to improve the sick system's performance and resilience via redundancy, extra processing power, and cluster upgrades
■ Declaring that since the dead or poorly performing system does not have to be operated and maintained, it is less costly, carries lower overheads and therefore contributes substantially more to the enterprise's bottom line than working systems
■ Finally, initiate the search for the guilty, punishment of the innocent, and promotion of nonparticipants; standard "failed project" practice in many installations

---

P.S.: If you don't understand this IT take on Dakota wisdom, or you think it is untrue, you probably haven't been in IT long enough. If you aren't yet in IT, remember this section.

---

* If you need to be *au fait* with this language, study *The Official Politically Correct Dictionary and Handbook* (HarperCollins). It could save your job or even get you promoted.

Moral: Better to do nothing than do the wrong things when such actions compound a problem. Albert Einstein once wrote that a definition of madness is when a person repeats the same experiment and expects a different result.

Learning Skills

It is better to keep your mouth shut and to appear stupid than to open it and remove all doubt.

Mark Twain

Introduction

Learning a new skill or subject can be difficult, as I and many other have discovered. There have been acres of trees sacrificed in making books on this subject, which I won't refer you to. I have my own method, forced on me by being unable to master a topic in the traditional way, grinding through a detailed exposition of it. An analogy of this method, outlined next, is not being taught to swim the breast stroke initially, but being made comfortable in water from which other swimming skills follow. The diversity of material on any given topic is usually large, but a double-edged sword with both benefits and drawbacks as explained next.

My Take on Learning

It may be unique to me, but I am a great believer in learning by immersion in any subject. What I mean by that is that to pick up a topic, it is better to tackle it piecemeal than in one marathon effort with all the information about that topic in front of you. Why do I say this? Some years ago, I was placed on a course at an IBM education institute in Belgium. The course was on scientific computing, run by a fanatic who drove us 12 hours a day for a week. We had lectures, mock sales calls, and were making presentations, running until about 9 p.m. each night. Great you may say; what a fantastic way to learn a subject. I thought the same until about 2 weeks later, when I found I couldn't remember anything at all about the course, except that it was hard work.

By experience, I found the best way to learn a new subject was by approaching it from different angles and levels of complexity. Let me present an analogy of this. If you wanted to know your way around London or New York and what went on in those cities, you might buy a detailed guide and a map then study for days. You might even walk around both cities, but you would only get one perspective of them and very sore feet.

The best way, I think, would be to walk some, ride about, take a look from the air, read a few articles about the cities, watch a video, and so on. Eventually, everything will click into place and you will feel confident, though not expert, in those places. Taxi drivers in London have to acquire what is known as *the knowledge*, an ability to navigate from almost anywhere in London to anywhere else in that city. This can take 2 to 4 years to acquire and many potential cab drivers use a scooter to traverse London to be able to achieve the knowledge. I know of nowhere else that has this level of qualification demanded of a taxi driver.

To summarize, I think learning in this piecemeal way, using different levels of material written by different people is the way to go. It works particularly when you come across a presentation or paper that makes everything click into place. After reading other tracts you may understand all the words and features of a topic but not fully understand the topic. This is a common problem similar to that where a person can see all the trees around but doesn't know he is in a forest. You must have attended presentations or read books where you understand every page but at the end still have no idea what it's all about. I certainly have.

"Little, varied, and often" is my learning motto, which incidentally is also the dietary advice given by specialists if you have a hiatus hernia. Small world.

Concentration (and Time) Stealers

There are a number of things that can divert one's mind from learning the job at hand, and a useful article outlines many of these and, more importantly, suggests remedies (*fixes*) for them.* These diversions are as follows:

- Social media
- E-mail overload (and addiction)
- Mobile/cell phone
- Multitasking (dealt with in the section above)
- Boredom
- Nagging thoughts
- Stress, fatigue, and depression
- Hunger
- Effects of medication
- Attention deficit hyperactivity disorder (ADHD)

It will pay for you to scan and read this article, especially if you are wondering why you aren't getting anything done despite the hours spent doing it. (You may have to register with WebMD, but it's free.) You cannot only save time but also put what time you have to more effective use.

---

* http://www.webmd.com/add-adhd/ss/slideshow-top-concentration-killers

Lunchtime Briefings

You may have seen the concept of lunchtime briefings elsewhere, but before accusing me of plagiarism, let me tell you where I came across idea. At IBM internal meetings, a technical person would sometimes give a presentation, often on something topical and not as a learning exercise. A good presenter could get across quite a few ideas to a receptive audience in 20 minutes. I thought about this and came up with the idea of lunchtime briefings, no more than 20 minutes long, given by various people on topics of interest but not known by the audience.

Lunchtimes of 1 hour usually has about 30 minutes of idleness, unless you have a gargantuan feast each day. Idle time, except for destressing and leisure, is a time waster. When you are struggling to finish a piece of writing in time because of the need to research something you should know, you may regret this lost time.

Time to Reflect

It is often a refreshing change to sit back and consider on how you, your team, or IT department are faring in your development and planning. My time in IT showed me, sometimes in retrospect, the value of *time to reflect* on things. Two things were of value; the *annual appraisal* and counseling (A&C), and *account reviews** and plans at the beginning of a financial year. In the general IT world these might be translated as

- An annual strengths, weaknesses, opportunities, and threats (SWOTs) analysis; self, team, or department (A&C)
- A review of plans and personal, team, or department development (annual review and planning)

Two things are needed to make these happen: (1) a facilitator/scribe and (2) the determination to make them work by documentation and follow-up. They need not be too formal and might cover:

- A review of the previous year's major activities, noting what worked (strengths) and what didn't (weaknesses) with a simple plan to capitalize and correct, respectively
- An idea of what support is needed for the customer in the broadest sense, for example, for a vendor, this might be sales potential, for an IT department, the next year's new applications and other changes, and so on
- Any education, training, and additional support needed to ensure success

These activities needn't be onerous, complicated tasks, and are really just times to reflect as the title of this section suggests. If you don't already do them or do the

---

* These were usually held during a very long day in early January in a local hotel room with gallons of coffee consumed during the sessions; not very good for the night's sleep I found.

equivalent, then try them and they should become second nature to you, your team, or department. The department one will need some management approval and would then split into team development anyway, except where management decides to do a similar exercise at a department level.

Note: This description is general and if you get the drift of what I am saying, you can tailor the activities to suit your circumstances.

Support for My View of Learning

I couldn't believe my eyes when I came across the following extracts on the Internet about the best way to learn. I banged on about the immersion technique in my book *High Availability IT Services* and to anyone who would listen. These quotes support my view 100% and it is from a university student.*

1. *Immersion through multiple, different sources.* Don't rely solely on repeated encounters with the assigned text(s). Get a bunch of input from different sources. The basics will be redundant, helping to solidify your learning foundation, but because the delivery of info is varied, you're much more apt to remain an attentive audience. You're looking for "resonant" descriptions that leave an imprint on you, like that oh-so-special teacher you had in grade three. This is important because so many textbooks suck at delivery, but not all in the same ways. A particular (or peculiar) diagram in a book you found on your own at the library could be the answer to your dream of an intelligible exposition/illustration of Concept X.
2. *Mind maps.* Sketch, doodle, devise insane visual or auditory or tactile correlations. A series of dry interrelated concepts could become a banana tree whose hanging fruit are yellow trucks, high heels, jewels, and oak saw horses. Absurdity makes abstractions memorable.
3. *Frequent re-visits.* Like with your sick friend, or mom, frequent, but brief touchdowns signal the importance you place on the nearness of your interrelationship, in this case, with knowledge.

Check out another interesting article "Making Learning Stick."† The following is a pertinent extract:

> Consequently, Ebbinghaus proposed that people need to continuously review what they learn. He suggested that, with mnemonic techniques

---

* "How Can I Study Effectively?" https://www.quora.com/.
† "Making Learning Stick," https://www.mindtools.com/blog/corporate/2015/12/11/making
-learning-stick/?utm_source=nl&utm_medium=email&utm_campaign=15Dec15.

and *repetition** based on active recall—especially "spaced repetition"—an individual could reduce this loss. Later research suggested that, in addition to these two techniques, higher original learning is forgotten more slowly.

Other learning wisdom prescribes short bursts of 25 minutes work before taking a break, as the brain's absorption facilities deteriorate after that time. Studies have shown that most humans can only concentrate fully for approximately that time, so any time after that is quite unproductive without the pause.

Many lectures are 40 or 45 minutes long acknowledging the same principle, although there might be classes that are too long without a break. Marathon learning sessions saturate the brain and do nothing for information retention; that is the message from erudite studies on the topic and my own brain saturation experience.

William Shakespeare, Too

Dear old Bill has also written about this way of learning[†]:

> Shakespeare's education was simple, as Elizabethan education was. While it sufficed and stood him in good stead, Shakespeare was never persuaded by scholarship as such. He clearly expressed his attitude in:
>
>> Small have continual plodders ever won
>> Save base authority from others' books.

I take this to be verification of the idea of modular, frequent learning spells and rest my case.

Checklists: Use Thereof

People often think that if they have a detailed checklist for doing things, then they don't need to study or know too much about the subject to get it right. I dispute this on the grounds that a knowledgeable checklister will beat an indifferent checklister. Let's take a medical analogy: You enter hospital to have a heart operation and hear the surgeon muttering his way through a checklist and making comments on it:[‡]

- First find the heart; it is somewhere on the left just behind the breastbone … think I can manage that.
- Check if it's still beating … must read up how to do that.[§]

---

* My emphasis.
[†] "Shakespeare, Newton and Beethoven—A Talk by S. Chandrasekhar," http://www.parrikar.org/essays/shakespeare-newton-beethoven/.
[‡] Before you are anaesthetized.
[§] Remember Groucho Marx taking a prostrate man's pulse: "Either he's dead or my watch has stopped."

- ■ Mark off the incision area … wonder what I do that with. Pen? Pencil, marker … it just doesn't tell me. Nurse!
- ■ Choose correct scalpel … how do I do that? Must be extra details somewhere in this list.

By this time, you will be signing yourself out of the hospital and going to your local vet instead.

The point I am making is that checklists are backup to your knowledge and personal list and could make your tasks easier by embedding other peoples' experience in it. There are nonsensical items in some checklists that your knowledge will expose and therefore avoid.

Conclusion: Know your subject, even if you have a detailed checklist, is the key message here.

Some Winning Techniques

These are things I have picked up in my sojourn in IT; some I developed myself, others I picked up from others working alongside me. Many of these tips are applicable to jobs other than those in IT and can be a shortcut to looking wise beyond your years in almost any environment. Some of them need subtle application since getting them wrong could earn you a punch on the nose from an irate person on the receiving end of your efforts.

Spotlight technique. Sometimes there are issues when two sides disagree and you need to break the deadlock. Often, the disagreement is caused by the view of one person in the opposing camp. A technique of resolution is to identify and isolate that person from the rest of his team and query the validity of his argument and spell out the consequences of following it. A sales example is a situation we had in IBM where the customer has apparently decided to buy look-alike pieces of equipment from elsewhere to save money. The equipment ran on microcode and needed updating every so often and it was not certain that the competitive equipment would do that in time to benefit from the upgrades. There was no certainty that their upgrades would work correctly. Having identified the proponent of this move, we went on to show the issues that might arise as a result and made it obvious to the opposition who would be responsible if these terrible things happened. Eventually, they backed down.

This is I suppose a rather selfish example but, if you are convinced your argument is right, it is a powerful method of winning the day; isolate their champion and put the spotlight of consequences on him and his supporters. This is similar to the technique used by a U.S. marshal faced with a mob. He eyeballs the mob leader and says, "You may get me but I'll get you and a few others first, Kincaid." The "others" often turn on Kincaid.

Aunt Sally* technique. It is usually bad business and manners to openly criticize your competition and their offerings, but there is a subtle way around this that I have done in preparing proposals. Let's imagine the opposition is, for example, proposing a distributed system as the solution for the customer. You could tell the customer that his proposal is nonsense, but there is a better way. Your proposal is for a central system. In your proposal (or at a presentation), you explain that you considered two options seriously: distributed and central. You then "examine" both solutions and demolish the distributed one, showing the prospect that this is why you think the central solution is best for their needs. As an aside, it also indirectly sabotages the competition's solution.

Self-examination questionnaire technique. This is similar to the Aunt Sally ploy but involves a self-examination of your own solution or idea, again involving competition or opposition of some sort. This is best illustrated by, again, a real example when IBM was having difficulty selling against competition in the mainframe arena. The survey revolved around the MVS operating system and its interface with the mainframe microcode to provide function and be upgradable in tandem without a hitch. The survey took the form: (1) Does your OS have the published interfaces with … and support for … regular updates, etc.? (2) How often is the microcode updated and is it upward compatible? The questions are pseudoquestions but illustrate the survey format. IBM would fill this in with all necessary details and present it to the customer or prospect, hinting that perhaps he ought to put the survey to X, the competitor.

If the IT section is unwilling, talk to the finance guy, saying how important it is to his applications that the things in the survey are done correctly by their supplier. If your case is solid and your survey true, you will probably win the day; IBM did on that occasion. The competitor was the now-defunct Amdahl, a formidable adversary.

The magician technique. When selling to or trying to convince a non-IT person, particularly a senior business manager, about computers and your solutions, this ploy is useful, as I have tried it. Ask him what would he like most for a magic computer to do for his business for it to succeed. You may get a few humorous answers but you will finally get a serious one, as per the example I give next. If it is amenable to an IT solution, go away and prepare a simple solution involving IT and ask to present it to him and others if you can.

This can be a winner, especially if he/she thinks IT is just an overhead. I was briefly involved in a situation with a very large airline and the manager in this case was connected with finance. His birthday wish was to know how much fuel was in

---

* Aunt Sally is a traditional English throwing game in which players throw sticks or battens at a model of an old woman's head.

all his aircraft at some point in the day or evening. It was something to do with buying fuel at the correct moment on the spot market. I asked him why it was important and he replied that if it could be done, he could save millions over the year. I was not involved much with that customer afterward and a simple solution may not have been possible, but it illustrates the point that if you hit what the industry calls that person's hot button, you are guaranteed his/her attention and support.

It was used elsewhere to tease out just what makes a businessperson tick. It's a simple application of the principle that if, for example, you talk to a golf fanatic about golf, you are sure to get their full attention. If you can design a system for their blue skies vision, you are a hero and a winner. Try it in difficult situations.

Specific body language. We have looked at body language before in a general way. However, long years of dealing with customers shows that there are sometimes specific body language signs that may be unique to a particular person you are dealing with. Watch out for them and make a mental note of what they mean for future encounters.

One customer I dealt with had a habit of moving his hands in circular motions, palms down, on his desk, as if polishing it. It took some time but I finally realized that he did this when he was lying and, in future meetings, I knew what to expect when he repeated this body language. This was passed on to others I worked with simply by telling them, "If he starts polishing the desk with his hands face-down, he's lying."

The unexpected presentation. This is less a technique but more of a warning. One Friday I was at a (rare) loose end and the salesman I worked with came across to me. He said, "I'm going to see Joe at X this afternoon for a meeting. Why don't you come along and listen as its your account?" I agreed, especially as getting home from the customer premises would be faster than from the office.

We sat with Joe at his desk and the salesman started, "Well Joe, today I'd like to see where we've been, where we are today and where we should go in the future … over to you Terry." When they picked me up off the floor, I mumbled a few words about this and that, mainly that, before I regained my composure and said something sensible (I think).

Moral: The message here is when you go to casual meetings, find out what is on the agenda from the organizer and check if it involves you! Do the same for official meetings too! You should never be surprised at a meeting.

Phone a friend. Most walkthroughs and reviews of projects, presentations, and ideas are carried out with peers who are involved in that particular situation. It is useful to have an outside view of it all from a person whose ability you respect but who is not involved directly. Believe it or not, a complete outsider can see things the involved team can't because of their myopic view of everything connected with it.

This is especially valuable when designing a human interface, the main one being web pages. Get this wrong and you will drive potential users/customers away from it and in the latter case, away from your company and its goods. Years ago, I knew of several companies who checked out the impact and usability of some of their public-facing websites by paying people off the street to come in and try to use the website unaided. It was easy money for someone just wandering around in London to get $250 (equivalent then) for playing about with a computer with no downsides. I wish I could get into that business myself now.

Pacing. Pacing is a winning technique that goes by different names but is dangerous unless you use it correctly and not in excess. It is a way of gaining the interest and confidence of someone unfamiliar to you who you are talking to. It means in essence copying the less exaggerated actions of the person opposite you but without making it obvious. For some psychological reason it seems to make the person opposite like you. I tried it for the first time on an account I'd never been to before and it worked. The IT manager who had asked for the meeting asked to continue our discussions over the next few weeks while they were evaluating IT equipment. I must confess I was very nervous before and during that meeting but didn't have to repeat the pacing exercise subsequently, as he thought I was a splendid chap.

Don't try this without practicing it on friends and peers or you will come unstuck in a big way.

Empathy. Reading the mood of a person you are dealing with and chiming in with it can have benefits. If the person is patently sad or morose, don't tell him how delighted you are to have won $1 million on a lottery. If you read his state of mind, be sympathetic even if you don't know the reasons. If he has a secretary,* when you arrive ask, "How is Dave today? Full of the joys of spring?" If she knows, she will tell you the reasons he isn't happy and you can act accordingly. If his cat has died and you hate cats, you will have to act I'm afraid, but I'm sure you get my drift in this matter.

On one occasion, an IT manager at a customer had ordered tape drives from a competitor instead of IBM. When trying to get them up some stairs to the machine room, some were dropped and crashed down the stairs. The IBM salesman heard about this and expressed his deep sympathy to the IT manager the next time they met.

Showing a little knowledge. One day, I was asked by a salesman if I would accompany him on a prospecting call on a water board person, a manager with a foot in both IT and business camps. I had some experience with the electricity and gas industries but none with water boards. I decided to learn a little about the industry before the call. The local library had a short book on the water industry and I scanned it over the weekend and picked up some pointers to what the industry was all about. The salesman and I went to the board's offices and met the manager. The salesman that day taught me a lesson; not what to do but *what not to do.* He was carrying his usual brochures and about to bury the prospect in them when I signaled him to wait a while.

The salesman started the discussion and I chimed in after a short time, asking about the issues that the manager and the board faced. He began to talk to us in that vein and mentioned a word or two that reminded me of the book I'd scanned. I asked, in query not knowledgeable mode, was that related to dry weather flow (DWF). He looked pleased and switched his gaze to me and off the salesman, and the discussion continued on the water man's terms.

---

* Secretaries are fountains of knowledge if you want to know.

At the end of this chat, he said something to the effect "Did we have anything that might help them?" The salesman jumped in and produced a relevant brochure and the guy was hooked. I didn't plan the whole of this in advance; after reading a bit about the industry and always thinking it was better to find the problem to which the brochures might be the solution, it just happened.

Moral: It is always advantageous to know a little about the industry you are dealing with but without pretending you are a know all. Talk initially about their needs and not your solutions; these should emerge as a result of the discussions.

A parallel situation to this one occurred when a prospect wanted to hear about possible IT solutions to their needs in some industry or other. The consultant who was working with the prospect took me aside before the presentation and said, "Look, whatever you say in the detail, the solution is UNIX." I passed this on to the IBM sales team before the presentation. Unfortunately, they were AS/400 salespeople and they presented this as the solution despite being told what the customer should hear. The result? We were blown out of the water and got nowhere near any business with that customer.

Sneaky skills. Although not part of any course curriculum or an approved skill, most salesman and systems engineering in IBM were adept at reading upside down, a useful way of getting information from letters and papers left on the desk of the person you are talking to. If your morality forbids your using this skill, it does no harm to develop it anyway—it may be a future Olympic Games event.

Listen to problems first, talk solutions second. Get things in that order and you have a chance of success in selling (in its broadest sense) anything, be it a product, idea, or course of action. You have been warned.

Meetings

Meetings can be the bane of people's lives when called at short notice, with no agenda and turn out a complete shambles. This is the norm in many organizations as I outlined earlier. Again, there are large tomes on running meetings with talk of objectives, expectations, mind-sets, psyche, and sometimes some bovine detritus. My thesis comes from what I've seen, done, and experienced.

Meeting Types

There are probably three basic types of meetings:

- *Urgent meetings*, called to address an immediate issue. These are usually called by someone deeply involved in the issue and the agenda may simply be "actions on system crash." For systems issues they could well be held in a war room where all relevant material is normally kept.

- *Regular meetings*, such as engineering reviews or program development checks and project meetings. They still need an agenda but often replay the same one from the previous meetings. This is OK but it does not add any value unless there is a review after each meeting and possibly an improvement suggestion placed on the next agenda. Without this, such meetings are what I call *sterile* and are often content- and ideas-free because of the familiarity of the agenda. Even for these types of meetings, the agenda should be a *living* one, not a cut-and-paste from the last one.
- *Exploratory meetings* to initiate activity in a new area or revise an old one, normally called by the person with responsibility for that particular area. This type of meeting definitely requires an agenda, objectives, and the reasons for this activity. This might overlap or be part of a quality circle.

The de Bono Six Thinking Hats technique is a useful tool in straightening out runaway meetings and I cover this later. First, I should point out that this method, like others, is not totally seminal, as it contains elements of SWOTs, Delphi, and normal common sense in the development.

The Typical Meeting

Before showing you the possible solution to meeting meltdown we will look at the structure of a meeting and where the Six Thinking Hats technique might help in such situations. There is a standing joke in IT that if you have nothing to do or want a good laugh, call a meeting. Unfortunately, this is not a very good joke because it is often true. Take a look at Figure 2.5, a representation a typical unstructured

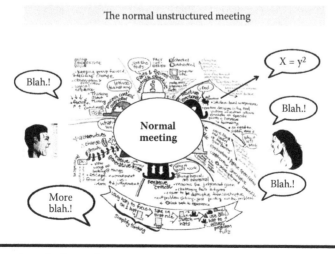

Figure 2.5 A typical meeting.

meeting. There will be people who are talking all the time, some who say nothing, some who spout nonsense, and those who are wondering if they are at the right meeting. Meetings, like living creatures, come in all shapes, sizes, and lifetimes. Some people live by meetings as it saves doing any real work.

- Meetings can in reality be effective and produce results if handled properly.
- They must have a defined purpose and expected outcome.
- They must have the right people there.
- They must be publicized and have an agenda.
- They must have a beginning and an end.
- They must have a chairman or gauleiter* to ensure order.
- They must be documented and minutes issued to the correct people.
- They must have any actions arising chased for completion.

People who have chaired meetings and pulled together people for the planning, design, and other aspects of some project will have learned by experience how to structure the proceedings of such events or perhaps from a technique they have learned. One such technique we will discuss next. There are numerous checklists for running meetings and the following link is a good, concise one: "Effective Meeting Checklist," http://www.itbusinessedge.com/itdownloads/staff-management/effective-meeting-checklist.html.

You don't have to read a whole paperback book on meetings; if you do, you shouldn't be in any meetings, let alone leading one.

Six Thinking Hats Technique

Edward de Bono proposed the Six Thinking Hats as a way of constructing interactive discussions of many sorts. The schematic of what the six hats mean in this context is shown in Figure 2.6.

These hats can be worn, not literally, in discussions where progress and an outcome are necessary, and they are different modes of contributions to the discussion, each with an objective in the proceedings. Also note:

- All hats need not be worn at all meetings/discussions.
- The hats should be worn as appropriate and not in some strict order although common sense will suggest a possible order.
- They need not be used in the same order each time they are employed.
- The time spent wearing each hat or using each hat at different sessions need not be the same.
- One hat (blue) implies the presence of a leader or organizer unless all attendees are 100% *au fait* with the technique.

---

* A term I use for a "fixer."

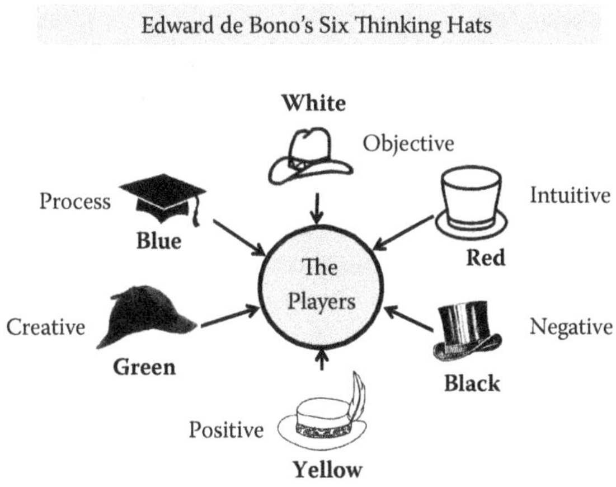

Edward de Bono's Six Thinking Hats

Figure 2.6   The Six Thinking Hats framework.

I think what I am saying here is that these hats are in essence colored paints to use on your discussion canvas and you can vary them in use and intensity.

Thinking Hats Outline

The Six Thinking Hats represented along with their primary functions (and associated colors) are

Blue—Managing and organizing the discussion, including "topping" and "tailing" it via the introduction and summary.

White—Facts, data, and requirements gathering from the assembled people.

Green—The ideas and relevant creative thinking about the issue(s), more than likely interspersed with the donning of yellow hats, the so-what test.

Yellow—The so-what test applied to ideas and suggestions as to the benefits of the proposal or idea along with the feasibility, sustainability, possible costs, and other real-life items that others might ask about when the plan is delivered.

Black—This is an interesting one as it smacks to me of the old walkthrough technique used in reviewing coding, designs, and the like for inconsistencies and other gotchas.* This is a devil's advocate role where constructive attempts are made to pick out areas that may cause issues or need reinforcement.

Red—The fire-at-will hat where people express ideas based on intuition, emotion, or simple gut feel about topics and might be positive, encouraging, or warnings from previous experience.

---

* Gotchas are unexpected things that come out of the project woodwork and bite you.

A Few Six Hats Notes

- Again, the frequency and order of use is dictated by circumstances but they shouldn't be used in tiny slices and mixed. For example, don't put your black hat on every time someone makes a suggestion and then pull it to pieces. Make a note for the black hat session when it arrives, that is, keep it under your hat.
- These components do not constitute a mandatory format but are valuable in structuring meetings and discussions, especially keeping people who scatter-gun the meeting with random ideas and comments.
- If attendees are familiar with the technique, don't even mention hats; just put them on at the appropriate times.
- There are obviously benefits to a structure that, though not rigorously pre-scriptive, has a tangible shape and allows for free exchange of ideas within the framework.
- Even apparently silly ideas may have a value if explored. My experience with intelligent people who send out ideas like bullets from a machine gun have approximately the following hit rate:
  - One-third are totally daft.
  - One-third have merit but are deemed not feasible because of other factors, like cost or manpower.
  - One-third are good and worth pursuing.
  So give them a hearing, especially if they arise in the red hat zone.

Six Hats Value

As I mentioned before, every facet of the Six Thinking Hats is not new; most of it represents common sense and discipline plus a few other existing techniques. Its value lies in its simplicity, discipline without force, and the ease with which it can be adopted and implemented. Other methods, such as PDWs (project definition workshops), Delphi, risk analysis, and others can complement the Six Thinking Hats method and results or even influence them. The hats can be used in solo thinking or, better still in a two-person discussion and then influencing techniques can also be used.

There are any number of articles, books, and reviews of the Six Thinking Hats technique to choose from, but a good starter is the *Wikipedia* entry (https://en.wikipedia.org/wiki/Six_Thinking_Hats). Another reference about some course/workshop prereading material that should prove useful if you wish to pursue the topic further is "The Six Thinking Hats: A Creativity Process for Results Driven Groups:" http://debonoforschools.com/pdfs/Six-Thinking-Hats-Pre-Reading.pdf.

Meetings Can Be Hilarious

Fun meetings. Meetings can be inspirational, boring, or hilarious, and an example of the last type occurred at a local government account meeting between IBM and a customer. First, it was an odd meeting because we were all seated on chairs (not desks or tables) in a circle from the beginning. This odd configuration got the gathering off to a bad start since it was impossible to see any material that a speaker wanted to show.

It was late afternoon and as is their wont, government staff like to go home on time or early; at least this group did. As the meeting (agenda-less) proceeded, the customer people began to drift away, saying they had to be home early or were in a car share scheme for transport to and from work. Eventually, the only people left were the IBM salesman and myself, talking to each other. This was ironic since the meeting was called by the customer.

Often, these meetings were arranged to be off-site and we thought this a bit odd but went along with it. After a time, we realized that the reason for this was that the customer staff could claim expenses for a lunch as they were "working away from the office"! This might account for the plethora of meetings we were invited to by this customer, most of which produced nothing worth documenting or following up; the classic nonmeeting.

Dining room course. While not exactly a meeting, I was giving an informal course of OCR programming to an electricity board to about 10 people. The course took place at about the time the breakfast trolley came round with drinks and food: coffee, tea, and sandwiches, including bacon sandwiches. One of the attendees, a voluminous individual usually had a small feast at this time of the day but was thwarted by his mandatory attendance at this course. Undeterred, he purchased six bacon rolls and ate three of them while I was giving the course. I asked him politely why he didn't eat the other three. In reply, he said he wasn't a glutton and was saving the others to consume at a break in the proceedings.

Moral: I think that the essence of these tales is that the organizer/teacher must take control of proceedings and steer them to a sensible conclusion, even if it means upsetting people a little. A trick to stop the backend of meetings becoming talking shops of any other business (AOB) is to put AOB first on the agenda. Make sure attendees know this and then chop the meeting at the end of the last item of the agenda. This clarifies people's minds and mandates saying things upfront and not mull over them during the meeting and bore everyone witless in AOB and use it as a grievance platform.

> Apparently, the world celebrates World Productivity Day on June 20 each year and the following blog post discusses why this is apparently necessary.* It certainly convinces me that I was right to emphasize meetings in this book.

---

* "Yes, I Fell Asleep during That Meeting!" http://www.infoworld.com/native?prx_t=bvMBAC 9IEAsSkMA.

Preparing for this blog post, I looked up some stats about unproductive meetings. Here are a few:

- Only 60% of the time you spend at work is actually productive
- Meetings of over 1 hour are usually considered unproductive
- The average IT staff member walks 42 km a year to start-up meetings
- 91% of professionals admit to daydreaming during meetings
- 39% of professionals have actually ever fallen asleep during a meeting

This underlines the need for planning and running effective and productive meetings.

A Last Word on Meetings

A nice article on the DZone website about scrum meetings suggests that to ensure short, intensive meetings, the participants should be standing.* In this mode, the meeting won't last that long. Sounds OK to me. (An IBM CEO some 35 years ago had a high desk and managed most of his morning correspondence and phone calls standing at it.)

Join Up! See the IT World

Some wiseacre once said "No man is an island," a phrase repeated ad nauseam in IT papers and books. However, it does have a meaning but in various interpretations. My take on this in IT learning is that you should learn and take advice from trustworthy sources, remembering the consensus rule in taking things as gospel from a single source:

- *People.* Peers, seminar presenters, meetings, topic groups, and so forth, and don't be afraid to ask questions, a thing you cannot do when reading some IT text.
- *Computer press.* I have found these quite useful and objective and the ones I tend to follow in the United Kingdom are *Computing and Computer Weekly* plus associated information sources. Subscribe if you can.
- *Normal press.* Beware here if you are a rookie IT person. Very often you will find articles in these august journals written by normal journalists who patently know nothing about IT. They pick up a hot topic, read something

---

* "How NOT to Run a Scrum Meeting," https://dzone.com/articles/how-not-to-run-scrum
-meetings-for-software-develop?edition=138252&utm_source=Daily%20Digest&utm
_medium=email&utm_content=Daily_Digest_A3&utm_campaign=dd%202016-02-04
&userid=1232889.

about it, and write their article, usually regurgitating from some report they have seen. I have read some outlandish nonsense in newspapers and have written to *The Times* (London) a few times and had letters published. There can be useful information there, but beware of opinions and conclusions drawn by first-class journalist who are at the same time IT illiterates.

■ *Websites.* These are my bread and butter sources, again taking care in reaching conclusions or believing statements made therein: disks are dead, the future is X, and similar prophetic outpourings. Use my consensus rule and, in addition, assess the status and possible vested interests of the writer of any particular text.

I have found *Wikipedia* an invaluable and mainly accurate source of IT information and information in general. Many people are wary of this source and don't trust it, but I have found spot on accuracy in topics I am very familiar with.

The websites I use most that follow my IT interests closely include the following:
- Availability Digest: http://www.availabilitydigest.com/
- Data Center Knowledge: http://www.datacenterknowledge.com/
- DatacenterDynamics: http://www.datacenterdynamics.com/
- Aberdeen TechPro Essentials: http://www.techproessentials.com/
- APMdigest: http://apmdigest.com/
- IT BusinessEdge: http://www.itbusinessedge.com/
- Computer Weekly: http://www.computerweekly.com/
- InfoWorld: http://www.infoworld.com/
- Wikipedia: http://www.wikipedia.com

There are a number of IT glossaries and dictionaries available on the Internet. Search "IT glossary" and "IT dictionary" to see what suits you in the resulting hits.

■ *Online presentation materials.* There are a number of very good presentations on the web, especially from Universities. When you search for hits on a particular topic, seek out these hits.

■ Don't pass over erudite *academic papers*; they often have abstracts which give a clue to the state of the art of some topic and sometimes give an overview without reading the sometimes impenetrable body of the paper.

■ *Sites* related tangentially to your interests, for example, DevOps, big data, and so on, but when they start to deliver content-free material, as many do, reconsider your subscription. I weary of articles with titles along the lines of "ROI of SCSI Channels," and "Finance Director's Guide to SCSI-2," when all I really want is an objective article on SCSI channels.

■ Join your *country's computer society*, the equivalent of the British Computer Society (BCS). You may need credentials or to pass a test of some kind to be accepted.

- Follow Gartner's *Magic Quadrant* assessment papers, which cover various products and groups of products such as data center infrastructure management (DCIM). They also contain the assessment criteria Gartner uses to evaluate product and product suppliers in its Magic Quadrant matrix. These assessment criteria can often be generalized for application to other products or services.
- There are other websites you may find useful and probably the best way to find them is to do a search on topics that interest you. Alternatively, just perform a search on the word or phrase you are interested in but be prepared for 301,867,103 (approximately) hits, of which only about 10 are relevant.

Communications Skills

Humans and even animals have been communicating with each other since learning to walk upright. From grunts to modern communication media and techniques is a long way to have come in a mere 100,000 years but to hear some presentations and read some reports you would think it has all been in vain. Remember that communication is very often two-way and the choice of medium may be dictated by the nature of this.

I have some personal preferences for communication media and if I had to choose only three, I would go for face-to-face with an expert, a good report/article, and presentations either by transparencies or suitable video. What I don't like are webinars, which I often find tedious, marketing-oriented, while masquerading as objective, and the inability to write notes or ask questions in a simple manner is frustrating. (Webinar devotees and promoters please take note.) Videos are useful if well structured and pertinent. I have found YouTube videos on aspects of using Windows 10 useful since the latter is a nightmare if you are moving from Windows 7. In summary, you can use whatever media suits your personal needs, but if you are communicating with other people, you need to select and master the appropriate media you use.

Writing Skills

This is not attempt to teach anyone how to write correctly, both grammatically and technically, since the former is country-and-culture dependent and the latter is topic dependent. Whatever you are writing in the IT arena will be read by people with different needs for understanding the messages you are projecting. A technical message will need manipulation if it is to be grasped by a nontechnical person. If it a purely technical message, then a single viewpoint is all the writing needs. If it is a technical message that relates to a business or science issue, then the message must be massaged to cater to those nontechnical viewpoints. Many scientific papers have an abstract at the beginning to tell a potential reader what the paper is all about and, normally, uses words that indicate the level of technical details in the paper. This is done to inform any reader what sort of skills he or she might need to understand the paper and to deter others from reading it and reporting it in a blog as rubbish.

Writing Skills Overview

This is not a language skills section; more a discussion of how to write, what to write, and what not to write. The main thing to remember when writing is a structure, the lack of which has caused me endless pain and extra effort. I had a Latin teacher at school who talked to us one day (in English) about writing books or sizeable reports. His advice was that before you write any text, think about and create a table of contents so that it flows logically and covers everything you want to say. Leave it at that for a day, then go back to it and you'll find that you don't quite like it and will alter it. A trick I've found is to write the sections as separate files and, when happy, embed them under the appropriate heading.

If you use a system where you can put an embed/imbed statement in the contents list that will automatically embed when you print the tables of contents, you are on a winner with this method. If you don't have this facility, just name the separate files suitably so you can find them to physically embed them in the growing document when happy with them. I use a naming convention like naming an embed file something like *performance-monitors-addon*.

You will of course need to make some changes when they are actually embedded in the master file, but it is safer than creating the text while in the master file. When it comes to the crunch, whatever you are comfortable with is probably the correct route.

Writing Hints

1. I have said somewhere that you have two ears and one mouth and, in normal conversations, they should be used in that ratio. A parallel law applies to writing. When I did some voluntary work at local schools, there were sometimes sessions where the pupils were asked to write about some topic using a computer text processing system. The pupils went straight to the computer and started pounding away at the keyboard, writing in the main disconnected ideas. This is a problem common to mankind, and that obviously includes myself. To get out the manuscripts for books, I had to finally knuckle down to handwriting ideas and headings on a piece of paper and play around with this until the ideas formed. You will rarely get an idea or a way of expressing yourself while typing, especially if it needs 100% concentration just to type correctly.

   Hint: Use the ratio 2:1 in thinking to keying (maybe 1:1) and certainly not 0:1.

2. Do your thinking in pieces, not one almighty meditation. You will find that different ideas come at different times. Certainly, in writing this book, my ideas and memories came at various times which makes for a richer written offering. Driving a car without the radio or any other source of noise is the most productive thinking environment I know, particularly on a long drive.

3. Carry a small notebook and pen with you—I have those items in all the top-coats I go out in—to jot down fleeting ideas and facts before they disappear. A large part of this book was conceived from notes I made while traveling on buses or even walking around town. A blank mind seems to be the most receptive to ideas and memories so they need to be captured at source. You cannot think clearly watching TV or listening to the radio, or at least I can't.

4. Bounce your ideas and possibly a table of contents off a friendly peer or even someone outside your IT environment if the writing is for general consumption. If you can get someone to read and comment on the actual text, possibly at various points in its development, so much the better. When you write, you sometimes become oblivious to errors in it since you know what it is supposed to say and convince yourself it actually says that when you proofread it. A common fault, probably invented by me, is to write along the lines "This is dealt with in Chapter 4" when either it isn't dealt with anywhere or it is dealt with but in Chapter 7. A casual reviewer will often spot this type of error.

5. The use of boilerplate material refers to stored fixed text for reuse by yourself and others. It saves an awful lot of time and a writer can concentrate on the variable, audience-specific aspects of the manuscript. Examples might be:
   - Company information
   - Product information
   - Services information
   - Terms and conditions
   - Other reproducible material, such as diagrams

All these can be modified as necessary.

Writing Reports, Tenders, or Proposals

The preceding rules and suggestions apply in this section too; in fact in my opinion, they are timeless universal laws.

Choose Your Weapons

In writing anything that is meant to convey information, a message, or to convince the reader of something, you will need to use all the means at your disposal. When I was with IBM, major sales losses (say, of system X) were followed by a review of the situation. One thing that was almost always asked was "Did you make use of all the resources at your disposal?" This meant did you use our X specialists, give the prospect a demonstration of X, outline the new leasing option for X, etc.? Negative answers spelled bad news. If you write an unsuccessful white paper, report, presentation, and the like, you might ask yourself similar questions. What are these resources? Don't use videos or media needing special software to run it unless the reader can access it. The basic message is KISS: keep it simple stupid.

First impressions count and if you want the reader to start your paper/article, it must look attractive. Acres of dense prose without headings or illustrations is a big turnoff as are papers with all known forms of visual formats known to man. It will make the reader think that it is probably beyond his capability to understand and move on.

With this in mind, what we need are at least the following:

- First, avoid byte-consuming pictures of people smiling and chatting, often round a whiteboard or a meeting table, resulting in a 5 Mbyte document with a mere 10 Kbytes of useful information. I usually bin these before I begin. If it does not convey information, leave it out. Art and pretty photographs are for galleries.
- Standard, well-constructed *prose*. This is a comfortable lead-in to your message(s). Try not to use trendy words or phrases to try to look with it, avoid overlong sentences, and break up long tracts of text with subheadings or similar break points. A sentence should ideally convey a single message and not be about 14 ideas in one fell swoop.
- *Bullet or numbered lists*, but not to excess. The output should not be littered with them as they are an adjunct to prose, which allows the reader to pick out points that might otherwise be buried in prose.
- *Diagrams and charts* to convey information, remembering that a picture is worth a thousand words.
- *References* to supporting sources of information. Frequent references to books is not advised as (a) the reader is unlikely to have access to them and (b) he certainly isn't going to buy the book to read 1 or 2 pages. Quoted text* and website links (URLs) are a good way of getting supplementary information across.
- *Date your paper* and give some sort of contact information for comments or other requirements generated by the report, article, and so forth.

One of the biggest headaches in my life in producing books or papers is the uncertainty about the currency of the information in undated written material, especially website material. Phrases like "A has the biggest share of the market" or "Y is the fastest processor available" can lead to lack of credibility if quoted elsewhere.

---

* You may need permission from the author(s) for this, but if you are advertising their wares there shouldn't be a problem.

The Viewpoint Approach to Documentation

The viewpoint approach to documentation is a topic dear to my heart. It recognizes that there are a number of ways of expressing things and presenting them to different types and levels of people inside and outside an organization. I have seen supposed IT architecture diagrams that look like NASA wiring diagrams for the Saturn rocket presented to a businessperson. At the other extreme is the sketch on a cigarette packet detailing the whole system and shown to the operations manager. This is, as the saying goes, not a good thing. However, it is a good thing to slant descriptions and diagrams to the intended recipient and not assume that one size fits all:

- Don't show the chief financial officer a diagram containing server and network components plus the relevant software, including release and patch levels, supplemented by microcode or netbios specifications.
- Don't show the chief operations manager a diagram containing invoice flows, expected return on investment (ROI), and Sarbanes-Oxley compliance status.
- Don't show anybody the network diagrams except people interested in networks.

I have seen these don'ts actually done to the detriment of the person and the project.

I think you get the drift: If you want to communicate effectively with someone, speak his or her language. What I am saying is that you need to understand the concept of viewpoints in all documentation or other media.

The next three points are areas where you must bear in mind what viewpoints you are trying to express; if there is more than one viewpoint being expressed, make sure that the text for each is clearly identifiable by the reader as being aimed at him or her.

Invitation to Tender (*ITT*). Many organizations are purchasing new systems to support new or migrated/modernized applications. In many such cases customers find the availability of numerous viable systems suppliers quite daunting. The question often asked is if they all the same. The answer will depend on a number of factors, including the customer's viewpoint and the nature of his requirements. No systems supplier is superior in all aspects of a solution as it applies to the requirements of a particular customer.

Preparation of the requirement specification or ITT should be based on customer requirements, volumes, and on user expectations for the new service. It would also include a specification of the appropriate environment (website, OLTP, science work, etc.). The ITT prepared in this way will contain a format to be followed by the responding vendors so that analysis and comparison of the bids is made much easier.

What it should not contain as the main thrust of the document are prejudged answers, powers, and so forth (e.g., we want 3200 GB of storage on a 120 squilliflops dual processor painted green). Tell them what you want and evaluate responses against your business requirements and then check for a viable supporting technical environment, even if you have a feel for it already. Two ideas are better than one.

Reports. The biggest fault in report writing, I think, is in the failure to identify who it is aimed at. It is essential in my mind to decide just what sort of people you are addressing with the report. Your peers within your skill group, you peers outside it, the CEO, the CIO, and so on.

Proposal response. This is a minefield I have negotiated many times, hopefully learning all the way and on which I am able to offer advice here. If the ITT or request for information (RFI) has a mandatory response format, you must follow it (see preceding ITT discussion). If you think you will be short-changing your solution, you should ask permission to add something to the response. The potential problem here, apart from a refusal, is that some customers feel duty bound to tell others bidding for the contract about it and allow them the same option.

This may not present a big problem but might well do if the reason for request was that something vital was missing from their ITT to fulfill stated business requirements. This then gives your opponents an opportunity to neutralize your advantage over them with your solution. This sort of fair-mindedness is typical of public sector procurements, as is the prejudged solution in an ITT.

Another problem I encountered in public sector requests was the number of function and technology must-haves increased each time you received a request, as each one purloined those from a previous request and added their own. With this kind of mega-requirements list, it was possible to select your vendor directly, even in what is an open tender, by making the specification such that only the favored supplier could match it. Clever ploy wasn't it?

Getting Information across Visually

Years ago, when operating systems were in flux and UNIX (Ken Olsen's snake oil) was coming to the fore, there were a number of related magazines in circulation. One I used to take was a workstation magazine and in one edition it was reviewing a new workstation in numeric detail and was written in the vein: "The Hokey Cokey 2000 is blazingly fast with a SPEC rating to die for and more than twice the storage of its nearest competitor. It features ultrafast graphics and ..." This belongs in a Shakespeare play or Hemingway novel, not a in technical appraisal. The phrase "a picture is worth a thousand words" was never truer than in the IT universe. You should make use of graphs, tables (as the writer above should have), and diagrams with the appropriate text appended. Although these visuals may be worth a thousand words, they will still need some explanation or a legend attached so the visuals don't look overbusy.

Attention to Detail

It is an unfortunate fact of life that to improve something by an extra 5% or 10% often takes an increase of 100% in effort expended. Sometimes it is worth that effort, sometimes not; it all depends on the task at hand. Let me illustrate this with a couple of examples.

■ I was once in a top-class restaurant and ordered the chef's signature dish, which was quite famous and popular. When I was served the dish, the signature part was magnificent but the vegetables were either undercooked or cold. Result? A potentially memorable meal spoiled and a question in my mind as to whether I would risk that restaurant again. Apply this experience to your customer and think about it.

■ The game of rugby in Britain is now fully professional with the top leagues in both codes of rugby very competitive. Some years ago, one team began to emerge as the top dog, winning most trophies that came their way. It revealed its secret some time later (when other teams had caught up). They had studied Australia's methods who, in turn, had previously studied American football methods of training and preparation. These methods upped the performance of the team by a few percent, enough to eclipse other teams in most games but involved a lot of effort to achieve but the returns were enormous. The method involved careful diet; a prescribed set of foods with high-energy foods the 2 or 3 days before a game, plus a scientific separation of methods for training (energy, stamina, speed, etc.). Today, most teams adopt this approach and the search goes on for getting that extra few percentage points over their rivals.

Lesson: The decision as to whether to invest this 100% for a 5% gain depends on the importance of the outcome to you and/or your organization. If it is an internal presentation, it can be less slick unless you have time to burn; a presentation to a potential customer who wants to spend megabucks may well repay any extra effort. Imagine the team charged putting men into space saying, after a rudimentary design and build, "That is a good enough job men, let's go have some beer." The improvement process is an ongoing task.

A Word on Documentation

If you use visuals or text from another source, cite the source and acknowledge it and ensure that you have permission from the author/source to quote these. Don't be afraid to contact the author(s), as they are mostly only too happy to help you with any queries about their work.

If you think the information presented is incorrect or misleading, try to contact the source and politely make your point, but make sure you are on solid ground. I have done this a few times and received an acknowledgement from that source.

One point I made was to the author of an article on IT queuing theory where he did not relate what he said to practical IT life.* The rest of the article seemed sound but did not involve lateral thinking outside the math of the subject—a salutary lesson.

Presentation Skills

Your presentation to an audience is your market stall; it should be set out attractively and contain what the customer wants to see and buy. It's as simple as that, assuming you know how to set out a stall and determine what the customer wants.

You may use presentations, or variations on one presentation, for different reasons:

- To tell people about yourself, perhaps in job seeking
- To educate people on a topic
- To sell something to people by showing it and explaining the benefits
- To update people on various topics, for example, an internal announcement or a staff reorganization update

You will want to vary how you do things depending on the audience you are addressing.

My Basic Rules

I was often baffled in presentations and by papers that described in graphic detail the wonderful features of some product or other and, very often, it was not quite clear what the problem was to which this product is the solution. I realized the solution when I was listening to a presentation on "application servers." First, I had heard this phrase before and thought aren't all server applications servers. No, the presenter was actually talking about a layer of software aiding access to various functions, as I soon discovered. The way he developed his explanation was by outlining what one would need to do in the absence of this software to achieve a certain result. This was done by explaining that one would first have to do X, and all that entailed, then Y, and so on. He then showed how this application server provided the function to enable the task to be done much more easily. In other words, he spelled out the problem to which the subject of his talk was the solution in one of the clearest expositions of a subject I have come across. We should all try to do this when presenting anything that provides some sort of solution; talk about the old world issues and then the new world with your solution.

Another similar situation arose when I was trying to grapple with a Sun Microsystems systems management product. The literature was full of information

---

* The case in point was a statement to the effect that the service time of a particular transaction was fixed, therefore I pointed out that in the case of a real transaction, the service (execution) time would depend on the many possible paths through a transaction depending on what it was invoked for.

on it being a three-tier solution, what it ran on, how it did things, and so forth but never actually said what it was actually doing and why such a product was necessary. In other words, the literature told the IT pro nothing of importance about the product and its functions. He couldn't really care less if it was a 3-tier or 56-tier product and the fact that it worked using optimized code and so on.

I am so hung up about this kind of literature that I actually produced a spoof data sheet showing exactly how not to produce a data sheet. At the time of this writing, I am looking for a site to publish it on.*

Presentation List

- Does your introduction grab participants' attention and explain your objectives?
- Do you follow this *presentation route map* by clearly defining the points of the presentation?
- Are these main points in logical sequence and don't cover, for example, consequences before cause?
- Are your visuals consistent in style, clear, and not overelaborate?
- Do the main points need support from visual aids?
- Does your closing summarize the presentation clearly and concisely?
- Is the conclusion strong?
- Have your tied the conclusion to the introduction?

Sample Presentation Rules

The base rule in presentations, at least the way I was shown, is to tell them what you are going to tell them, tell them, and then tell them what you have just told them. In other words, outline an agenda, present the body of the information, and at the end give a summary.

1. Know your audience's background and thus understand their expectations. If you use an industry analogy, make it their industry unless it is derogatory. If you use a dress retailer example when talking to a petrochemical audience they will unconsciously assume that what you are saying doesn't apply to them.
2. Try not to be nervous; the audience came to learn something that you are going to talk about, not trip you up. They are not TV presenters grilling a politician. They want you to succeed and they want to learn something; remember that.
3. Know your audience. Are they gurus or beginners? Plan accordingly and don't present intricate math about third normal forms to an audience of business managers. I exaggerate here but I've seen it done and I think you get my drift.

---

* If it does find a home, I hope nobody believes the spoof and tries to buy the product!

4. From the start and during the presentation, look at the audience in *scan mode*. This means looking at them, side to side and front to back to bring them into things. Don't look at the transparency or your notes except a glance for reference and position in your talk, in other words, address your audience and not your materials.

5. Seek understanding every so often by looking at someone and asking "Is that clear?" If he or she says not really, ask the rest of the audience if anyone feels the same. Often you will get a relieved yes, in which case cover the point again in a different way until you get the understanding nods from them.

6. Make sure you know the content and order of your material. Don't say "I will cover five main points" and put up a transparency with four or six bullet points on it. In addition, if you get the transparency order wrong and start talking about X when the transparency is about Y, then the audience will lose confidence in you.

7. If you have handouts for the presentation, give them out afterward, otherwise most of the audience will start reading them no matter what you say. If possible, choose a room for the event that does not have the walls covered in interesting pictures and large text, especially ones showing desirable vacation destinations. The audience might not spend much time reading them but their minds will be in Acapulco or Venice during your presentation. Not good.

8. Practice your rehearsal presentation in front of colleagues for feedback, especially if it is an important one.

9. Modulate your tone of voice to show enthusiasm or other emotion at the correct points, for example, "That is a wonderful feature of ..." (*elation*), "This will be the death of your project ..." (*sadness*).

10. Inject some humor where appropriate and germane to the topic, but don't give a one-man stand-up comedy show. Use humor to illustrate a point you are making. I used the picture in Figure 2.7 in the book *High Availability IT Services* to complement a discussion on disaster recovery (DR).

11. Be animated appropriately but don't look like an acrobat or give an impression of the wandering minstrel. Use facial features where possible to support your tone of voice, which in turn relates to what you are saying.

12. If you have a colleague watching, ask them to make a note of things that need attention (review, clarification, etc.) the next time you give that presentation.

13. Learn and use the signals to tell a fellow presenter that he/she is overrunning or should stop is a few tens of seconds. The first is achieved by making a wrapping movement with your outstretched hands (not arms) hands on top of one another, 30 cm from your chests and at that height; the second by moving hands, palms down horizontally, 10 cm apart and side to side in opposite directions. If you are at the back of the audience, these signals should be invisible to them.

14. Know your subject and materials. Make sure all the things to be used function correctly (pens, markers, projectors, etc.) and have backups if possible. Exploding projector bulbs were an occupational hazard in my early days with IBM.

Figure 2.7   Humor in presentations. (With permission from Cloudtweaks.)

15. If there is a key subject you and your colleagues would like to learn about and there is no course for it, formal or informal, organize one yourself. I did it many times, often as a simple lunchtime briefing if the speaker is local. All I did was find the speaker, book a room, and circulate details of it to assess the number of potential attendees. If I can do it, you can.

16. Make sure you arrive in good time, greet the audience as they arrive (if feasible), and that all audience members, wherever they sit in the room, can see and hear what you are presenting.

17. Don't overdo the tips given in the points above, especially the comedy (Figure 2.8).

Figure 2.8   Don't overdo the comedy.

However, here are some one-liners you might like to use in presentations but sparingly and at the appropriate moment and place in the topic.

- There is nothing like a good beginning to a presentation and that was nothing like a good beginning.
- This is a statistic and should be treated as such. Did you know that a man is knocked down by a car in New York every 8 minutes—and he's getting pretty fed up with it.
- I never forget a face, but in your case I'll make an exception.
- I was reading X's book on this topic and when I put it down I couldn't pick it up again.
- I'm not decrying X's work but the covers on his books are too far apart.
- I will take questions during the presentation but I must tell you there are three types of reply I give: type 1 are those I can answer; type 2, those I can't answer; and type 3, those I won't answer.
- A man asked another man, "Are you married?" to which the reply was, "Yes. I'm married to an angel." First man: "You are lucky, mine is still alive."

Having said all this, like many ointments, use sparingly.

The phantom presentation. I must have given the perfect phantom presentation at a data center event in Scotland many years ago. A delegate came up to me at about noon and said, "I enjoyed your presentation this morning; it was great!" I was very pleased with this compliment, especially since I wasn't due to present until 3 p.m. that same afternoon. He must have been psychic.

Keep 'Em Listening

One thing we've all done or been close to in presentations is falling asleep. There can be a lot of reasons for this: too much lunch and accompanying liquid, tiredness and the narcoleptic nature of the presentation material and delivery. This short presentation I came across says it all for me and I hope it does for you: "Why Do We Fall Asleep during Lectures?," (https://www.quora.com/Why-do-we-fall-asleep -during-lectures). Robert Frost, an instructor and flight controller at NASA, wrote an article on Quora on this topic.*

John Medina, in his book *Brain Rules*, introduces data that forms an "attention" graph, showing the degree of attention paid to a speaker over the period of about an hour. A schematic is shown in Figure 2.9. You will see that the attention flags after about 10 minutes, which is apparently normal.† The trick is to introduce some

---

* https://www.quora.com/, a Q&A website with lots of useful discussions.
† This is supposedly the reason that YouTube prefers videos that are less than 10 minutes long. Try to remember this in your presentations, perhaps marking your slides in some way to remind you.

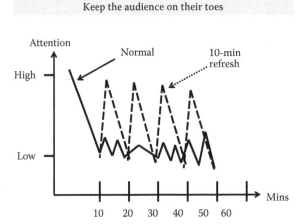

Figure 2.9 Audience attention spans.

variation in the presentation or lecture to reestablish the 10-minute *keen attention* period, also indicated in Figure 2.9. The dotted lines represent a return to near-full attention after a variation by the speaker, followed by another *stumble and recover*. The solutions to this *attention droop* can take several forms:

- Switch to an anecdote about the topic at hand.
- Involve the audience (or students) by seeking opinions or even asking someone a question directly. The latter is really a *sit up and listen to me* technique.
- Make the interaction between the speaker and audience two-way by any other means you can think of. A participating audience will remain awake.
- Remember that however knowledgeable you are, you can still render an audience comatose.

Don't just ramble, look at the faces of your audience for the telltale signs of *attention drift* and act accordingly. Another good way to make them pay attention from the beginning is by addressing every other sentence to a different person, looking directly at them. Cycle your gaze randomly round the audience so they don't know who is going to be next. It works; I know because I've been there.

Don't Shoot the Messenger

There will be occasions where the presenter is obviously a bit out of his depth on a subject you are familiar with; don't try to humiliate him or her by imperiously pointing out the errors he is making. Leave it to the end of the presentation or, better still, take the presenter aside at an interval and explain your concerns. A gentle middle ground is to speak up and add something to the topic in a helpful manner, assuming this is an appropriate option.

Communication Factors

When people write, all the communication delivered to the audience is in the words and pictures. In a presentation, there are several communication methods available to the presenter apart from the straight voice: transparencies, voice modulation, facial expression, and body language and movement. The factors that most influence a speaker's impact on the audience are as follows:

- 55% how you look
- 38% how you speak and sound
- 7% what you say, that is, content*

This list shows a basic split of the impact of communication on an audience. However, the interpretation of the 7% has connotations that are discussed and questioned in the paper "The Truth about 7%-38%-55%" and in a *Wikipedia* article where the effects on nonverbal and body language communication are discussed (with references), and points out that much communication (more than 7% that is mainly voice) is delivered via transparencies.†

Message: The top and bottom of this is that whatever figures are finally agreed on by the world at large, the fact is that your impact on an audience (or potential customer) will be influenced significantly if you use all the influencing delivery techniques. Whatever the percentages are, you will need to use the delivery technique spectrum effectively to convey your messages to the audience.

I remember my first basic class in IBM where we were all videoed while doing a very short presentation. My body and facial language was minimal as I kept wandering off the screen, in both left and right directions—exit stage left, exit stage right! I soon conquered my wanderlust in time to meet and present to customers.

Visual Impact Skills

The use and overuse of visual impact material can enhance or degrade your presentation, respectively. Subtle use of shapes and colors enhances; overelaboration and inclusion of irrelevant detail confuses. Variations of shapes is also an attention keeper, for example using different charts for displaying information instead of always using your favorite 2D pie chart in the 49ers colors. Some information

---

* Albert Mehrabian, *Silent Messages* (Belmont, CA: Wadsworth, 1971).
† "The Truth about 7%-38%-55%," http://www.speakschmeak.com/2007/08/truth-about-7-38 -55.html; "Albert Mehrabian," https://en.wikipedia.org/wiki/Albert_Mehrabian.

and data displays look better and convey more information when presented in an appropriate style.

There are various ways of representing data and numbers depending on the message you are trying to convey, four of them are covered briefly here. (Also see Figure 2.10.)

a. *Kiviat chart*—Also known as a radar chart, a kiviat chart is useful for showing multiple, related quantities in a radial form. The example shown in Figure 2.10 is illustrates the various IT resource utilizations that affect throughput and response times of a system. It's also useful in showing, say, the characteristics of two generations of a product. For an IT processor, these resources might be memory cache memory, MegaFlops, and so on. The older model will form a spider's web in the chart and outside it will lie the same characteristics for the new processor. This is a great one-stop way of doing a visual comparison of parameters related to two similar products.

b. *Bar chart*—This is an obvious chart and the simplest way to visualize discrete numbers that are related in some way, for example, the MIPs performance of generations of a product over time; vertical axis is MIPs, horizontal axis year of announcement.

c. *Sunburst chart*—The sunburst chart shows a hierarchy as a series of rings. Each ring represents the children of the ring it encloses and the area of each slice corresponds to its value. The outer ring can have a color gradient. Not every segment within a ring is expanded so that some are broken down further

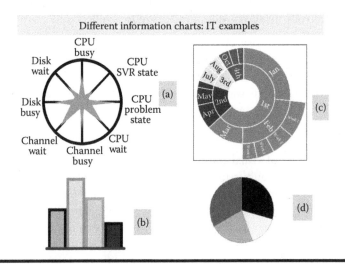

Figure 2.10 Visuals: Types of information charts: (a) kiviat, (b) bar, (c) sunburst, and (d) pie.

so they protrude more than other segments. They all represent some entity or other.*

d. *Pie chart*—A variation on presenting data about several items in the form of slices of a pie, either contiguous or broken out as if about to be eaten. They can be 2D or 3D. A typical pie chart might show the percentages of the working population in various trades, each slice differentiated by color or shading.

Equations are a special case of visual information. The main thing about using them is to ensure they are in a format that can be embedded in a text file for publishing purposes. The Windows Word Equation Editor is what is used but that does not mean it is the best.

Final Thoughts

If your presentation medium is transparencies and you wish to develop a theme, do not develop it by uncovering one line at a time; for some reason this irritates an audience intensely. If you are using electronic projection methods, present the theme one slide at a time, each with the extra line(s) as appropriate. Remember, once an audience has lost faith in you and established you are a professional bore, it is very hard to get them back on track. They switch off and dream of the next speaker.

Amusing aside. A speaker arrived at a conference and went to the room assigned for his talk. There was just one person, a man, seated ready for the start. The speaker gave his presentation just as if there were 50 people listening, a very professional approach. At the end, he addressed his audience of one and thanked him for his attendance and patience. "No problem," replied the *audience*. "I'm the next speaker."

Thinking Skills

Lateral thinking is a relatively new term in lifestyle literature and is often referred to as *thinking outside the box*. In essence it means looking beyond your immediate discipline or environment to solve a problem, even if it is outside your comfort zone. It is the equivalent of what I call lateral vision in the game of rugby. Lateral vision, in my terms, means knowing where other people on the field of play are, both your own team and the opposition. Knowing where the nearest opposition player is vital to avoid getting smashed receiving a silly pass of the ball from one of your own side.† Players with this vision know what is going on around them and can sense when the opposition is near and how they are moving so that he can offload the ball to someone of his own side in a position to make progress.

---

* See https://en.wikipedia.org/wiki/Sunburst.

† These are known in rugby as "hospital passes," a ball given to you when you are within thumping distance of an opposition player and when you are least expecting it.

Such a player also knows where the best-placed player in his team is and passes the ball to him and not just the nearest player to him. I played rugby for 30 years and never developed this skill, but it can be achieved to a certain extent by trying. Let me give some examples of lateral (outside-the-box) thinking.

Example 1—In about 1914, Niels Bohr,* a physicist, developed a model of the atom, based on Lord Rutherford's work, which comprised a central core (the nucleus) and a set of orbiting electrons. To calculate the particles' motions and other properties of this atomic model with classical (Newtonian) mechanics did not yield calculations that matched the results of various experiments. In particular, it was difficult to explain the photoelectric effect, a phenomenon where electrons are emitted from a surface irradiated with visible light. It was seen that however powerful the beam of light, the emission of electrons depended more on the wavelength of the light than its intensity. In a nutshell, this led to quantum theory and wave mechanics, which was an example of the lateral thinking about this issue, that is, outside the accepted classical mechanics of Newton and others.

Example 2—U.S. engineers were trying to develop a pen or biro to write with in the weightlessness of space; as we know, writing with one of these implements upside down loses the ink flow. Apparently they managed a design after spending $2 million. The Soviets had a similar project but it cost far less than that; their solution was to use pencil.

Example 3—I watched a TV program about the Colosseum in Rome. The crew and engineers were trying to reproduce the manual elevator that the Romans apparently used to lift animals, gladiators, and other items from the basements to the arena. This was proving difficult using manpower and pulleys only. After a while, someone thought that a technique used in Roman ships for lifting masts and other heavy items might be appropriate. It was.

One technique for streamlining thinking in meetings is to employ the Six Thinking Hats methodology of Edward de Bono and is a boon to personal thinking, covered earlier in the section "Meetings."

Listening Skills

I don't need to learn about listening; I do it all the time, and my hearing is perfect. Probably, but where does the information you receive go after passing your auditory membranes? It may sound trite but there is a knack to listening to maximum effect, which involves a few "blocking" techniques.

---

* As an aside, it is interesting to note that Bohr was an avid fan of Western movies but could never understand the plots. Friends used to accompany him to the cinema to explain things as they happened.

Learning to ignore extraneous sounds may sound impossible but can be learned. Many years ago, my parents and I moved to a house on a main road that carried a lot of traffic, some of it very heavy. I thought I'd never be able to read a book in peace let alone sleep with all the noise outside. After a week or so, I realized I couldn't hear the noise as my brain must have filtered out that distraction. My hearing was perfect and recognized the noise but my brain was having none of it.

A similar thing happened when I moved with my family more recently to a house near a major freeway. Although it was distant, the buzz was audible, particularly in the morning and evening with rush-hour traffic. Again, this noise faded after a week or so. A man visiting the estate where I lived was asking about the neighborhood before buying a house nearby. He asked if the freeway noise bothered me and, surprised, I said I didn't hear it but could if I tried and listened for it. Enough of this and I hope you are convinced that extraneous noise can be filtered and blocked.

The other blocking technique is to try to ignore people around you when you are listening; they may be talking, fiddling with their iPhone/iPad or even their tie *a la* Oliver Hardy. Block them out. The next blocking technique is to *listen fully* and not start preparing your retaliation before being attacked as soon as you hear an issue you want to counter or were wondering about.

You may be listening to a presentation, in which there may be areas that need clarification in your mind. This, believe it or not, is why questions* were invented. So that you don't appear to be a wally asking something stupid or irrelevant, you need to use the listening skills outlined above. Ask relevant questions at the right time, not on an item covered by the speaker 10 minutes earlier, or that you anticipate will be covered in 10 minutes time. When you ask a pertinent question of the speaker, you may get a sigh of relief from the rest of the audience who didn't understand the point either but were too shy to ask. Fear of looking like a prize wally shouldn't prevent you from asking about something you truly do not understand.

Moral: If you don't ask questions, you will spend the rest of your career struggling under an ever-increasing burden of ignorance.

Listening Duties

It is an unfortunate part of life that one sometimes has to listen to a bore; not the social bore whom you can escape from quite easily but the customer bore who insists on telling you all about his or her job and its trials, tribulations, and critical importance. In many cases, the subject matter may be a key part of IT and you

---

* I was once on a month-long IBM course in Belgium attended by people from all over Europe. One man, a German, stood out from the rest. In every presentation we were given, he said nothing until the very end when the instructor had wound up and we were all weary and preparing to leave. "Pleece, I haff a kvestion …" to a chorus of groans. He was not a popular person and only escaped persecution and possible assassination because the rest of us subscribed to the UN Charter of Human Rights.

must listen and show interest, if at all possible, but don't overdo it by swooning with feigned delight at certain junctures.

On one occasion, I was asked by the customer to talk to the ledger application man, ledger being very important to this particular company, which was part of a group of dissimilar companies. I seem to remember his pet ledgers were general and bought ledgers and he dragged me through every nook and cranny of both of them during a 2-hour one-way talking session. I gritted my teeth, bore it stoically and even managed to be *compos mentis* enough to thank him afterward and say how interesting it was. Sometimes you need to be economical with the truth in the interests of progress.

The Mind Tools site is very useful for learning this type of personal skill and the article on listening can be found there.* You will find other useful coverage of several more personal skills on its website.

Listening to Advice

You may be the whiz at your subject, but often it is useful to ask for an outsider's opinion of your paper, presentation, or design. From my experience of IT and other, unrelated topics, it is often the untrained eye and mind that can see things that the trained eyes and mind miss. This is not a criticism, but it seems to be a fact that the trained mind follows his training and the established facts and laws within that discipline, whereas the outsider may have to think laterally. Being unaware of any restrictions taught in the topic at hand, he can let his mind wander and explore any avenue he chooses and sometimes strikes gold.

I have been that ignorant person on several occasions, the latest being a medical matter. The doctor involved had written an erudite article on some topic regarding a medical problem, but in it confessed that solutions were hard to come by. My mind wandered onto a possible solution, based on observation of the world in general and not any medical training. I made the suggestion in an e-mail and received a "I never thought of that … Good point" reply.†

Moral: Involve others in a review of your offering, not just your peers in that subject. You may be surprised what transpires when the interlopers play devil's advocate in the review of the project.

Influencing People

Influencing people means either bringing them round to your way of thinking, to do something for you, or reach an agreement on a course of action. These normally come under two headings: persuasion and negotiation. Short of beating them over the head, you will need some subtlety and guile to move some opposition. The use

---

* *Active Listening*, https://www.mindtools.com/CommSkll/ActiveListening.htm?#np.
† It's so hard to be humble when you are so great!

of some body language may also help. To be successful in this arena you should know or research the power and influence profiles of the people you are going to meet. Do this via a power/influence table as in Table 6.1 (Chapter 6).

Persuasion

Persuasion is the development of a reasoned argument with positive language, not "it is obvious to even an idiot." You will need to back up any points you make with logic or some kind of proof, such as "95% of CIOs do it this way and it is the IEEE standard for doing X" (positive response) and not "you will regret not doing as I say" (negative response). In short, stress the positive aspects of your thesis.

You should present your points at a steady pace, in a calm way but assertively. Don't look exasperated as if to say you are fed up with his silly views, so let's get on with it. Concentrate of showing how following your way of doing things in beneficial to him or them rather than to the whole world in general. Your argument then looks as though you have thought it through with them in mind and is thus a tailored solution.

Your body language should reflect you calm approach so don't lean forward staring him or them in the face in aggressive fashion. Similarly, don't lean too far back as if you are on the point of giving up in exasperation. Keep a calm open face without grinding your teeth and don't clench your fists or worse, bang them on the table.

If you are talking to a group of people, try before the meeting to have a casual chat with any friendly member of that group who you feel will support your argument, try to convince him or her and you might get support from him or her when you meet the whole group. You will then have what is called a mole in their camp.

Negotiation

Negotiation is not my forte as I didn't have to do much in my IT life, but I've picked up the rudiments from various salesmen. First thing to do is understand their side of things and this means listening, only speaking to ask for clarification and not to counter each point with your response as you go along.

You will almost certainly have to make concessions to reach an agreement but make sure they understand it is a concession and you expect one in return (meeting halfway). One way to make concessions is to present in your argument something you are willing to forgo and then (reluctantly) give way. Do not however lose your calm, as shown next.

This is the technique I recommend to newlywed men I know.* Tell your new wife that you want to go out with the boys 3 nights a week and fishing 1 day each weekend. When she objects, declare your undying love and sacrifice a night with the boys and make your fishing once a month. This is a powerful weapon in your negotiating armory, made more powerful if you don't fish anyway and you haven't get any friends to go out with.

Make your body language support you and sigh resignedly when you concede things. They will then think their powers of persuasion have won the day and this will take their eye off other things you want as they retrospectively gloat mentally through your next points.

Team Building

All that we've seen previously may involve people other than yourself on either a consultancy basis or as a team of peers with a common objective. The reference at the end of this section is a useful guide to team building and the assessment of the compatibility of team members.

A team of brilliant individuals with their own minds is not necessarily a good team. The article referenced at the end of the list makes some good points about team members, supplemented by my own observations:

■ Does the team have a sponsor, that is, a senior person who will benefit from the output of this team and can be called upon to resolve disputes?
■ Do the team members get on with each other?
■ Is there a team leader who can actually lead?
■ Do some members focus on their own success and harm the group as a result?
■ Are the team communications mechanisms adequate?
■ Do the team members understand the function of teams?
■ Do any of the team members have traits that militate against teamwork and progress, for example, individualism, resistance to change, mood swings, and so on?
■ Do members of the group need a boost to their morale?
■ Are the team members full-time or are they involved in other activities?
■ Are the skills present in the team complementary and adequate for the task?
■ If you are forming, or are just part of the team, employ your body language knowledge to assess members' attitudes and their mind-sets. It will pay dividends when dealing with them in later encounters.
■ It may be wise to do a short *SWOT analysis* when the team is formed and either iron out any "creases" or reconstitute the team, using the sponsor as a lever if necessary.

---

* Other advice I give premarriage is to get married very early in the morning so that if it doesn't work out you haven't wasted the whole day.

There is a lot of other useful teamwork material in the Mind Tools article "Team Building That Actually Builds Teams" and on the Mind Tools website in general.*

Spotting Phonies

In IT, as in every walk of life, one needs to be able to recognize people who mainly talk hot air and act (or not) accordingly. Watch for these species:

- *Flower hoppers*—They are bursting with ideas, tell everyone in sight about them but never achieve any one of the activities in question. They jump from one idea to the next with great rapidity, like a bee landing on flower after flower in search of pollen. A common phrase from a flower hopper is "Someone ought to do …" but that someone is never them; they are too busy.
- *Management-speak experts*—This incarnation walks around and attends meetings, talking like a mobile glossary of management terms: CSFs, KPIs, objective-led functionality, empowerment, going forward, getting a result and similar phrases. They may be surprised if you ask, "Could you please repeat that in English, Bill?"
- *Tunneling bore*—This creature has tunnel vision and only knows one subject that is the solution to all known problems. Best dealt with by agreeing with him and then ignoring what he said but using some of his terms where possible so he feels included.
- *Meeting hijacker*—This one tries to take over a meeting or discussion group and, despite knowing very little about what is going on, keeps butting in on people who do know. Response? "Would you like to chair the meeting then Bill?"
- The *dreamer* is on a different cloud from everyone else but wakes up every so often to speak, usually about a topic long past in the meeting. Harmless but occupies a chair.

The ways to deal with these people are complex, depending on the type, situation, and seniority. The main thing is to keep calm and be patient, treat what they say with due deference, and then try to expunge it from the proceedings.

Problem Solving

There are two basic methods for solving any problem:

1. Run a round in circles in a flap, looking concerned (Figure 2.11)
2. Use a structured methodology to bottom the issue and solve it

---

* "Team Building That Actually Builds Teams," https://www.mindtools.com/pages/article/new TMM_52.htm?utm_source=nlsignup&utm_medium=email&utm_campaign=tour3#np.

Figure 2.11 Problem solving: Method 1. (Courtesy of Cloudtweaks.)

Before looking at this methodology, it is instructive to ponder a couple of phrases coined by Albert Einstein who, I am told, was quite a clever chap.

- Anyone who repeats an experiment and expects a different result is insane. (Paraphrased)
- The significant problems we face cannot be solved by the same level of thinking that created them. In other words, don't repeat your mistake in trying to solve it.

These sayings, in essence, mean to think laterally when trying to solve a problem, otherwise you will end up in the same big hole you dug for yourself first time.

Many years ago, there was a process in IBM called Intensive Planning developed in the main by a single person, a registered sadist, and was aimed at examining a single major issue in some area or other. It may have been developing an account plan, system management issues, and so on. Each topic session ran for 2 weeks, started at 8:29 a.m. (not 8:30), and anyone arriving after that was banished from the meeting until the first break. It ended each day when the first delegate collapsed from either exhaustion or terminal boredom.

It appears to have originated with IBM and is not well documented anymore, but I will add the comments made on it by an ex-IBM friend who suffered the process:

> The original sessions were 2 weeks and started at 8:29 and other –:x9s times during the day which was an excellent idea. Late arrivals were excluded from that session. Each session posed a question and couldn't end until there was unanimous agreement. One of the main things was to agree on the real issues ... not necessarily the obvious ones. (I seem

to remember it was called the Kluge although I can't find any reference to that term elsewhere.)

My main memory is that it was a very wearing 2-week experience.

However, one startling good thing came out of all this after at least a 3-hour discussion in the first day's session: What is a problem? The answer turns out to be a simple one, like $E = mc^2$, but has similarly far reaching implications.

A problem is something that prevents you from achieving an objective.

An obvious corollary (follow-on) is "If you don't have any objectives, you can't have any problems."*

The development of this theme implies that no issue in itself can be a problem, only when it prevents someone from meeting an objective. Let's look at a day when it is pouring rain. For the man who sells umbrellas or the gardener who has planted crops that need lots of water, the rain is a godsend, not a problem. For the man who organizes outdoor parties for children, it is a serious problem since it prevents him reaching his objective of earning money to live. I hope this clarifies what I have just said.

The Simplex Method

The Simplex (type 2) process, the brainchild of Min Basadur, appears in his book *The Power of Innovation*. It comprises eight steps that I have listed next as an *aide memoire* and added my comments to the steps based on my experience, good and bad, with problem solving in general.† In this short discussion I have slanted the process toward IT and rolled in techniques I have included in this book.

1. *Problem finding*—How does the problem manifest itself? You should be aware of the difference between chronic and acute problems of which customer complaints about the website and a system outage are examples respectively. They need different teams and different actions.
2. *Fact finding*—What do we know about the problem, especially if it has happened before, and what are the potential/previous solutions? This assumes they have been documented.
3. *Problem definition*—Specify the issue in such a way as to choose the right people or method to eliminate the issue, perhaps by tracking the problem from earlier events. This might include monitor and operating system logs, probably in a war room environment.

---

* This mirrors the G. K. Chesterton paradox: If there were no God, there would be no atheists. There are atheists, therefore …
† I am veering toward the acute problem aspect, mainly with service-level agreements (SLAs) in mind.

4. *Idea finding*—This is the discussion of avenues of solutions that, in my view of the world, is a turbo-Delphi technique. The success of this delving process depends on your selection of the correct mix of people in the war room; you are on your own in this matter since it is organization and system dependent.
5. *Selection*—I diverge from the discussion in the reference at the end of the list and hone in on IT concepts and ideas. At this stage, or earlier, a component failure impact analysis (CFIA) should be carried out, which, in essence, is a list of knock-on effects that are caused by this particular issue. For example, the loss of some component(s) in the IT system might cause the loss or degradation of the company website. In addition, it is important to examine the possible knock-on effects of the solutions put forward; a solution might cause another problem!

   Root cause analysis (RCA) is an important phase in this whole process. The documentation listed in the reference at the end of this list puts this process in this phase. For acute IT issues, I would place it in step 3, perhaps refined in step 4. (See Appendix A for a discussion of RCA and CFIA.)
6. *Planning*—For acute issues, a rapid action plan and assignment of responsibilities is necessary for resolution. For solutions to longer term issues, change management should kick in and possibly formal project management. For the latter case, communications to all involved or affected will dictate the success or failure of the solution.
7. *Sell idea*—This step in the process is superfluous for acute problems—it has to be done—but for solutions to longer-term issues, consensus of those affected may be required. This often involves influencing people to convince the over-my-dead-body persons of the benefits of the proposed solution.
8. *Action*—An obvious step but there are some additional aspects other than fixing the symptoms of the problem; the RCA may dictate other fixes to prevent reoccurrence. The other aspect, often neglected, is documentation of the issue and its solution for future use in similar (hopefully not the same) situations (see point 2).

   I would add a *consolidation* phase to this step where an examination of past issues is performed to see if there is an overarching problem of which these issues are a subset. For example, it may transpire that power fluctuations have been a major factor in many of the problems examined and that power supply replacement or intermediate voltage smoothing equipment is required. Such actions on common factors in problem areas solves and sometimes prevents other problems. If this can be done in an earlier step (war room), then so much the better, but the short-term fixes need to be done first and cemented by attention to the overall contributory factors.

The Simplex process is introduced in the following article, expanded upon, and gives seminal references to the technique, which, quite frankly, is not rocket science; it is just that someone has thought it through for you. It is useful nevertheless as long as you translate generalities in it to IT-specific activities. See "The Simplex Process," https://www.mindtools.com/pages/article/newCT_10.htm.

> *Outcome*: Have objectives for anything important that you undertake and use root cause analysis (RCA) to clarify exactly what is causing the problem. You can obviously avoid problems completely using my definition but that means having no objectives, which is not a good thing.

Other Skills and Techniques

Assume nothing. I have said several times in this book to assume nothing and I say it again here. A perfect illustration of this is the tale of a car park attendant at a municipal site in England. In this affluent southern English town, people got used to the polite, elderly man who collected their money, said good morning, and pointed out where they might best park. He was the only attendant people ever saw and were impressed by his dedication. Some 15 years after his appearance, he suddenly disappeared. People were disappointed and wrote to the local council, expressing their thanks, asking that the council pass on their thanks, and hoped the car park attendant had a happy retirement. The bemused council replied to the well wishers telling then they never had an attendant at that car park, which was free anyway and always had been.

Challenge things. If you have proof, or even a gut feeling, that something being said or written is not quite right, challenge it in the politest possible way, giving your reasons for your doubts. This does not mean challenging everything and everybody as a matter of course; it should be a productive, air-clearing activity. There are people in IT who write and speak as if they know everything about everything; I know, I've met them. When challenged, they either ignore your message (shyster) or respond with an explanation or acknowledgement that you have a good point (true professional).

If you come across one, challenge anything you feel is not quite right but do it in a professional manner. This is best done by a question, for example, "Does that mean then that …?" drawing what seems to be an illogical conclusion to what he has said/written. In math, this is called *reductio ad absurdum* (reduce to an absurdity). There are other ways but the main rules are don't be afraid, be polite, and be sure of your ground.

Mapping Your Future

Your IT future depends on several factors but mainly yourself, although there may temporarily be situations you cannot influence. An example might be a manager who doesn't like you, probably for little or no reason. I had two of these managers in my time. In the main you can be the driver of what happens to you. Whatever the IT environment you find yourself in, it will change and if you don't change with it, you are redundancy fodder.

*Evolve or Die**

- Work within the ethos of your company except where it clashes with legal or moral principles. I have only come across one such person, not so much a conscientious objector; more of a bone idle bloke.
- Remember that one of the most valuable assets an IT company or IT organization possesses is its people. You are part of that asset and it behooves you to keep it valuable and, if possible, increase the value of that asset. In this way, it is a win–win situation for you and your company.
- One avenue open to any employee in a company is the ability to suggest a quality circle (QC) to solve a specific issue or devise a new way of doing things. An example is the circle formed when I was at Sun Microsystems and called by management to suggest reasonable criteria for some senior promotions. Such a circle is not meant for immediate operational issues (that is the war room's function), though it might well meet to improve system monitoring and analysis, for example. The QC is a type of Delphi technique but more interactive since it takes place in the form of a meeting of suitably qualified people. In a good company, such initiatives should form part of any reference given about you should you ever need it. Some hiring companies don't want references and some won't give them for people who are leaving them but you should add this initiative to your CV.
- While on the subject of leaving a company, the best time to think about a new job is when you have one; not when you lose one. This is not to say you should be planning to leave as soon as you are hired. No, what I mean is develop the skills that make you an asset in the IT world and that means doing quality work, keeping up to date, and showing initiative. This activity can form the basis of a live, rolling CV where you capture key events and demonstrations of forward thinking, problem solving, and other things that are mentioned in this book. This is easier than sitting down and writing a CV

---

* I saw a paper on security and part of the heading struck me as appropriate in thinking about the future in IT and your part in it "Evolve or Die." I think that it's a perfect phrase for IT people (and anyone else) to ponder.

from scratch, trying to remember what you did over the past years to show your star quality.*

■ However young you are, the pundits say you should be planning for your retirement by investing in a personal pension scheme. You should keep an eye on the state of IT (assuming you want to stay in it) and back what appear to be winners in terms of techniques and technology. I say this because the world changes and evolves and you need to evolve with it if you want remain a marketable commodity. If you plan to work after official retirement you will need to leave with a current portfolio of skills to do contract work, part-time work, or become a consultant. If you opt for the latter, my recommendation would be to develop a skill that is (a) in demand, (b) will remain so, and (c) is light on experts. My skills at IBM's Card BPS operating system fulfill (c) but fail (a) and (b) miserably. I am still available for hire in this vital area of IT expertise though.

■ Leave an IT legacy you can be proud of each time you move on in the company or achieve promotion, and also when you finally part company. A good legacy in an IT environment is a quality job, sustainable without massive reworks, and one about which your successors say something along the lines of "This is a superb system/program/design. Who did it?"

■ Before you move anywhere, do an analysis of your skills and nonskills, and compare them with the environment you plan or hope to move into. This is in essence a personal SWOT analysis (Appendix A) since any move may well be a one-way ticket.

Justifying Your Existence

You will in your journey to that great data center in the sky be asked by a manager "Why do we spend all this money on IT on availability, performance, and other expensive stuff? Everything runs OK as it is without you and your mates crawling all over it." Tell them this story:

> A man was walking round my hometown of Warrington, UK, scattering a green powder. A second man saw this and asked the first man, "Why are you scattering that powder?" to which the first man replied, "To keep the elephants away." The second man looked puzzled and said, "But there are no elephants in Warrington." "No," said the first man, "this powder is very effective isn't it?"

An equivalent objection was raised against the brouhaha about Y2K saying it was a big trick designed to make money. The fact it didn't happen in a serious way was due to diligence and this elephant story fits there too.

---

* As Muhammad Ali used to say, "It's hard to be humble when you're so great!"

Keeping Up in IT

The following suggestions are taken from an Extrahop blog on this subject,* which summarizes nicely what I am trying to say.

Here are a few steps for figuring out what you need to learn in order to stay ahead of the IT curve:

1. Hang out and listen for awhile, and you'll quickly get a sense of which topics are worth your time, versus passing fads or some random guy's idea that doesn't jive with the industry as a whole.
2. Choose some specific topics to dive into. After you have a good idea of emerging topics and some context for why they're important, you're in a much better position to drill down into specific training.
3. Research your continuing education options. Most people can't ditch the day job to go back to school, but these days you hardly need to: local evening classes are cropping up everywhere, and online learning has become sophisticated enough that you can cover a lot of ground independently, at your own pace. And you don't necessarily need to enroll in a larger program—often it's just the matter of taking a workshop or a couple of courses to brush up on particular skills. High-quality courses are becoming increasingly accessible, in everything from programming languages to conceptual topics like big data or cloud integration.

IT Jobs

Given the speed of change in technology and the skills needed to support it, it would be foolish of me to spell our particular jobs that are winners, especially as it might be 2 years after I write these words that you read them. The broad skills I see with a longer-term future are based on experience, recent publications, and the technology that is evolving to meet user needs and, more recently, fears due to security breaches are

- The cloud and directly related technologies
- Security
- Storage, including backup and recovery and big data
- Internet skills including web design, remote working, and the like

---

* "3 Steps to Keeping Up in IT," https://www.extrahop.com/community/blog/2015/3-steps-to-keeping-up-in-it/. Extrahop (http://www.extrahop.com) specializes in the analysis of wire data from communications connections and has given kind permission to quote this text.

- Network skills, which are in short supply as I write; networks are going to get a hammering when big data transfers and remote computing by everyone and everything gets up to speed
- Systems management skills in the various areas (performance, high availability, etc.); power and cooling are growing in importance as processors get smaller and more closely packed
- Operations skills in, for example, data centers
- Social media, gaming, and similar areas
- Design/architecture skills in all these areas, including the use of simulation tools in design
- Education and training (schools, universities, freelance)
- IT management skills in PDWs, Delphi, change management, and so forth
- Probable need for skills in artificial intelligence (AI), cognitive computing, and similar
- High-performance computing (HPC) in the science world and increasingly in other areas of work, such as economics, finance, and biosciences

You will also need the overarching personal skills like giving presentations, listening, writing, ongoing learning, and so on, which will put the final polish on your CV to see off competition for the job you covet.

Managers: Know Your Staff

If you've ever worked for a boss who reacts before getting the facts and thinking things through, you will love this. Arcelor-Mittal Steel, feeling it was time for a shakeup, hired a new CEO. The new boss was determined to rid the company of all slackers. On a tour of the facilities, the CEO noticed a guy leaning against a wall. The room was full of workers and he wanted to let them know that he meant business. He asked the guy, "How much money do you make a week?"

A little surprised, the young man looked at him and said, "I make $400 a week. Why?"

The CEO said, "Wait right here." He walked back to his office, came back in 2 minutes, and handed the guy $1,600 in cash and said, "Here's four weeks' pay. Now get out and don't come back."

Feeling pretty good about himself the CEO looked around the room and asked, "Does anyone want to tell me what that goofball did here?"

From across the room a voice said, "Pizza delivery guy from Domino's."

Key Reference Sites

Webopedia, http://www.webopedia.com/
DZone, http://www.dzone.com. Offers reference cards on multiple IT topics, including cheat sheets (http://www.dzone.com/refcardsz), topic guides (http://www.dzone.com/guides), and a portal to information elsewhere (http://www.dzone.com/portals).

Chapter 3

Technical and Management Skills

Knowing is not enough; we must apply. Willing is not enough; we must do.

Johann Wolfgang von Goethe

As with most human endeavors, there is a right way and a wrong way to do things. You might do all the right things but possibly in the wrong order.* The phased and sensible approach is shown in Figure 3.1, where, with a little hard concentration, you will discern the right way from the wrong (hint: look for ticks and crosses).

I have alluded in the "Preface" to the vast chasm between *using* and *employing* technology and it is pertinent to cover it again here. There is a supporting report by Bitdefender.† It contains a chart, sketched in Figure 3.2, showing the benefits to organizations who have a "high maturity" in these two areas. The paper works on the principle I outlined in the "Preface": know the mistakes, avoid them and you are doing the right thing. It is not only executives who risk irrelevance, it is you as well.

If you grasp what I have said (and had corroborated), you are 50% on the way to a successful IT career. If you fail to grasp it, you are condemned to eternal "geek-dom," which is fine and noble if that is what you aspire to.

---

* A member of a UK comedy duo (Morecambe and Wise) once attempted to play Grieg's Piano Concerto along with a studio orchestra conducted by Andre Previn. There was a predictable mess-up and the conductor told him he was playing the wrong notes. His reply was, "I am playing the right notes, but not necessarily in the right order!"

† "Top 5 Ways IT Executives Risk Irrelevance," http://resources.idgenterprise.com/original /AST-0151221_BitDefender_eBook_Spreads_v6c.pdf. BitDefender website, http://www.bit defender.co.uk/. I found this paper after I had written about use and employ it in the "Preface," so absolutely no plagiarism is attached. In fact, I have been preaching and boring people with this sermon for many years and have had many a run-in with geeks.

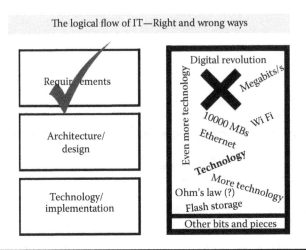

Figure 3.1 The flow of any major IT project.

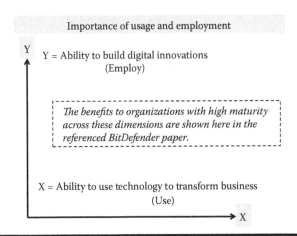

Figure 3.2 Use versus employment of technology.

IT Control

In the flurry of progress and invention, 10-year-old children becoming PC experts and IT articles by journalists* who wouldn't know a gigabyte from a grand piano, we risk losing perspective. The reason is that technology, instead of being viewed as a tool, is touted as the be-all and end-all of computing. This is a big mistake. In my view, this accounts for the plethora of screwball projects that infest the IT world; the unmanageable designed by the unthinking.

---

* Anyone in journalism writing about IT should have a formal qualification in it. I will be happy to devise such a scheme.

Management of IT

This section suggests areas where installations might improve the level of service of various IT initiatives. These areas are what I loosely term *IT management*. What follows are specific areas where activity needs to be focused and are basic to IT whatever the underlying technology. They don't age, only increase in importance as clouds, virtualization, and the Internet descend on IT systems and threaten to bury them in complexity.

Some installations I have come across used to try to buy their way to success by purchasing expensive software to do the management tasks involved in IT to design, implement, and operate projects. For XYZ Management they would purchase The Ultimate XYZ Management Package, light the blue touch paper, and stand back. This would be repeated for managing work types ABC, DEF, and so on. This sounds fine and might be the correct option if:

■ It has a pedigree but doesn't break the bank.
■ You know how to use it and employ it (*use* and *employ* are not interchangeable, as we have seen ad nauseam).
■ You understand the subject it addresses.

Regarding this list, there is a saying "a fool with a tool is still a fool" and unless the third, and most important, point above is fulfilled, the chances of success are greatly reduced. If this point is fulfilled, you can almost certainly manage XYZ and the rest using a school exercise book as your tool project documentation better than you could mishandling a software package.* In the Appendices, we will examine some of the tools and techniques that might add value to almost every IT project.

The following management disciplines and techniques are of prime importance in managing IT systems in every area of endeavor (those marked with a double asterisk [**] are not covered in this book, although they may be mentioned in outline):

■ Preliminary activities
  – Preproduction activities
  – Business plans and requirements
■ Management disciplines (methods and techniques)**
  – Service-level agreements (SLAs), explicit or implicit
  – Project definition workshop (PDW)
  – Delphi technique and group planning
  – Failure mode effects [and criticality] analysis (FMEA/FMECA)**

---

* Circa 1985. A customer I dealt with had a performance person in IT. His office wall was covered with multicolored charts of *anything* versus *everything else* plotted on them. One day I plucked up the courage and asked him what they all meant (the so-what test). He wasn't really sure, although we both agreed they were very pretty and covered the ugly wall nicely. This is a true story; only the name of the man has been left out.

    – Component failure impact analysis (CFIA)
    – Walkthroughs**
    – War room
■ Implementation and operations
    – Some of the disciplines above
    – Change management
    – Problem and fault management**
    – Risk management
    – Security management**
    – Availability management**
    – Resource management**
      • Performance
      • Capacity
      • Network
      • Data and storage
      • Software
      • Assets
      • Other factors

When these disciplines are ignored, skimped, or used with no understanding, problems, including disasters, will ensue. That is the only guarantee this book offers by an author who hates to say, "I told you so."

IT Project Flow

There are a number of flowcharts outlining various aspects of IT management and I'm not attempting to reproduce them here. A general project or piece of work can be described as a journey from A to B with various stages, including a costing exercise if this is needed. The start of most exercises is

■ Where are we today? (A Point)
■ Where do we want to be? (B Point)
■ How do we get there from where we are? (Project items)

This is pretty simple isn't it? You'll be amazed how many people get it wrong, mainly because they don't start at the beginning and only have a hazy notion of where the end is. Check out the flow diagram in Figure 3.3.

The IT options might be the subject of a Delphi exercise and the overall flow carried out via a project definition workshop (PDW). I have had people say to me, "Oh we don't need a PDW. We have our own project management standards." This is a silly statement. A PDW finds out and specifies what needs to be done; the project manager and any project software or techniques get it done. If a proper PDW or equivalent is not done, it is likely that the project manager will deliver a "pup," but deliver it extremely well.

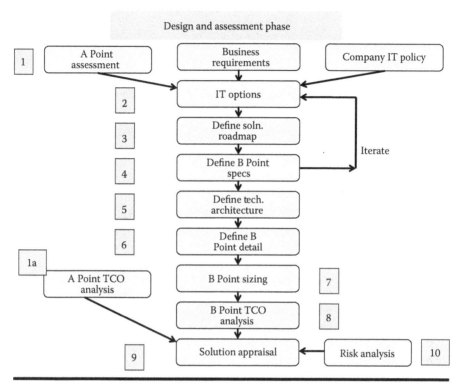

Figure 3.3   Project design and assessment: Reminder.

Out of this flow of activity will come other subprojects that will have their own flows and methods. One phase is the detailed solution and selection of specific technologies and vendors moving on to pilots, benchmarks, and any other *proving* necessary to ensure the success of the project. Once you reach the destination, there is no retracing your steps to fix it.

Note: Many organizations have templates for these types of development; a good idea to stop maverick projects, but clever organizations will also allow some variation to suit special needs brought about by a project.

Technical Horizon

General IT World

Here, I am trying to outline the generic world of IT, as it has been since the dawn of (IT) time; the latest fads and fashions live within these general boundaries, but it is instructive to start with the latter.

IT Architecture

IT architectures are specifications of configurations presented in such a way as to allow different implementations. Thus, if I sketch out the architecture of a simple house, you might be able to decide to implement it in brick, wood or stone.

Service architectures covering the diverse areas that can have an impact on quality of service (QoS) are discussed in Appendix B.

Service and Systems Management

Service management is the set of activities that allow the smooth running of IT-based business systems. These activities include monitoring and reporting on SLAs, developing processes for the running of business applications, a service (help) desk, and anything generally outward-looking toward the customers' needs. In essence, it is all the things necessary to offer a high and improving QoS to the end users.

Systems management is the management of the computer infrastructure (system) that underpins the services offered to the users. This will include:

■ Network management
■ Systems (processors) management
■ Storage management

which together with management and reporting on factors of importance across these elements:

■ Availability of the system elements of a service
■ Performance and capacity of a service
■ Security of everything, which is confidential to the company
■ Other activities vital to services: audits, upgrades, assets, etc., management

In short, both management disciplines cover the design, implementation, and operation of business IT services across processes, people and products.

The *major resources* of interest in providing a quality service to users are

■ Processors and main and cache storage in them
■ External storage, such as disks, tapes, solid-state devices (SSDs), and flash memory devices
■ Networks and components that make them up as well as pure transport "wires" and fiber
■ Application software (programs)
■ System monitoring software
■ Procedures to report on the whole service at two basic levels: the IT level and the business level viewpoints (see Chapter 1, Figure 1.8)

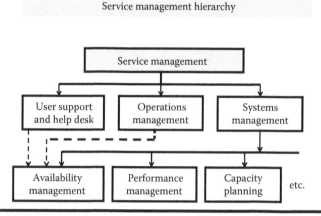

Figure 3.4   Service management component hierarchy.

To manage these resources, we need to measure them, compare them with a baseline dictated by the SLA, and take action on out-of-line situations. The phrase I always use is *if you can't (or won't) measure it, you can't manage it and if you can't manage it, you are probably in trouble or soon will be.*

Systems management then is the management of resources that impact QoS and probably other things as well. The whole point of this management is to stabilize performance in the areas of response time for a transaction and throughput of work. If a service-level agreement (SLA) is in place, the management supports the reporting of response and other targets agreed between IT and the business. See Appendix A for a detailed discussion of SLAs.

The management of a service to a business unit is quite a complex task and involves the following functions (see Figure 3.4):

- User support, which is an interface between users and IT, usually staffed by people who have a foot in both camps
- Help desk, which is the first port of call for users experiencing difficulties with a service
- Operations, which run the systems on a day-to-day basis
- Systems people who design, implement (alongside operations), and monitor/ manage the quality of the service(s); performance, availability, security, etc.

These functions have communications between them. In particular, the help desk will need to call on operations and/or systems to resolve any problems that come their way.

What Do I Mean by Management?

Systems management is the measurement (monitoring), analysis, and control of various components (resources) that comprise a system. These are mainly processors, storage, and the network, but it is important to note that monitoring is not the same as managing since monitoring is passive, whereas management is active, using information from monitoring activity. The following equation, which we have seen previously, illustrates this principle:

$$\text{Management} = \text{Design} + \text{Measurement} + \text{Analysis} + \text{Action}$$

This equation is the IT equivalent of Einstein's $E = mc^2$ in physics and about as well understood. Learn it.

Management of a particular resource, such as storage, starts with the design of the resource's configuration, the measurement (monitoring) of the parameters that define its purpose, the analysis of this data, and the taking of any actions deemed necessary by results that are out of line from an established base determined at the design stage.

What Do We Manage?

First, we manage to *objectives* and if you don't have any objectives, there's no point in worrying; let the system look after itself. However, in most cases, there is a contract between business and IT, and this is called an service-level agreement (SLA), which covers factors dictated by the business to ensure a QoS that supports their working adequately.

SLAs are covered in Appendix A and it is this that tells IT what control it needs to exercise over system resources to meet the criteria set out by the business in the SLA.

Systems

A system in our context is the end-to-end setup of resources that support the business service: resources such as processors, storage, network links, tapes, printers and so on. A modern system is illustrated in Figure 3.5.*

The *main characteristics* of the system resources (many illustrated in Figure 3.5) that are important in providing a quality service to the users are

■ *Availability*, that is, what percentage of their operating time to deliver a service is actually usable. Thus, a service that is supposed to be available for 180 hours per month and is not functioning for 30 minutes will have an availability of 179.5/180 × 100% or 99.72%. The more that business depends on IT, the more important availability becomes.

---

* If you are a potential IT person, don't worry about this figure. You'll meet it when you join the IT fraternity.

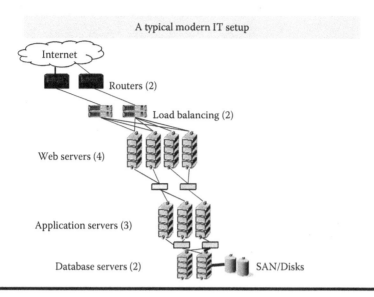

Figure 3.5   An example of a system today.

- *Performance*, in terms of the time taken to do certain things like run a job or handle a transaction of some sort (response times) or how many jobs/transactions get through the system in unit time. This might be transactions per second (tps) or jobs per hour. These numbers are known as *throughput*.
- *Capacity* management of system resources supporting the applications. This involves predicting when extra resources are needed to avoid degradation of the business service. This has been the subject of much attention and analysis using intelligent methods acting on operational data to make capacity predictions.
- *Security* in terms of outside intrusion, deliberate malicious damage, and loss of data. This aspect is now as important as any in the management arena.
- *Networks* in each of the areas deemed necessary for the processors: performance, availability, and so forth.
- *Key QoS characteristics in other areas*, such as printing, data backup and recovery, SLA reporting, and many other entities.

Processors

Processors are the main brains of the system although there are some clever components that support them. Modern systems often have multiple processors in a single frame and several systems might be linked to form a cluster of processors for performance but mainly availability of a service.

Networks

Networks are the glue that hold separate systems together, carrying data and information from system to system and system to people. The physical composition of networks is metal or fiber but there are logical and abstracted layers above this. These layers form a model of the whole network, one of the earliest defined being a *seven-layer model*. The purpose of the layers is to insulate the user* from changes in the other layers so that changes in those layers only impact the one above and the one below. This allows a network setup to be modified for functional or performance enhancements. To traverse these layers, one needs a protocol or a set of communication rules of engagement known as *protocols* and these vary depending on requirements or preferences.

Networks, in a nutshell, consist of transmission "wires," various "boxes" at both ends and along the data route, and "packets" (the transmission units of data) and control information flowing through them (Figure 3.6). A *network protocol* defines rules and conventions for communication between network devices, at end points, and in networks boxes.

Network types are configurations that normally come in two flavors:

1. *Local area networks* (*LANs*), used by workgroups or across a building
2. *Wide area networks* (*WANs*), used for distance transmission

Network Protocols

A protocol is a set of rules for any form of communication between two or more entities. For example, the protocol for speaking to the Queen of England is only speak when you are spoken to, not to interrupt, and so on. One of the best definitions of network communication protocols I have come across is the following:

> A network protocol can be formally defined as a set of rules, conventions and data structure which is used by network devices to communicate with each other across a network. These rules govern the syntax, semantics, and synchronization of communication, and how data is packaged into messages, sent, and received. It includes mechanisms for devices to identify, control and make connections, communication, and data transfer between computing endpoints. Tasks such as data representation, authentication, and error detection are also performed. Network protocols are intended for the secure, fast and error free data delivery between two communication devices. Protocols may be implemented by hardware, firmware, software or by a combination of them.[†]

---

* This might be a person at a workstation, an application program, or a device.
† "Introduction to Network Protocols and Algorithms," MacroThink Institute, http://www.macrothink.org/journal/index.php/npa/article/download/239/153.

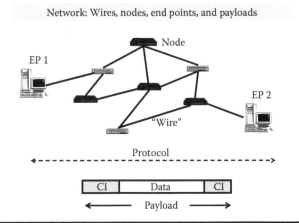

Figure 3.6   Network components and communications.

The common network protocols are covered under "Network Protocols" in Chapter 4.

There is also Multiprotocol Label Switching (MPLS), which is a type of protocol for speeding and shaping network traffic flows but is not the same type of formal protocol as those in the transmission list mentioned above. There are other examples of this in networking.

Networks can be the bottleneck in a rapidly changing environment since in general it isn't possible to do a live plug in of extra resource as one often can with a processor or storage unit. It is therefore important to do your homework on the network part of the service chain. In addition, it would be wise to anticipate an upgrade path should demand exceed supply. This is done by calculation or simulation and there are several tools that can help in this part of the project.

References

- A presentation with good, simple outlines: "Computer Networks: Introduction," http://research.microsoft.com/en-us/um/people/pcosta/cn_slides/cn_01-hand out.pdf
- A useful WAN starter pack: "The 2015 Guide to WAN Architecture and Design," http://www.webtorials.com/content/2015/06/2015-guide-to-wan-architecture -and-design.html

Storage

Traditional Disks (HDD)

Most people know what a disk is without seeing a detailed diagram: it consists of magnetic platters or disks, connected together on a spindle and accessed by read/

write arms that traverse these platters from their outer to inner extremities and back looking for requested data. The characteristics that dictate the performance, read/write accesses/second, and data transfer rate, are as follows:

- Disk diameter: From about 14 inches in the old days to 3.5 inches now
- Number of access heads (disk surfaces): Typically 8
- Rotation speed: 7200 rpm (revolution per minutes) or 15,000 rpm

In the IT Stone Age, these and tape drives were the main online storage media and 100 Mbyte drive was mind-blowing. Believe it or not, tapes were often used as the medium for application data and also for doing sorting of data.* Today, single disks are boasting 4 terabytes and probably more by the time you read this.

Other Storage Media

Today, the media used in online and other time-critical work are[†]

- Traditional hard disks (HDDs), introduced to the world via IBM's RAMAC
- Solid-state devices (SSDs)
- Solid-state flash storage
- Magnetic tapes, normally now used for backup and restore
- CDs, optical, floppy, stick, and other devices, used mainly for backup or transportability but rarely on larger systems

The battle between which of the first three media (Figure 3.7) is the most effective for data used in real time was still raging at the time of this writing. There are advocates for each one, some favoring mixtures, others either one or the other. Take care when reading recommendations for one of the media since you may find that the company writing the article only sells that particular medium.

Presently, the consensus is for a mixture, often in *tiered mode* with the fastest media front-ending slower media as a cost-effective way of getting performance and capacity at a reasonable cost. It also protects investment in older storage for some time further. Geeks like the latest technology, but finance people want to "seat" their current assets before kicking them out and writing them off.

---

* This was amusing to watch as two or more tapes would oscillate back and forth sorting data using a mathematical function called a Fibonacci series.

† The days of storing information on punch cards expired with the demise of Thomas J. Watson Sr. because of pressure from his son, Watson Jr., who believed in tape storage.

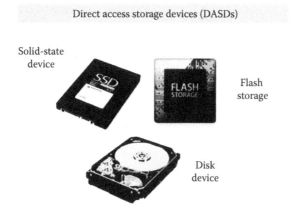

Figure 3.7 **Storage: Disk, solid state, and flash.**

References

- "Storage:" Techtutorials: http://www.techtutorials.net/tutorials/computer_hard ware/storage.html. *There are a number of tutorials at this link—some elementary, some more advanced—but there are 39 of them (at the last count) so you will find something to help you in whatever area of storage you wish to pursue. This link will be of use to existing IT people as well. (Note: You may have to register [free] to access these tutorials.)*
- "Computer Data Storage," *Wikipedia*: https://en.wikipedia.org/wiki/Computer _data_storage
- "Introduction to Computer Information Systems/Storage:" https://en.wikibooks .org/wiki/Introduction_to_Computer_Information_Systems/Storage

Elementary Math Skills

Summation, Products, and Integration

This does not mean a course of study but simply the recognition and interpretation of some math symbols (Greek in the main). They shorten the space needed to explain something involving many elements or entities. Conversely, they allow you to understand some things expressed in this fashion more quickly. This is a short discussion of some of the main ones you may come across, and inability to understand their meaning may jeopardize your comprehension of the message an article or presentation delivers. Don't be frightened off a paper or article because of a few occurrences of this type of math.

These notations are sometimes used to shows sums of quantities, for example, across a network and through the network components in it. The time taken to traverse the network is the sum of the times resident in all those components plus any waiting time due to queuing. In the sample below, a_i might be the sum of normal transit time through the n nodes in a network plus any queue time.

The symbol Σ, Greek uppercase *sigma*, denotes a summation of items, and Π, (Greek uppercase *pi*) denotes a product or series of multiplications of items. The following examples should make these functions clear, for example, a *sum* of several terms a is

$$a_1 + a_2 + a_3 + \dots a_n \ (is \ written \ as) = \sum_{i=1}^{n} a_i$$

and a *product* (multiplication of several terms) is written as

$$a_1 \times a_2 \times a_3 \times \dots a_n \ (is \ written \ as) = \prod_{i=1}^{n} a_i$$

where a is a property of a component for which there are n values.

Often there are summations and products of quantities where there are numbers attached to different entities, say, delays in a network transmission of data. If there are several units, say, 1, 2, 3, 4, and 5, making up the network, each with a delay, D, of its own, then the total delay in transmitting a piece (packet) of data across a network will be the sum of all these delays:

$$Total \ delay = D_{unit1} + D_{unit2} + D_{unit3} + \dots$$

which in shorter form might be written $D_1 + D_2 + \dots$ and in math summation form

$$Total \ delay = \sum_{i=1}^{n} D_i$$

The summation and integration signs are also used to express the area under discrete and continuous distribution graphs (refer to Figure 3.8).

Mathematical Distributions

The total area under the discrete graph is the sum of all the elements. The area is the ith element, starting at t_i, is height times width, which is $F(i) \times \delta t_i$ for all elements 0 to infinity and $F(i)$ is the value of F at point t_i. We will call this area A_D:

$$A_D = \sum_{0}^{\infty} F(i).\delta t_i \ (sum \ of \ the \ areas \ of \ the \ elements)$$

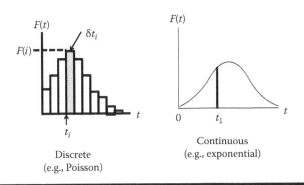

Figure 3.8   **Areas under discrete (A_D) and continuous (A_C) functions.**

I have used "·" (middle dot) in the preceding equation to represent multiplication instead of "×" (multiplication sign) and will do so where confusion with a variable called "x" (lowercase letter x) might occur, as it does in the following integral area.

As δt_i approaches zero, the discrete graph becomes a continuous curve and the area under this curve, instead of being a discrete summation as seen earlier, it becomes an integration, area A_C, thus

$$A_C = \int_0^\infty F(x)\,dx$$

Refer to the graphs in Figure 3.8 again to understand these areas.

Sometimes, as we will see later, difficult or unfathomable integrals are often approximated by a summation using a series of discrete "chunks" instead of a continuous curve. We have already seen that areas under curves, for example, the probability density function, have a meaning when applied to reliability and hence, availability. Cast your eye over these symbols and their meaning again and you will be able to follow the subsequent usage of equations better.

Figures derived from such distributions feature prominently in systems design and sizing, and the areas under curves or discrete distributions have various meanings depending on the subject at hand. For example, the total area under a curve/distribution for the probability of something happening or having a certain value has to be one, which is the total certainty. Other total areas of curves and distributions have other meanings. The various distributions have sometimes frightening names, particularly in queuing theory, but don't let that put off nonmath people; just remember the interpretations given earlier.

Chapter 4

The IT Universe Today

There's a long, long trail a-winding, into the land of my dreams.

"There's a Long, Long Trail A-Winding," World War I song
Words by Stoddard King, music by Zo Elliott

You will inhabit the IT universe, at least for the next few years, and presented here are the main components of that cosmos; what you need to know or be aware of in your work and dealings. This section is not a detailed tutorial but an outline of the world of IT as it is evolving. Depending on your job, responsibilities, and preferences you will need to know about some of them in detail and some in passing. You should not be in a position to say "I've never heard of that"* on many occasions.

Chapter Components

The IT field consists of, in my view, two sets of knowledge:

- *Type 1*—That which has been here since the dawn of (IT) time; eternal knowledge
- *Type 2*—That which is invented, appears, evolves, develops, becomes a standard, and sometimes disappears; semipermanent and transient knowledge; this is the world of technology

---

* A phrase I use when told about a modern pop group or hit.

Type 1: Eternal Knowledge

There are four things I think will always be with us while IT is around as a business service:

- Users (clients) with business needs
- Computer systems of some sort (servers plus peripheral devices)
- Layers of complementary hardware and software between the systems
- People

The last three items provide services to the first item—the users, customers, or clients.

These services, which are usually coded applications to aid the users' jobs, are developed, implemented, maintained, and replaced in an eternal cycle, shown in Figure 1.7 (Chapter 1).

Knowledge Needed in a Type 1 World

The skills needed in the Type 1 environment can be broadly classified as management skills, which means managing the whole cycle of IT development from requirements to retirement of applications.

The A Point–B Point terminology is part of the project definition workshop (PDW) output, which is covered in Appendix A. This A Point and B Point philosophy can be applied to any change in IT: configuration changes, new systems, software changes, and so forth. It is particularly valuable in complex projects involving critical systems, for example:

- Code conversions or replacements
- Migrations and modernization, especially "legacy" modernizations, which are the easiest thing in the world to foul up
- Rationalizations of hardware, software, and the environment
- Other radical changes, such as using a new supplier and transitioning across

Many IT projects, large and small, involve a change or migration as opposed to implementing a brand new application or system. In such cases, it is vitally important to consider the environment in which you are operating in (*modus operandi*) and not just the code or hardware involved. The management and development environment may have to change and, in addition, maybe the *modus operandi* of the system operation. The change from state A to state B is illustrated next.

Change management is the vital ingredient in all such undertakings, especially those involving business critical applications.

Type 2: Evolving Knowledge

The IT world today is complex and can be viewed in many ways, a sure recipe for confusion. What I have done in what follows is to categorize the moving target of technology into two parts:

1. The physical universe
2. The logical universe

These universes, like those propounded in modern cosmology, live in parallel, develop in parallel but with a clear relationship between them. This relationship is called *abstraction*. Abstraction is manifest in many forms with different names as we will see.

IT Abstraction

IT abstraction is a way of hiding the true complexity of something by some kind of front end that is comprehensible to the end user who is not familiar with the underlying components. The abstraction layer acts as an interpreter between end user and the underlying (complex) system. The Application Programming Interface (API) is the way one accesses the physical infrastructure without knowing the details of it. Refer to Figure 4.1 and the next section "Application Programming Interfaces (APIs)."

In the nonabstraction world, the access from layer 1 to layer 3 would be direct, with no intervening "insulation" layer, layer 2.

An analogy is a situation we are all familiar with is electrical power. To most of us, the world of electricity is a plastic socket in the wall and a plug that fits into it. The ensemble is completed by a switch that activates the flow of power. If you were

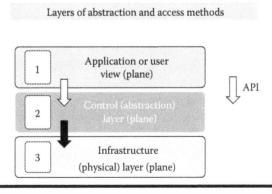

Figure 4.1   Configuration abstraction in IT.

showing this facility to a man from another planet, this is the scenario you would show him and explain its operation so that he could use it if necessary.

Neither of you have (or need) any idea of the physical world behind that socket: the world of cables, pylons, transformers, and power plants. In addition, you need not (in most circumstances) be aware of a change in this configuration, for example, if the driver for the turbines providing the electricity changed from coal to natural gas. Your abstract view of the power supply remains the same and you interact with it in the same way.

Application Programming Interfaces (APIs)

This isolation of the end user from the underlying complexity is the basis of programming APIs, which can survive changes to this underlying structure. To take a trivial example, imagine your program wanted to obtain the time from the operating system (OS). In the old coding days, you might access a control block and pick the time from, say, the nth position in that block. If the operating system is advanced in function, the time might no longer be where it was before and your code would then return some odd value. This could be avoided by the operating system providing a GET-TIME command, which could be used in a program and the OS would find the time wherever it might be.

This GET-TIME is an example of an API and, in fact, a form of abstraction as it dispenses with the need to understand the composition and location of the data block containing the time.

Abstraction Examples

IMS PSB   IBM's Information Management System (IMS) was a transactional system with a database component. The database component was (originally) a hierarchical one with a root from which associated data components flowed. The physical layout could be drawn to show all the data elements in this hierarchy, for example, the explosion of a motor into subcomponents and so on down to the basic units that make up the motor. The levels in this hierarchical diagram might be three or four (described by a Database Definition or DBD).

Programs written to run against these hierarchical databases might have functions that only required parts of the database to operate, so leaving the poor application programmer to find his way around the database for the bits he needed would be time consuming and error-prone. The solution was a logical hierarchical view of the database that the programmer used for his database navigation.* This view was called a Program Specification Block (PSB), which defined the whole database

---

* This *navigation* is too complex and possibly confusing to fully explain here. A simple way of showing how the programmer found his way around is to imagine talking someone through a hierarchy on the telephone "Starting at the top (root), go down one level and take the second segment from the left. Within that segment, take the first segment on the left ..." and so on.

as far as the programmer was concerned and he didn't have to know what the real, physical layout was. For a physical database, there would typically be several PSBs, each designed for different applications, which needed access to different parts (segments) of the physical hierarchy.

The true underlying physical structure of the database was described by the DBD, and the abstract PSB views were specific subsets of the DBD structure. Thus, if the program using PSB1 tried to stray into other parts of the database it would get a "not found" message. This is illustrated in Figure 4.2.

Early Virtualization and VM   Virtual machines (VMs) can be traced back to IBM's Cambridge Scientific Center, a research and development lab that pioneered virtualization with CP/CMS. CP, *Control Program*, was the original hypervisor component that created multiple independent virtual machines, each a full virtualization of the underlying hardware, and CMS was a lightweight, single-user operating system. CMS at the time stood for Cambridge Monitor System, renamed Conversational Monitor System.

Someone using a virtual machine would have a view of IT resources such as a processor, storage, and memory, which he considered his own physical machine. In fact it was an abstraction of parts of the real physical resources (real machine) assigned to him. Thus, he might have 30% of the processor power, 40% of the storage and memory, and might ask for other resources to be assigned to him on a temporary basis. This is a parallel to the PSB concept described earlier.

Such a resource might be a real tape drive to back up some data every few days, which might be used (assigned to him) and released when he had finished with it. There might be a pool of four physical tape drives shared among many virtual machine users to be accessed on demand.

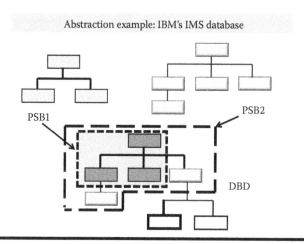

Figure 4.2   Abstraction illustration using IMS.

Summary: The concept of machine abstraction has been around a long time and the development where resources are assigned dynamically as required from a pool of systems is what is today called *the cloud*.*

The Physical Universe

The physical universe is the sphere of what are known as "feeds and speeds," especially to writers of business IT proposals.[†] These are subject to inexorable increases in speeds, capacities, and capabilities of

- External storage
- Main storage (memory)
- Processors
- Networks
- Other devices supporting these resources

I don't intend to cover these, since you will be bombarded regularly by product announcements, followed by "me too" announcements as others catch up with the leaders in these fields. Suffice it to say that the IT universe has changed from 11 and 28 Mbyte disks to 4 and more terabyte disks and processors from an arbitrary unit power of 1 to 100s. Memory storage of processors has progressed from a "massive" 16 Mbytes[‡] (IBM 3033 system c. 1977) to many gigabytes.

The memory on the PC that I am writing on now (8 GBytes) was unavailable on a single processor when I started in IT and if it was, it would have cost millions of dollars. My PC costs me about $45 for a 4 Gbyte upgrade or did a year or so ago.

Graphics

Full function graphics is a specialist subject, but the IT all-rounder should understand the basics of graphics.

Graphics functionality in its simplest definition is the visual display of information, new or previously obtained, in the form of tables or lists in a meaningful form to the observer. This form can vary from a simple two-dimensional line graph of sales against calendar months to a complex three-dimensional graphics representation of an object with multiple colors, shading, shadows, animation, and other esoteric ways of observing data and information. It depends on the business or aesthetic purpose of the display.

---

* "z/VM—A Brief Review of Its 40 Year History," http://www.vm.ibm.com/vm40hist.pdf.

† Those who put feeds and speeds upfront, before the business requirements aspects, usually lose IT bids.

‡ The IBM 3033 processor, announced in 1977, boasted this main storage. A caption contest in my branch "What on earth can one do with 16 Mbytes?" was won with the answer "1 user of VSPC," an ill-fated IBM time-sharing product of that time.

The speed of manipulation and display of such data will depend on the complexity of its representation and the speed of the hardware and software delivering it. It will also depend on how efficient the software is. There are standards for graphics software and, like other standards such as OSI and TCP/IP, there are *de jure* and *de facto* forms.

Graphics performance is often taken to mean the speed at which the workstation graphics hardware can create visual images on the screen once the data is handed to the adapter to be drawn on the screen. Sometimes it is interpreted as the speed at which the CPU can handle the user requests to generate graphics output and present it to the screen for viewing. The combination I suppose is what we would call the *graphics response time.*

There are dozens of books on graphics but for the IT all-rounder, the following two sources will be useful. The first one does an introduction and had a useful side panel where you can choose a graphics topic at will. The second is a general discussion on Wikipedia.

- "Introduction to Computer Graphics:" http://ecomputernotes.com/computer -graphics/basic-of-computer-graphics/introduction-to-computer-graphics
- "Computer Graphics:" https://en.wikipedia.org/wiki/Computer_graphics

The Logical (Abstract) Universe

We have already seen what abstraction is in general terms and now is the time to outline some implementations of the concept. In a nutshell, abstraction is the hiding of complexity behind an intervening layer of software, rather like an interpreter between two speakers of different languages.

The logical division of a physical machine into multiple *virtual machines*, called VMs or sometimes *guests*, is the basis of virtualization. The VMs are controlled by a *hypervisor*, the big *boss* which oversees them and the VMs in turn control the applications running on them.

Virtualization

Partitioning: A Precursor

As systems became more powerful, the need for multiple machines to provide a certain level of power diminished. Fine; or was it? When there are multiple applications sharing a system, they can get in each other's way and cause all-around slowdowns.

There are some applications that can't coexist peacefully, for example, five I/O intensive applications battling for supremacy over disk accesses or five processor intensive jobs with deadlines to meet fighting over processor cycles.

I worked in IBM so I will outline partitioning as they did it but other vendors offered similar functions on their systems.

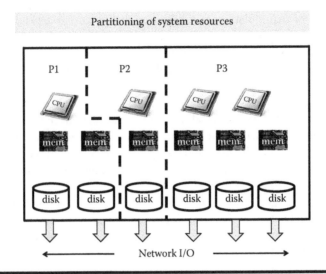

Figure 4.3 Partitioning of system resources.

Resource *partitioning* is the dividing of the resources on a system between applications or users on that system (see Figure 4.3). The dotted lines in Figure 4.3 show the boundaries between the three partitions assigned to three workloads. This ensures they don't tread on each others' resource toes, as was the case previously.

Thus, the processor power, main storage, and disks would be assigned in chunks to these users. Initially, these slices of the resources were fixed, but later it was possible to alter them dynamically without bringing everything down and restarting the system. Similar partitioning could be applied to network I/O resources (not bandwidth, as that is a separate issue).

One difference between a *partitioned* mode of operation and *virtualization* is that the former has a single operating system, which along with microcode handles the division and distribution of resources in each partition. The virtualization environment can have several. In addition, they need not all be the same operating system.

Virtual Systems

The concept of virtual systems came mainly from ideas developed in the 1960s and made into a time-sharing software product called Control/Program Cambridge Monitor System (CP/CMS). CP/CMS became CP-40 and evolved into CP-67, which appeared in 1967. (It also owes something to MIT's Multics, 1969.) IBM eventually announced its virtual storage software (VM/370) in 1970, along with the System/370 computer series.

A computer systems' resources (processor, memory, and storage) are partitioned to emulate multiple logical systems, each with its *own operating system*. The

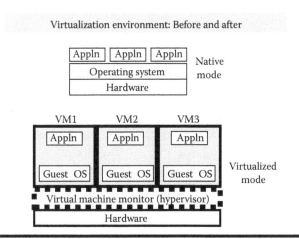

Figure 4.4   Virtualized and nonvirtualized (native) environments.

operating systems (guest OSs) on the VMs are unaware that they have been "virtualized" and are completely isolated from the underlying hardware. They "think" they are accessing and controlling the hardware themselves. In fact, their hardware requests are handled for them by the hypervisor and mapped onto the physical resources of the system. In cloud situations, virtualization may be spread across multiple systems and resources (Figure 4.4).

A good definition of *virtualization* is provided by PCMag.com.*

Virtualization: A variety of technologies for managing computer resources by providing a software interface, known as an *abstraction layer*, between the software (operating system and applications) and the hardware. Virtualization turns *physical* RAM and storage into *logical* resources.

A simple *analogy* is the division of a large classroom with many desks and chairs divided between several study groups who have the impression of having their own classroom, but they are only sharing a single classroom and its resources. The isolation would be even more evident if each group was surrounded by partitions. If the needs of the groups change, the "allocator" might shift desks and tables around to meet those needs, calling on spares in an adjoining store room if necessary.

This division of resources is the basis of the cloud systems that are so prevalent today. The cloud user buys a service from the cloud supplier, which is delivered from a virtual machine he knows nothing about (in theory).

In this crowded area of abstractions, there are variations of Figure 4.4 as to how the hypervisor (supervisory) function is placed relative to the native operating system and you will come across terms like

---

* "Virtual Machine," http://www.pcmag.com/encyclopedia/term/53927/virtual-machine. The web page also has brief but useful pieces of more information about the subject.

- Paravirtualization
- Containers
- Dockers

which are variations on the configuration of the virtualized environments. These you can pick up on a need-to-know basis.

References

- "Virtualization for Dummies (Cheat Sheet):" http://www.dummies.com/how -to/content/virtualization-for-dummies-cheat-sheet.html
- "An Introduction to Virtualization:" https://software.intel.com/sites/default/files /m/d/4/1/d/8/An_Introduction_to_Virtualization.pdf. *This is an excellent introduction to virtualization with terms explained with the use of very clear diagrams.*
- "Introduction to Server Virtualization Technology and Hypervisor Types:" http://www.thegeekstuff.com/2014/01/virtualization-intro/. *This is an introduction to virtualization but also describes the virtualization of networks, storage, and servers.*
- "Virtualization and the Cloud—Tutorial:" http://www.edn.com/design/wireless -networking/4421896/1/Virtualization-and-the-Cloud-A-Tutorial-Part-I

Virtualized/Abstracted Environments

One paper on the topics in this section states that "the world has gone *software-defined* mad." Not 100% true, I'm sure, but very close to the truth and moving closer. The only possible issue might be the old adage if something looks too good to be true, it probably is. The main thing to remember is that very few things in life are free and abstraction may incur cost and performance overheads. In addition, there is still the hidden infrastructure to be managed whether or not it is visible to some people.

Don't just dive in; put your toe in the water first and remember to put requirements before technology.

Software-Defined Data Center (SDDC)

According to *Webopedia,*

> Software-defined data center (SDDC) is the phrase used to refer to a data center where all infrastructure is virtualized and delivered as a service. Control of the data center is fully automated by software, meaning hardware configuration is maintained through intelligent software systems. This is in contrast to traditional data centers where the infrastructure is typically defined by hardware and devices.

Software-defined data centers are considered by many to be the next step in the evolution of virtualization and cloud computing as it provides a solution to support both legacy enterprise applications and new cloud computing services.

There are three core components of the SDDC: network virtualization, server virtualization, and storage virtualization, which means that access to them is via an abstraction, outlined previously.*

Software-Defined Storage (SDS)

Software-defined storage is the pooling of physical storage from multiple network storage devices into what appears to be a *single storage device*. The physical configuration is managed from a central console as if it were a single device. Storage virtualization is commonly used in storage area networks (SANs).

By separating the storage hardware from the software that manages the storage infrastructure, software-defined storage enables enterprises to purchase heterogeneous storage hardware without having to worry as much about issues such as interoperability, under- or over-utilization of specific storage resources, and manual oversight of storage resources.[†]

Software-Defined Network (SDN)

Software-defined network (SDN) is a general term for the abstracted view of a network's components.

Software-defined networking (SDN) is an architecture purporting to be dynamic, manageable, cost-effective, and adaptable, seeking to be suitable for the high-bandwidth, dynamic nature of today's applications. SDN architectures decouple network control and forwarding functions, enabling network control to become directly programmable and the underlying infrastructure to be abstracted from applications and network services.[‡]

---

[*] "Software Defined Data Center (SDDC) Definition," https://www.dmtf.org/sites/default /files/standards/documents/DSP-IS0501_1.0.1a.pdf.

[†] http://www.webopedia.com/TERM/S/software-defined_storage_sds.html. There are a number of other terms for abstracted resources defined with links to information on them. Also see "A Guide to Software-Defined Storage," http://www.computerweekly.com/guides/A-guide-to -software-defined-storage. This link is a discussion document on SDS in its own right but has links to more details throughout.

[‡] https://en.wikipedia.org/wiki/Software-defined_networking

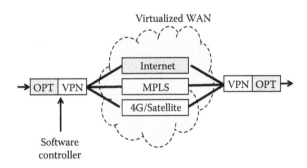

Figure 4.5   SD-WAN and software controller.

Advanced. Should you need it, there is a free online course titled "Software Defined Networking" provided by Princeton University (https://www.coursera .org/course/sdn1). There are other computer courses at Coursera.org and other sites. You can search for them with a simple search for "free online computer courses" or similar keywords.

Storage-Defined Wide Area Network (SD-WAN)

A storage-defined wide area network is a subset of the general software-defined network concept.

> The WAN is no longer a single pipe, it's a fabric of multiple types of links, everything from 4G LTE, DSL, cable … and the [software-defined WAN] SD WAN will offer customers much more intelligence allowing them to prioritize traffic and apps based on policies they just couldn't do before," said Jason Rolleston, Cisco's senior director of product management for WAN enterprise networking. "The WAN has always been a bottleneck and a problem area in terms of complexity— software defined networking can take away a lot of those issues.*

The concept of a software controlled WAN is illustrated in Figure 4.5 where a software controller stands in for individual connections to the WAN. Other functions and *performance enhancements* can be implemented via this controller as follows:

- Application bandwidth priority assignment to give preference to key work
- Measure real-time performance in both directions: across the WAN and back

---

* http://www.networkworld.com/article/2893390/lan-wan/what-network-technology-is-going -to-shake-up-your-wan.html

- Implement business polices on link types and usage (prioritization)
- Implement *protocol acceleration*, *data compression*, and *caching* to improve application performance (response time and throughput)

The take-up of SD-WAN is relatively slow but pundits expect it to continue to grow in the next few years. Its benefits are numerous according to nearly all reports and universally achievable.

References

- "Citrix SD-WAN Introduction and Overview:" https://vimeo.com/152852142. *This Citrix video provides an excellent introduction to SD-WAN with clear diagrams. Other sources I've checked are mostly diagram-less and/or marketing fluff. I rarely attempt papers or articles on network topics that don't contain diagrams.*
- "Technology Overview for SD-WAN:" https://www.gartner.com/doc/reprints. *A Gartner paper (2Q 2015) that covers some of the nontechnical aspects of SD-WAN that businesses need to consider in assessing SD-WAN in their circumstances.*
- "Talari Blog:" http://www.talari.com/blog/category/software-defined-wan-sd -wan/. *Talari has published several papers. They include a look at SD-WAN take-up over the next few years and the future-proofing of a WAN, a very desirable thing.*
- "Posts Tagged 'Software-Defined Networking:'" http://zkresearch.com/blog /tag/software-defined-networking/. *Some blogs and useful information on software-defined networks and WANs, but not for the beginner.*

Other IT Concepts

Many terms in modern IT do not always represent new concepts or products; they are often a combination of things that are involved in some particular aspect of IT. An example of this is bring your own device (BYOD), a term applied to remote or casual users of a system(s). This type of access brings other factors into account, such as performance and security, and so putting all these similar eggs in one basket and giving it a name makes some sense.

Application Performance Management (APM)

APM is sometimes taken to mean application performance monitoring, but there is a wider meaning. Monitoring, of any resource, is part of management, which I define as follows:

$$Management = Design + Monitoring + Analysis + Action$$

Having said this, a definition of APM, commonly accepted, comes from Gartner:

> Application performance monitoring (APM) is one or more software and hardware components that facilitate monitoring to meet five main functional dimensions: end-use experience monitoring (EUM), run-time application architecture discovery modeling and display, user-defined transaction profiling, component deep-dive monitoring in application context, and analytics.*

But, always remember that full management of a resource, including applications, covers all that I have put in the pseudoequation discussed above, whatever words are meant by the acronym APM.

The measurements of importance will depend on the person's viewpoint. The systems man will be interested in utilizations of key resources (CPU, disk, etc.), whereas as the network guy is interested in numeric properties of the network. The end user (or business user) is interested in

- The *response time* (speed) of the transactions and their variability as seen at his point of access. These are usually expressed as *percentiles* (see the Glossary).
- The *throughput*, that is, transactions per second or jobs processed per unit time.
- The *availability* of the service. This means working when it is meant to be working and not just the hours the service is scheduled to be available.

The end user is also interested in *security*, but this is less a tangible measurement than the others listed.

These factors of interest to the user are often enshrined in an agreement between business and IT, which is called a service-level agreement (SLA; for details of this, see Appendix A). It is the standard against which the service to the users is measured, often called quality of service (QoS).

A good starting point is the *Wikipedia* entry for "application performance management."† There are numerous other articles on APM, mainly by vendors and some, though not all, have useful generic information on the subject. If you are looking at such literature, ensure you understand exactly the measurements involved and if they fit your requirements.

Bring Your Own Device (BYOD)

In today's proliferation of IT, BYOD is a phrase that has become widely adopted to refer to employees who bring their own computing devices, such as smart phones,

---

* http://www.gartner.com/it-glossary/application-performance-monitoring-apm/
† https://en.wikipedia.org/wiki/Application_performance_management

laptops and tablets, to the workplace for use and connectivity on the (hopefully) secure corporate network.

One issue when such devices are used remotely by employees is security of access over networks. Without adequate measures to ensure that only bona fide employees can access various parts of the system, it is wide open to cyberattack and data compromise. See the two references at the end of this section.

The second reference in the following section suggests a number of job types that would benefit from, or need as a necessity, BYOD accessibility:

■ Millennials (young people who can only communicate via such devices)
■ Technical staff
■ Executives (business and IT)
■ Older workers
■ Salespeople
■ Hourly workers
■ Other, mainly moaners and the disgruntled (why them I don't know)

References
■ "BYOD—Bring Your Own Device:" http://www.webopedia.com/TERM/B/BYOD.html
■ "All about BYOD:" http://www.cio.com/article/2396336/byod/all-about-byod.html

Unified Communications (UC)

According to *Webopedia*,

> Unified communications is a phrase used to describe any communications system, usually a business system, that encompasses a broad range of technologies and applications that have been designed, sold and supported as a single communications platform or as one entity. Unified communications systems generally enable companies to use integrated data, video, and voice in one supported product.

According to *Wikipedia*, UC is not a single product but a collection of elements that includes:

■ Instant messaging
■ Unified messaging
■ Speech access and personal assistant
■ Conferencing (audio, web, and video)
■ Collaboration tools
■ Mobility

- Business process integration (BPI)
- Software to enable business process integration
- Access to other services

References

- "Unified Communications:" https://en.wikipedia.org/wiki/Unified_commu
nications
- "Unified Communications for Dummies:" http://www.dummies.com/how-to
/content/unified-communications-for-dummies-cheat-sheet.html. *A useful
cheat sheet and an excellent introduction to UC.*
- "Art Rosenberg:" http://www.ucstrategies.com/unified-communications
-professionals/art-rosenberg.aspx. *The coiner of the phrase "unified communications," Art Rosenberg has written papers on the topic, which are listed at this link.*

OpenStack (b. 2010)

OpenStack is another "collection" entity as opposed to an architecture or product
set.

> OpenStack is a global collaboration of developers and technologists
> producing an open source cloud computing platform for public and
> private clouds and consists of a series of interrelated projects delivering
> various components for a cloud infrastructure solution.[*]

It has three major components (all of which are explained in the link https://en
.wikipedia.org/wiki/OpenStack):

- Compute
- Image service
- Object storage

OpenStack has attracted more than 500 member organizations, including Dell,
Cisco, Citrix, HP, EMC, VMware, Red Hat, IBM and Intel, and the project is currently managed by the nonprofit OpenStack Foundation (http://www.openstack
.org/foundation).

Colocation

"A colocation (colo) is a data center facility in which a business can rent space for
servers and other computing hardware."[†] "Colo" facilities offer organizations a secure

---

[*] http://www.webopedia.com/TERM/O/openstack.html
[†] http://searchsoa.techtarget.com/definition/collocation

place to physically house their hardware and equipment, as opposed to locating it on their own premises where the threats of fire, theft, or vandalism are much greater.

Converged Infrastructure

Converged infrastructure is one in which multiple IT components are combined in a single, optimized computing package. Components of a converged infrastructure may include servers, storage devices, networking equipment, and software for IT systems management and operations. It is rather like buying a complete piece of furniture instead of a self-assembly flat-pack.*

Reference
■ "Converged Infrastructure:" http://www.convergedinfrastructure.com. *Also at this site find the link for the article "Best Practices for Implementing Converged Infrastructure in the Data Center."*

Clouds

Clouds is a huge topic, but its basic ingredients are abstraction and virtualization. Think of it as a serve-yourself restaurant where you take what you need when you need and pay for it afterward. There is not only yourself doing this, but other people sharing the food on tables, in containers, and so on. Refresh yourself on virtualization and I'm sure you'll get the picture.

The following is the NIST definition of cloud computing:

> Cloud computing is a model for enabling ubiquitous, convenient, on-demand network access to a shared pool of configurable computing resources (e.g., networks, servers, storage, applications, and services) that can be rapidly provisioned and released with minimal management effort or service provider interaction. This cloud model is composed of five essential characteristics, three service models, and four deployment models.

Cloud Characteristics

On-demand self-service. A consumer can unilaterally provision computing capabilities, such as server time and network storage, as needed automatically without requiring human interaction with each service provider.

---

* Especially if you become homicidal, as I do, when faced with a flat-pack where the instructions don't match the units in it.

Broad network access. Capabilities are available over the network and accessed through standard mechanisms that promote use by heterogeneous thin or thick client platforms (e.g., mobile phones, tablets, laptops, and workstations).

Resource pooling. The provider's computing resources are pooled to serve multiple consumers using a multitenant model, with different physical and virtual resources dynamically assigned and reassigned according to consumer demand. There is a sense of location independence in that the customer generally has no control or knowledge over the exact location of the provided resources but may be able to specify location at a higher level of abstraction (e.g., country, state, county, canton, arrondissement, or data center). Examples of resources include storage, processing, memory, and network bandwidth.

Rapid elasticity. Capabilities can be elastically provisioned and released, in some cases automatically, to scale rapidly outward and inward commensurate with demand. To the consumer, the capabilities available for provisioning often appear to be unlimited and can be appropriated in any quantity at any time. However, there's no such thing as a free lunch and in general you pay by resource consumed.

Measured service. Cloud systems automatically control and optimize resource use by leveraging a metering capability at some level of abstraction appropriate to the type of service (e.g., storage, processing, bandwidth, and active user accounts). Resource usage can be monitored, controlled, and reported, providing transparency for both the provider and consumer of the utilized service.

Note: In addition, a search on "cloud computing" with a vendor name will yield a lot of information, assuming you can sort the educational wheat from the marketing chaff, unless you like the latter.

References

- "NIST Cloud Computing Program:" National Institute of Standards and Technology (NIST): http://www.nist.gov/itl/cloud/index.cfm
- "Cloud Computing—Primer:" http://www.cisco.com/c/dam/en_us/about/ac123/ac147/archived_issues/ipj_12-3/ipj_12-3.pdf. *A very good introduction to cloud computing.*

Data Topics

Data and databases housing this data are the backbone of modern IT as it was in the dawn of IT; only the format has changed. In addition, today's IT world has data volumes on the order of magnitude greater than those of 20 years ago—the so-called *big data*. This necessitates a change of direction in storing and accessing this data.

The older database systems are still around in various hidden corners of the IT universe:

- Simple flat or sequential files
- ISAM/VSAM, index databases

- DL/I, IBM's hierarchical database, often used in conjunction with IBM OLTP
- Company DIY databases (I've come across a few of these)
- Network databases, for example, a materials one for "composed of" and "where used" queries in bill of materials (BoM) processing and similar

Databases

Wikipedia has a list of databases, past and present, and some of the former are predecessors of some modern versions.* The main relational database management systems (RDBMS)† in use today are

- Microsoft SQL Server
- Oracle
- Oracle MySQL
- IBM DB2
- IBM Informix
- Ingres
- Sybase
- MySQL, named after someone's daughter called My
- MongoDB, a variety of NoSQL and used in document storage
- NoSQL
- NonStop SQL

Most of these databases are listed in the *Wikipedia* link in the footnote and there are links within the article to nearly all of them should you feel inclined to pursue them further.

Big Data

According to IBM,

> Big data is being generated by everything around us at all times. Every digital process and social media exchange produces it. Systems, sensors and mobile devices transmit it. Big data is arriving from multiple sources at an alarming velocity, volume and variety. To extract meaningful value from big data, you need optimal processing power, analytics capabilities and skills.

---

* https://en.wikipedia.org/wiki/List_of_relational_database_management_systems
† Standard RDBMS are databases using tables that can be linked to give the impression of a single table that can be accessed in various ways. It is totally different in structure and access methods from hierarchical databases.

Hadoop is a clustering process for handling big data and structured or free from data. An e-book on it (*Hadoop Illuminated*) can be obtained from various sources via a web search using "hadoop illuminated, e-book" as search terms. This e-book defines big data as a "very large, loosely structured data set that defies traditional storage." According to this source, big data arises from multiple sources, some unheard of years ago:

■ Web data
■ Photographs, music, and videos
■ Social media data (Facebook, Twitter, LinkedIn, etc.)
■ Clickstream data (when users navigate a website, the clicks are logged for further analysis which is important for online advertising and e-commerce)
■ Sensor data from numerous sources including road traffic analysis, petroleum production, and weather forecasting

Examples of big data given in the Hadoop e-book are

■ Facebook has 40PB of data and captures 100TB/day
■ Yahoo has 60PB of data
■ Twitter handles 8TB/day
■ eBay has 40PB of data and handles 50TB/day
■ U.S. Library of Congress has 235TB of stored data
■ Boeing collects 640TB per flight
■ Wal-Mart has 2.5PB of stored data

Add to this the normal business data—databases, e-mails, documents, and so forth—and that archived for various reasons and you have the picture of a world drowning in data when it wants information. Information in my book is data, trimmed and cooked, ready to eat and easily digested.

See also http://hadoop.apache.org/.

One question some people are asking is "Do we need it all in raw form?" To which I answer, "I don't know. It's an organization's business requirements issue." Maybe they do, maybe they don't.

Systems and Service Management

The management of the IT resources that support business applications is known as *systems management*. The management of the IT services that support the user and his

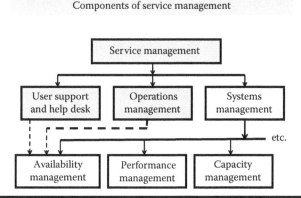

Figure 4.6   The components of service management.

application is known a *service management*. The latter includes systems management but also things like help desks, service-level agreements, and other overarching functions (Figure 4.6) to *keep the user show on the road*, which is a key business objective.

Remember, management is not the same as monitoring and encompasses design and action phases as well as simple monitoring (measurement).

There are some details on service management in Appendix D, mainly in the form of topic lists that comprise the various parts of service management.

Malware

Malware is a generic term that covers software that finds its way onto your system with malicious intent; sometimes for mischief, other times for financial gain or political attacks by one faction or nation on another. There are various types, each with a name* but in essence, they all do harm in one way or another to your system, your bank balance, or both. Similar terms are cybersecurity and cybercrime.

Some malware encrypts files and demands a ransom to obtain a key to decrypt them, others might destroy them altogether, and some may just steal bank records for account access. Whatever form these attacks take, they need to be countered and there are numerous products out there that purport to do this. The problem is that however clever the countermeasures, the perpetrators always seem to go one better, so it is a constant cat-and-mouse game.

This phenomenon started with PCs but now affects large corporate and government systems and has moved on to mobile devices. As well as using antimalware products, personal vigilance is needed; the watchword is if in doubt delete (IIDD).

---

* Worm, virus, phishing, ransomware, trojan horse, or just malicious executable files with innocent-looking names.

It may interest you to know that a large proportion of malware damage is done by internal staff in an organization.

The following link is an introduction to malware and contains onward references for you to follow if you wish: "Introduction to Malware," https://www.cert .gov.uk/wp-content/uploads/2014/08/An-introduction-to-malware.pdf.

Note: Despite this being a short introduction, the topic is of immense importance and growing.

Network Protocols*

We have dealt with network protocols earlier but we will add some details here, mainly to put the various protocols into perspective against the OSI network communications model.

The OSI 7-Layer Model

The original seven-layer model (or stack) was introduced by IBM in 1974 with the announcement of its Systems Network Architecture (SNA). The model defined the functions of each layer from the application to the physical transmission media. The function layers were designed to effectively isolate changes to one layer from all but the adjacent layers. The seven-layer concept was adopted by IEEE in defining its standard Open Systems Interconnection (OSI) model.

There are several implementations of this model, as shown in Figure 4.7. Some implementations span layers and some appear as four- or five-layer models but are based on the defined function of the OSI model. The difference lies in the boundaries between the layers, and sometimes the names of the layers, in the OSI, SNA, and Transmission Control Protocol/Internet Protocol (TCP/IP) models.

The model and implementation depend on the requirements: performance, security of transmission, controllability, and so on.

There are a number of names of protocols that may confuse you (they certainly did me) but remember the following:

- There are several protocols that operate at different levels in the stack.
- Some of these protocols only work at certain levels/layers in the stack.
- Protocols can cooperate in a stack, performing their allotted function, and interfacing with the layers above and below.
- Application layer protocols cover
  - Application
  - Presentation
  - Session layers

---

* Wannabe IT people might want to skip this section.

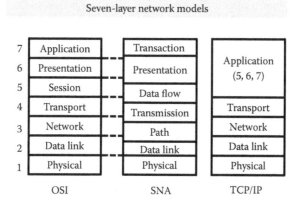

Figure 4.7 Seven-layer network models.

- Transport services cover
  - Transport services layer
- Network services cover
  - Network layer
  - Data link layer
  - Physical layer

References

- "Introduction to Protocols:" http://pluto.ksi.edu/~cyh/cis370/ebook/ch06b.htm
- "List of Network Protocols:" https://en.wikipedia.org/wiki/Lists_of_network_protocols

Wireless Protocols

In addition to traditional wired transmission protocols as covered here, wireless networks also contain protocols dictating how they operate—often in terms of the range, frequency, and transmission methods of wireless communications as well as the security of the network and the speed at which data can transmit. The Institute of Electrical and Electronics Engineers (IEEE) creates standards for multiple protocols that deal with larger wireless networks (*de jure* or "official" standards). Short-range wireless protocols (such as Bluetooth) exist to regulate communications between devices at short ranges, usually for purposes such as voice transmission or wireless accessory use (*de facto* or "everyone uses it" standards).

Protocol Security

In modern times, security is a prime concern for both private individuals, the public sector, and companies. Most protocols were designed 40 years ago when *phishing* was something you did with a rod. Security is now of paramount importance and some protocols have amendments to cater for this concern, for example, Secure Sockets Layer (SSL). The advent of *wire data* access (see the Glossary) offers the opportunity to examine a network at its most basic level and check for pattern irregularities that might identify attempted malicious access to services.

DevOps and Continuous Delivery

DevOps is not a new technique or piece of hardware but a grouping of activities with a common goal. The literature on it varies in definition but agrees on the essence of it. The need for speed of development and implementation (agility) has impacted the traditional way in which software is developed and dictates collaboration between *developers* who wrote the software and the IT *operations* team that maintains an organization's hardware infrastructure.

The skills for this might seem specific at first sight but development and operations involve different skill sets, but the DevOps environment might involve anyone in the IT department. Whatever your chosen job spec, you will need to be aware of the use of DevOps in your company. It is more than likely today that DevOps will function in a virtualized environment, hence extra skills are involved in the rapid development cycle.

References

- "An Introduction to DevOps:" https://insights.sei.cmu.edu/devops/2014/03/an-introduction-to-devops.html
- "Introduction to DevOps:" https://channel9.msdn.com/Series/DevOps-Fundamentals/Introduction-to-DevOps
- "An Introduction to DevOps:" http://devops.com/2014/04/02/introduction todevops
- In addition, as usual, you will find a trusty article on *Wikipedia* in any "DevOps" search.

Data Centers and Environment

There is a lot of talk today about aspects of data centers that were minor issues many years ago. Cooling of smaller multicored processors and other compact but high-performance/capacity devices plus concern for the environment in general—the green data center—occupy planners and operations staff. There are dozens of sources of information on planning, designing, operating, and migrating to data centers. It is pointless my referencing all of them here since all organizations' needs and requirements are different, so my choice may not be your choice.

However, search terms like "data center," "migration," "best practices," "rationalization," "consolidation," "modernization," "legacy migration," "legacy modernization," together with other qualifying terms will yield a lot of information sources. Having said that, I will mention a few key documents in some of these areas because they are well written, mainly objective texts that cover topics that will apply to most installations.

References

- "Green Data Center:" http://www.greendatacenternews.org/
- "Use Best Practices to Design Data Center Facilities:" http://www.it.northwestern .edu/bin/docs/DesignBestPractices_127434.pdf. *Mainly cooling and power related.*
- "Data Center Design and Implementation Best Practices:" https://www.bicsi .org/uploadedfiles/BICSI_002_Sample.pdf. *A heavyweight look at details of a design: space, power, cooling, and safety.*
- "Best Practices in Data Center and Server Consolidation:" http://gartnerinfo .com/futureofit2011/MEX38L_B4%20mex38l_b4.pdf
- "Cisco Best Practices Data Center Operations Management:" http://www .cisco.com/c/dam/en_us/about/ciscoitatwork/downloads/ciscoitatwork/pdf /Cisco_IT_Operational_Overview_Data_Center_Management.pdf. *This is a look at the management of a live Cisco data center; always better than a theoretical treatise.*

Green Data Centers

Green data centers is a relatively new slant on data centers, coming off the back of facilities design and management. A green data center is a repository for the storage, management, and dissemination of data in which the mechanical, lighting, electrical and computer systems are designed for maximum energy efficiency and minimum environmental impact. The construction and operation of a green data center includes advanced technologies and strategies.*

Data Center Infrastructure Management (DCIM)

The general topic of infrastructure—heat, power, space, and other environmental items—is collectively known as DCIM. Here are two links to discussions on the topic: one a Gartner "magic quadrant" evaluation of DCIM tools, the second is a general discussion of the DCIM field, which contains some supporting onward links:

- "Gartner Magic Quadrant for DCIM:" http://www.gartner.com/technology /reprints.do
- "Top Five Data Center Issues: DCIM to the Rescue:" http://www.datacenter knowledge.com/archives/2013/01/08/top-five-data-center-issues-dcim-to -the-rescue/

---

* See http://searchdatacenter.techtarget.com/definition/green-data-center.

IT Operations Analytics (ITOA)

In ye olden days, operational data for performance, capacity, or other management disciplines was often retrospective with people browsing monitor data after the event. This relied on the skills of the interpreters of the data to produce key indicators and suggest any remedial action thought necessary. It was generally impossible to measure trends and connections between results in this mode of operation.

In today's vastly more complex IT environments, such *modus operandi* are not adequate or even feasible and other methods have evolved. They go under the general name of *operations analytics*, often prefixed with the word *real-time*, and software does a heap of work analyzing monitor output to produce key indicators of QoS in the measured areas (performance, availability, etc.). The software can often make predictions, especially where erratic system loads occur as, for example, on public websites.

The definition of ITOA given by *Wikipedia* is roughly as follows:

> IT Operations Analytics (ITOA, also known as Advanced Operational Analytics or IT Data Analytics) technologies are primarily used to discover complex patterns in high volumes of often "noisy" IT system availability and performance data.

Forrester Research defines IT analytics as "The use of mathematical algorithms and other innovations to extract meaningful information from the sea of raw data collected by management and monitoring technologies."

ITOA solutions aim to analyze the masses of data accumulated by monitors in IT operations and turn it into relevant information and areas of remedial or preventative action.

Such analytics solutions use *intelligent* computing capabilities to understand IT systems behavior over time and provide early warnings of out-of-line situations, assuming you have a baseline to work from.

IT operations analytics solutions can

■ Predict problems before they impact service and possibly result in outages
■ Search quickly across operations data for faster problem resolution
■ Provide information to aid optimization of IT and application infrastructure to meet the specifications of service-level agreements (SLAs) for quality of service (QoS)

There are a number of suppliers of ITOA solutions, including products, for instance:

■ IBM
■ HP

- Teamquest
- Extrahop
- Other organizations

A search for "ITOA solutions" and a vendor name and you should get all the extra information you need about this topic.

*Performance Benchmarks**

The prediction of the performance of systems (including networks) and applications today is done in various ways:

- By calculation, if the workload characteristics and volumes are known
- By software simulations, which are, in essence, rolling calculations that measure performance metrics by math carried out at short intervals to simulate a workload; this is quite sophisticated for network loads
- By using standard, bespoke, or specific *benchmarks* and trying to relate the results to your own workload
- By actually running your workload somewhere on some other system and extrapolating or interpolating the results to the system you are interested in

Performance numbers, in various units and derived from benchmarks, are known as *metrics*. Sample metrics are

- Transaction or query response time and range of variation
- Throughput: data rate, jobs completed per unit time, or the elapsed time for a large job
- Input/output operations per second (I/Os per second or IOPs) for storage devices
- Graphics write speed and other metrics related to graphics displays
- Other metric numbers for special workloads

Thus, it is now easy to see why single or even multiple metrics do not fit all workload types. You can find many common benchmarks by viewing the TPC and SPEC organizations listed later in the section "IT 'Standards' Bodies."

Other system metrics, including performance, and their measurements are covered in Appendix D, which deals with systems management. Performance was introduced here to introduce the concept of benchmarks.

---

* A test used to compare performance of hardware and/or software. When comparing benchmark results, it is important to know exactly what the benchmarks are designed to test.

Aside: Benchmarks flew like arrows in the 1980s benchmark wars, and vendors were not averse to minor fiddles in their pursuit of being hailed as the performance king. I have seen benchmarks run by vendor 1 on his and vendor 2's equipment and vice versa. You would not believe the results obtained and neither did the public.

Information Sources

There are some sources of useful and impartial information that you should be aware of and search for on current topics.* You will probably need to perform a subject search and which ones you use will depend on what depth you need to take in any subject. This is the technique I use and often add the vendor names of IBM, Cisco, and Microsoft to the other search terms, simply because I have found that much of their material is generic and educational as opposed to marketing fluff or candy floss (informal IBM terms) found in some search hits.

Useful search terms, apart from the topic itself, are "tutorial," "overview," "definition," "white paper," and similar fluff excluders. These can yield good educational material, much of it from university sources in the form of presentations, although some of them are impenetrable jungles of jargon and graphs.

There is some useful material from sources other than vendors or specialist organizations, particularly universities. There are often good presentations, usually at undergraduate level, that are very clear expositions of various topics. I have relied heavily on the information in some of them for my own understanding.

One high-class source is the Webtorials site where detailed analysis and instructions on many topics, mainly network related, can be found.†

Another source of useful information is *Wikipedia*, despite some publishers and others decrying it as having articles lacking peer review, of dubious origin, and so forth. I have found it excellent in its presentation of topics I am very familiar with, often taking me beyond what I already knew, and I also believe that the same quality exists across other topics. Where a topic needs clarification or expansion, this is clearly stated.

You may also find books and chargeable papers helpful and if the benefit outweighs the costs, then go for it. Libraries tend to be very slow in putting up-to-date books on their shelves,‡ so the purchase route, e-book or paper, may be your only option.

---

* At a first pass, I stick to impartial sources and not vendors since many slant "vital requirements for X" to "what our product does is X." I have nothing against them but if you do use them as a primary source, try to get a consensus across vendors when trying to understand a particular topic.

† See "Category Archives," http://www.webtorials.com/content/category-archive-summary.html; "Infrastructure & Performance at Webtorials," http://www.webtorials.com/content/subject -area/infrastructure-and-performance/. Much of the material, though first class, is not beginners' fare and may cause intellectual indigestion.

‡ My local library is so dated it still has books recommending trips on the Titanic and some others as current as *Modern Americans: Abraham Lincoln*! (only joking).

IT "Standards" Bodies

This heading may be a misnomer as there are technical bodies that are not *de jure* (official) bodies but develop ideas and make suggestions for standards and best practices as well as providing resources such as white papers and checklists. Often they are treated in a *de facto* (widely used) way as the leaders in a particular field, though some would dispute this.

If you are coming into IT or even already in it, an occasional scan of some of these websites will yield vital information for you as part of the "little and often" style of learning. The ones I have come across in my work and in writing are listed next but should not be taken as either definitive or exhaustive.*

- National Institute of Standards and Technology (NIST), IT section: http://www.nist.gov/information-technology-portal.cfm. *There are IT subareas covered in this section, for example, Cloud Standards can be found at* http://www.nist.gov/itl/cloud/upload/NIST_SP-500-291_Jul5A.pdf.
- Storage Performance Council (SPC), storage benchmarks: www.storageperformance.org/home
- Transaction Processing Performance Council (TPC), commercial benchmarks: www.tpc.org/
- Standard Performance Evaluation Corporation (SPEC), a range of benchmarks on processor power and throughput in various areas: http://www.tpc.org/
- Storage Networking Industry Association (SNIA): www.snia.org/
- IT Infrastructure Library (ITIL): https://www.axelos.com/best-practice-solutions/itil
- Institute of Electrical and Electronics Engineers (IEEE): http://www.ieee.org
- American National Standards Institute (ANSI): http://www.ansi.org
- W3C: www.w3.org
- Web Services Interoperability Organization (WS-I): http://www.ws-i.org/
- Internet Engineering Task Force (IETF): www.ietf.org
- International Organization for Standardization (ISO): http://www.iso.ch
- International Telecommunications Union (ITU), with subsections: http://www.itu.int
- Telecommunications Industry Association (TIA): www.tiaonline.org/
- Network Standards (Data Communications and Networking): http://what-when-how.com/data-communications-and-networking/network-standards-data-communications-and-networking/
- The Open Group: http://www.opengroup.org/

---

* There are numerous national bodies, too many to mention here, but a good source for these is: https://en.wikipedia.org/wiki/List_of_technical_standard_organisations#International_standards_organizations.

- Linux Standard Base (LSB): http://www.linuxbase.org/
- Object Management Group (OMG): http://www.omg.org
- Distributed Management Task Force (DTMF): http://www.dmtf.org/

There are many other bodies dealing with various specific aspects of IT, in particular availability and security:

- "10 IT Organizations to Help Your Career:" http://www.networkcomputing .com/careers/10-it-organizations-help-your-career/22319024
- "High Availability Organizations:" http://www.availabilitydigest.com/public _articles/1010/availability_organizations.pdf
- Cyber Security and Information Systems Information Analysis Center (CSIAC): www.csiac.org
- Cloud Security Alliance (CSA): www.cloudsecurityalliance.org
- InterNational Committee for Information Technology Standards (INCITS): www.incits.org

Other bodies will make themselves known if you search on a topic or subject. For example, NIST has a security section as well as a cloud section referenced elsewhere in this book.

Chapter 5

Roles and Responsibilities

There is often confusion about the words *role*, *responsibility*, and *accountability*. A *role* is a job within a specified environment, for example, network (environment) specialist (job), MVS operator, or mainframe sales. In a technical environment, *responsibility* is the area you work in, functionally and possibly location: "I am responsible for the running of MVS batch jobs." *Accountability* is the onus that lies with the person who, in the words of an IBM U.S. manager, "gets his ass nailed to the wall if things go pear shaped." This may be the overall manager of the responsible people but operating under his control and guidance or it may be the same person responsible for the task. It all depends how the working scheme is set up and organized. In the sales arena, responsibility and accountability often rest with the same person, the salesman (or woman).

The IT Role*

Some pointers to making it in IT, most of which I didn't know until later in my career. Absorb them and use.

- Learn from the past, peers, and, if you are an IT vendor, the competition. You can learn from almost any situation where things have gone right and especially on occasions where they have gone wrong. Just like the saying that there is no bad publicity, there is no such thing as a totally bad experience.
- Try to apply the so-what test to things you say and write. A manager I knew, very nontechnical, when faced with abstruse technical jargon from someone would respond thus: "What does it mean to the end user?" which is often a

---

* Do you mean me? Yes.

killer punch to the speaker. Try it when someone tells you that their Hokey-Cokey 2000 runs at 50 squilliflops and, unless he/she is user/customer aware, he/she will retire crushed.

■ No ATTAM projects: All Things To All Men. They all fail miserably. Set for yourself and the customer realistic and phased goals—no *Star Trek* stuff on offer.

Larger projects should be phased in design and implementation so that iterative amendments can be made before commitment to the final operational system. The key elements of project success I have found in my old acronym FUMP (c. 1994), expanded for today's services, to be borne in mind in any development aimed at end users and the service factors they care about:
- Function/functionality
- Usability
- Manageability
- Performance
- Availability
- Security

These are all or nothing for success.

The M covers availability as well as other things and P, U, and F are also vital. Availability, for example, if it can't be used properly, as per expectations and need, it isn't available. Security is the buzzword today—it wasn't 20 years ago when FUMP was all you needed. How IT changes its emphases as it progresses.

The classic example of an ATTAM project was the United Kingdom's National Health Service (NHS) system to put all patient records on a centralized system for security controlled access by different medical staff. It failed and was scrapped at an estimated cost of more than £12 billion ($18 billion). I realized something was amiss when the overall manager of the scheme jumped ship 2 years before the balloon went up. The debacle was reported in the press, hands raised in horror in Parliament, and then all was forgotten. Forgotten! £12 billion of *my* money (me being the UK public).

Apply FUMPAS to all designs and their implementations—functionality, usability, manageability, performance, availability, and security. Miss one of these and you are as good as dead, in the medium term anyway.

■ Strive to be a *trusted adviser* to the client/user on IT architectures of various types (see Appendices). If the CIO calls you in for advice, you've made it. If he doesn't, work on the points in this list. Gray hair and adequate gravitas helps enormously.

■ Develop communications and rapport with the business units of your customer, not just with IT people and with developers, implementers, and operations.

When I worked at Oracle, I was assigned short term to a large multinational company that was implementing a large new system. I will not name it but tell you it sold cornflakes. There was a well-known consultancy involved and I came across them while they were having a meeting in a room where it was possible to pick up conversations from outside. They were throwing management-speak phrases around like confetti—objectives, timelines, CSFs, expectations, endgame, and so on. Being ex-IBM I tuned in nonchalantly* and soon got the picture. When they emerged from the room, I introduced myself to the person who looked like the leader of the session, saying I was from Oracle. He looked bemused so I said, "This system is based on Oracle. Have you talked to us yet?" No was the reply at which my grimace told him all I was about to say. I don't know how the project fared but I imagine not very well.

If you are part of a multicompany, multidiscipline project, you must be on cooperative terms with the other people in that project. If there is a disjointed feel about the whole affair, tactfully suggest a joint meeting to take place every so often, that is, you take the initiative. If that does not happen, reach for your tin helmet and write backside-covering e-mails and memos.

- Develop architecture viewpoints for different parts of the business: businessperson, architect, operations, deep techie, tyre/tire kicker. Viewpoints are covered under "Service-Level Agreements" in Appendix A.
- Sell architecture (and hence IT) as a business benefit and not an overhead. There are numerous papers on this topic that you might find useful if a nontechnical manager says, So, what about the work at hand?
- Be a listener not a brow beater. Use the 2:1 rule, you have 2 ears and 1 mouth (unless you are very odd). Customers warm to listeners, especially those who have taken the trouble to learn a little about their business and the project at hand. However, don't try to be too clever with what you know; just say something like, "I know a little about that and does it mean …?"
- Anticipate needs of businesses and seek opinions, then, if appropriate, offer advice, especially about relevant technical points and the possible applicability of newer technology and techniques. Take the lead but not in overt *selling* mode.
- Isolate technology from architecture; the same technology and configuration can display differing viewpoints. Similarly, an architecture can be implemented in different ways with different technology.

---

* I also learned to read documents that were upside down across a desk as well. Not part of official training but expected of you. A useful skill you should practice, alongside hearing when apparently not listening in.

■ Be adept at resolving disputes (use the Delphi technique where possible). Try to see all sides of the dispute and politely point out that the end point is a system/project that fits the end users' needs, not the implementers' preferences.

I have been a member of a rugby club for many years and for several of them I sat on the committee. There were often discussions, even arguments, about the way forward: should we build squash courts to boost revenue, change the color of the kit, run dances, and so on. When things got too hectic, I would take out my membership card and read aloud a sentence. That sentence was: "Rule 2—The object of the club shall be to further the interests of Rugby Union Football," giving a perspective against which to judge the merits of the different proposals and ideas. The same logic will apply to IT disputes if the end user or business objectives are substituted in the appropriate places.

■ Develop and maintain 180° vision* of what is going on. You may want to plow your own furrow but there are others plowing theirs and they may cross paths at some point, causing chaos and arguments. Refer to the preceding bullet point to resolve these and to the Six Thinking Hats discussion (Chapter 2 under "Six Thinking Hats Technique").

■ Mentor/educate others involved; be mentored and taught by them as well. You can pass on to the junior IT people what I am trying to pass on to you in this book.

■ Manage risk with and for the customer (see "Risk Management" in Appendix A).

■ If you have time, do a "coffee call" on the customer. You'll be surprised what you can dig up in casual conversation and how they appreciate seeing you around. They may even think you are doing something useful!

■ Read voraciously and keep learning. Anyone who thinks they know it all, or even all they need to know in their environment are fooling themselves.

■ Finally, the golden rules: "Assume nothing" and the Boy Scout motto: "Be prepared." "Oh, I thought you were doing job A, not me" when B, C, and so forth, can't start until A is complete.

The Role of an IT Architect

■ The general rules for the IT person apply equally to any specialist discipline.
■ Learn from the past; reuse any architectures or subarchitectures. An example of reuse is a diluted version of a high availability configuration to cater for an application of lesser importance.

---

* A 360° vision is not recommended as it means looking over your shoulder all the time.

- Apply functionality, usability, manageability, performance, availability, and security (FUMPAS) to all designs and their implementations, as stated previously. If you don't, a reviewing manager might.
- Vet the final implementation plan for adherence to the original architecture design. If necessary, examine any pilot scheme too.
- Develop architecture viewpoints for different parts of the business. Non-technical people don't want to read technical material about their business project, capacity planners are not too concerned with troubleshooting and trouble tickets, and so on.
- Be a trusted adviser on architectures of various types. Know your stuff and check its validity and feasibility before visiting it on the world in general.
- Be honest about what you know and don't know. Someone will soon find you out and blow your cover, which means loss of credibility.
- Develop communications with the business units in your organization or customers if you are with an IT vendor.
- Develop communications with your customer developers, implementers, and operations.
- Sell architecture and demonstrate how it fulfills business needs, showing IT as a business benefit, not an overhead.
- Be a listener.
- Be an assertive leader but not a browbeater.
- Be a business communications earpiece for IT, coffee calling on anyone you can collar.
- Anticipate needs of the business and seek opinions of your understanding of them before proceeding.
- Isolate technology from architecture; many technology configurations can usually fit a single architecture.
- Resolve disputes (Delphi or Six Thinking Hats techniques).
- Develop and maintain 180° vision (360° only if you are a frog).
- Mentor/educate others.
- Leave a solid architecture legacy to a company.
- Manage risk as an integral part of any IT project.
- Assume nothing; same rules as for the generalist.

I've said some of these things before but that is a deliberate part of the immersion process (although occasionally it may be done unconsciously).

Rules for Everyone

- Set business units' expectations, no *Star Trek* stuff on offer, which means being realistic about the technology and, more important, what you can do to streamline the business you are involved with.

Never forget that technology is rarely an end in itself, except for geeks and anoraks, and is there simply to enervate business processes.

- Understand and support company goals and where IT can influence them.
- Provision of "timely" management information as per requirements.
- Concentrate on information needs, namely, data into information, which is "cooked" data served with recommendation trimmings.
- Make suggestions and innovations, but think them through first and implement, perhaps, via a task force or quality circle.
- Instill confidence in business over IT's role in aiding it to function more effectively and profitably. Some business managers see IT as a necessary evil and IT must dispel that myth (unless it is actually true).

A colleague of mine, a long, long time in IBM, was assigned to a large bank as trusted adviser. I knew him well and knew that he knew as much about current technology as my cat and was nervous about that assignment. He was the typical English gentleman who exuded confidence and panache, even though he knew little about IT. He had gravitas and a wise, avuncular appearance for which the young IT people loved him. He was involved in all sorts of things, encouraging and cajoling but stayed well away from any technical issues and was always on hand to smooth furrowed brows. Nice work if you can get it and if you have done your bit in IT for your company, you may be entitled to spend your declining years in such a state of nirvana. However, for the cut-and-thrust, dynamic powerhouse (as I know you are), this is a long way away and maybe not even desirable; you may want to die in harness as I plan to do.

- Inform business users what architecture is and what benefits it offers their part of the business, where appropriate.
- Be a good listener (2-to-1 rule: ears-to-mouth ratio); can't say this too often.
- Keep up *skills development*; see what the future holds in terms of users and technology then plan to be able to meet it head-on. There is a tendency for some vendors of say, technology B, to try to convince everyone that A is dead and B is the future and we just happen to have B.

At the time of this writing, a current theme is disk (HDD) is dead, so is solid state (SSD), long live flash storage. They said cinema was dead when TV became popular, records were dead with the availability of music downloads, books were dead with eBooks … RIP. Those media are having a resurgence. Cinema movies are far more enjoyable than watching a TV version alone, records/DVD I don't know the reason, books are a thing of beauty and handling them far superior to staring at a screen. There may be a lesson here for us all when reading such crystal ball forecasts.

■ Keep up to date with relevant non-IT standards, such as financial changes, that affect you or your customer's business. There may be help needed on the IT front or, if your company sells IT products, opportunities for business. An appropriate variation on the British Special Air Service (SAS) motto might be: "Who watches, wins."

■ Every so often, *stop*, *think*, and *take stock* of whatever you are doing, especially in a team environment—take a halftime break for a team talk and a review of the game plan. At the beginning of the new financial year, IBM encouraged account teams to spend a day off-site developing a plan for the upcoming year. Believe me, if done properly these sessions, lasting from about 8:30 a.m. to 6:00 p.m., were hard work but produced results.

■ If you skipped them or didn't do them properly, you would be found out when your manager or his manager asked you to present your plans. If your management doesn't check on plans, do it anyway if you want to be a true IT pro. "Who skips, loses."

■ If you are doing nothing and need to look busy, rush around with a sheaf of papers in your hand, bumping into people and apologizing saying, "Sorry, in a hurry, lots to do ..." I knew people who carried out this charade for years and even gained promotion. "Search for the guilty, punishment of the innocent, and promotion of nonparticipants" (an old IT saying after a disaster).

■ If harassed and pushed for time:
  - Stop, put your brain on hold, and look out of the window for 5 minutes. If there is no window, stare at the ceiling. If you haven't got a ceiling, get a job somewhere else.
  - Prioritize work *a la* Alan Lakein.*

Prioritizing Tasks

Lakein is a great believer in priorities. He suggests that you sort all of your possible to-do's into three piles—A, B, and C. Then you break it down further by assigning priority numbers within each category. You end up with separate lists of coded to-do's: A-1, A-2, ... B-1, B-2, ... C-1, C-2, ... This is more methodical than I can normally force myself to be, but I acknowledge that it *would* be helpful if I did use it.

One key thing that this priority listing achieves is that you can take the list of C-priority items, put them in the drawer, and forget them. If they're *really* important, you put them on one of the other lists, or else you find somebody else to do them, by delegation or by hiring them out. You can set the B list to one side, too, because Lakein would have

---

* Alan Lakein is a well-known author on personal time management, including *How to Get Control of Your Time and Your Life* (ISBN 0-451-13430-3) which has sold over 3 million copies.

you focus on the A list to the exclusion of everything else for as long as you can. If you get tired of doing your A-1 project, that's fine; switch gears and work on some other A-level project to refresh yourself.*

Delegate where possible ("Jim, could you do X for me please?") but don't look as though you are abdicating. I found the book *Going from Undisciplined to Self-Mastery: Five Simple Steps to Get You There* by Harris Kern very useful.†

---

* http://tewalkerjr.com/blog/2006/10/06/notes-on-alan-lakein-how-to-get-control-of-your
 -time-and-your-life/
† http://www.amazon.com/Going-Undisciplined-Self-Mastery-Simple/dp/1940192706/ref=sr
 _1_1?s=books&ie=UTF8&qid=1446537565&sr=1-1&keywords=harris+kern. You might be
 better searching Amazon under "Books," then search "Harris Kern," looking for the title.

Chapter 6

Fun, Mottoes, and Gaffes

I'll never forget my first fight … all of a sudden I found someone I knew in the fourth row. It was me.

Henny Youngman

I'll never forget my boxing days. I was carried out of the ring so often they put handles on my shorts.

Les Dawson
UK comedian, alas no longer with us

A key part of any job is the ability to have fun without jeopardizing the work you do. Having fun in this context can actually boost your ability to do your job. My three employers—IBM, Oracle, and Sun Microsystems—all had "fun days" in one form or another, usually involving beer!

Laughs aside, I think you will learn much about the IT role from the incidents and accidents I outline next.

Instructive Incidents

There are a number of incidents and situations I have come across in my decades in IT; some are simply amusing, some have fairly serious implications but nevertheless can raise a laugh. The essential message emanating from most of these incidents is that mistakes were made and can be learned from. I certainly did and never repeated any of them. You can perhaps learn and not even make the types of mistake that my colleagues and I did.

The OCR caper. I was assigned a role as the optical character recognition (OCR) guru in the branch I was in and this involved optical mark reader (OMR) as well. One customer, a public utility, installed an IBM 1287 OCR machine and "driver" computer (IBM 360/22), which I oversaw and provided a bespoke course on programming and running the system. The system was running smoothly until, one day, I received an urgent call from the operations manager at the utility.

"We have a problem with the 1287 …" Without hesitating, I launched into my vast repertoire of possible causes: "Was it an 0C4 data check?" "A CCW chain over-run?" "Buffer overflow?" "Documents too small?"

"No," came the impatient reply. "None of those; it just caught fire!" This nearly spelled the end of my OCR career. This is a true story, at least from my end of the telephone line.

Moral: Problem determination—assume nothing and listen to the symptoms before putting your big foot in it.

There is an amusing corollary to this tale involving the actual installation of this 1287 OCR. The machine is very big, some 4 meters long, nearly 2 meters high, and about a meter deep, which necessitated breaking it up (it was designed this way) and taking the two pieces into the machine room before reassembling it. The individual pieces were still very heavy and were transported into the room on a wheeled "bogey."

On this occasion, one piece of the machine gained momentum as it was being pushed and smashed through the half-open machine room doors, putting one of them on the floor and leaving the other hanging drunkenly at an angle. A min-ute or so later, a customer IT manager arrived, surveyed the scene and let out an anguished cry. I looked at him and realized he wasn't looking at the recumbent door and its sibling, but the disk drives of the system, which had colored panels at the front. This time, one panel was red, the other blue: a configuration mess-up to say the least.

I tried to calm him then took one of the odd panels (red), jumped in my car (it wasn't in the machine room but the parking lot) and drove furiously back to IBM base in Manchester, some 60 miles away. In that machine room there were disks identical to the customer's so I swapped panels with the one I had, leaving the IBM disks with odd panels, and returned to the customer with the blue one. The cus-tomer was placated, particularly since in my absence the machine room door had been rehung.

Moral: If it is your "baby," check the configuration before installation at the cus-tomers or in your machine room for internal use.

The weakest link. Just after my "1287 period," I was involved with the use of an IBM mark reader (cutely named a 3881 OMR) used in a UK Examination Board. It was employed for marking multiple-choice questions from school examinations after a successful experience using an IBM bureau 1287 OCR. Part of the system design was the use of a mechanical numbering unit on the reader and these printed numbers formed a vital part of the whole marking system and subsequent results processing. On discussing this project informally with an engineer, he pointed out that the numbering unit on the mark reader was added as a design afterthought and was the least reliable part of the whole system. We quickly changed the process flow of the marking system before we were confronted with irate parents complaining about botched exam results for their little Cyrus Jasperberger II or Peggy Sue.

Moral: Don't base your design of service processes, even non-IT ones, on a single point of failure (SPoF), especially one that is unreliable and cannot be duplicated for redundancy. We got away with this one by what was essentially a walkthrough of the system with an expert in component failure impact analysis (CFIA), a topic discussed in Appendix A.

Examination miracle. In my early days in IBM, I had to learn programming along with every other rookie and one of the languages we were taught was report program generator (RPG), a parameter-driven coding method. I was assigned the task of writing a program for a local examination board. The program was to examine exam marks and create a table containing numbers of entrants in each examination grade: A, B, C, and so on. I ploughed through the program and delivered the requested table of grades. I never really examined this output since I was just pleased that the program actually did something. When a person from the examination board examined the output, he pointed out that more people attained an A grade than the number of people who entered the exam!

Moral: Make sure you understand requirements and check your output. This applies to nonprogramming work, too.

Shock, horror—cannibal code. In my early days in IBM, I also had to learn assembler code and I was assigned to a customer to write an assembler program for, I think, an electricity board. The program was constructed and when I tested it, it crashed and the system died. I tweaked a few things and tried again—same result. I then took a core dump (as the spewing out of the whole contents of main storage was called in those days). I looked at the dump and saw that the main storage consisted wholly of "0000 ..." until near the end where the diagnostics indicated it had died. It ceased at a ZAP (delete) instruction and I then realized it had crashed when it tried to ZAP itself! The reasons were twofold: First, the operating system was very, very basic. Second, I was trying to blank out (zap) a particular data field by it deleting piece by piece, using a data header that contained the field length and stopping the deletions when I reached the end. I was thus merrily zapping for what I thought was just the field length but somehow I picked up the wrong header length and carried on zapping everything in my path until I tried to zap myself. The picture of that core dump could have won a Turner Prize (an art award), especially if it had been titled *Man's Stupidity*.

Moral: A little coding knowledge is dangerous.

Amusing Incidents

The disappearing channel. IBM systems attached its storage via *channels*, today's equivalent being SCSI and similar. There were three types, one of which was a block multiplexor channel (BMPX) allowing concurrent transmissions by interleaving different data streams. One of the IBM engineers in Liverpool left a BMPX by the side of his desk when he left work one evening. The next morning, the BMPX had disappeared. Panic inquiries showed that one of the cleaners has assumed it was rubbish and put it in with the rest of the cleaning rubbish that evening and that, in all likelihood, the BMPX was on a municipal tip (dump) near the office. The customer engineers (CEs) swarmed over this tip like flies and, I believe, eventually retrieved the channel. It was rumored that after this channel was installed, each time a storage I/O took place there was a faint smell of fish bones!

Smartness can kill. IBM customer engineers (CEs) often worked alone, sometimes at night. In the old days, everyone in IBM wore suit and tie to comply with company standards. This included CEs and one day a CE was working alone in a machine room. He was leaning over an IBM golf ball* typewriter console when his tie became entangled around the rotating metal rod supporting the golf ball. He managed to free himself with some tool or other which was to hand. An edict was issued shortly afterward banning solo working and excusing CEs from wearing a tie while working on machinery.

I had to work alone in machine rooms, as did many other IBMers and if it was at a time when nobody else was around, you needed a partner. It was unlikely that a colleague would spend several hours sitting around doing nothing while I worked so I "employed" a rugby friend to sit around reading his newspapers. I paid him $15 (this was about 1974), which I reclaimed on my expenses. Company, my friend, and myself all happy.

Keep it clean. Another CE tale involves an IBM 1403 line printer, a popular workhorse that made a lot of money for IBM. The front of this printer opened to reveal the band containing the character set employed, and to print, these characters were pressed against a black ribbon to pick up the ink. While doing work with this front panel open, the CE accidentally pressed his white shirt against the character chain and got a line of type across it. He tried to claim a new shirt on expenses, but this was turned down and CEs were advised to wear protective clothing in such situations. I think some of them wore their wives' pinafores when working in such circumstances.

Dangers of transcription. Anyone who had had dealing with IBM's Job Control Language (JCL) will know it can get quite complicated. The following example is just part of the JCL stream preceding a batch job for execution on an IBM

---

* The one with a revolving head containing the characters, housed on a rotating metal axis. The golf ball moved back and forth on this axis, rotating to choose the required characters.

mainframe: get it wrong, or drop a comma or two and who knows what will happen to the job or jobs.

```
//TMEIIN    DD   UNIT=SYSDA,DCB=(BLKSIZE=0,LRECL=132,RECFM=FB),
//               SPACE=(TRK,(500,100),RLSE)
//TMEIOUT   DD   DSN=*.TMEIIN,DISP=(OLD,PASS),VOL=REF=*.TMEIIN
//EIDAIN    DD   UNIT=SYSDA,DCB=(BLKSIZE=0,LRECL=32,RECFM=FB),
//               SPACE=(TRK,(500,100),RLSE)
```

An IBM systems engineer I knew was a poor typist and, in the days before computer word processing, such work was handed to a secretary to transcribe via a typewriter. The poor girl of course did not realize that every comma and asterisk was very significant and gaily bashed the stuff into a set of instructions written by the systems engineer for other people to use.

The said systems engineer read the output and exploded: "This will never work. All secretaries should be sent on a JCL course as part of their training!" This advice, of course, was ignored by IBM management.

Moral: Transcription can be dangerous and more chains in the transcription may lead to exponentially increasing errors in the final content. Witness the old UK message about this in a spoof army message undergoing transcription and retransmission:

> *Original message*: Please send reinforcements, we are going to advance.
> *Transmitted message*: Please send three and fourpence* we are going to a dance.

Communication gaffes. IBM used to employ quite a few temporary[†] staff, often as secretaries. Some were very good, others not so, and their effectiveness depended on what other experienced secretaries told them about the job before they started. IBM secretaries who were replaced on a temporary or job-switch basis produced what was known as a "will." This explained the job, deadlines, and recurring activities for the new person to use until they got the hang of the job.

Some, however, never got the hang of it. One of the temps left me a message one day when I was out. It read: "Terry, please ring Brussels." So I went to her and asked if I was to ring everyone in Brussels or someone in particular. She didn't know.

The same secretary gave me another message that said, "Please ring Amen Jones." Baffled, I had visions of a Wild West preacher carrying a Colt 45 to reinforce his heavenly message. It turned out she meant "Eamonn Jones," who I knew about, but she probably couldn't spell Eamonn.

---

* Three shillings and four pence, a UK predecimalization amount of money, equal to about 20 to 25 U.S. cents.
† Some not all that temporary. I know one temporary secretary who retired recently after more than 30 years as a temp! She was working at IBM longer than I was.

A different temporary secretary once took a call, obviously from a potential customer as she shouted out across the room (without shielding the phone) "Do we sell System 370s?"!!!

The female role in IT. As my stint with IBM rolled on with the years, more women joined the company and often made customer calls, either alone or with a colleague. One particular customer manager in Northwest England, while not an outright woman-hater, had firm opinions as to their station in life. On one occasion, a female systems engineer came to join an existing meeting between IBM and the customer, poked her head round the door, and was greeted by her IBM colleague. Unfazed, the customer manager said, "Hello Miss, the typing pool is to your left, just down the corridor." There was then an irate IBM female and I was not privy to what happened next. On other occasions I'm told he would redirect female IBM and other lady employees to the kitchen.

Bye-bye! I switched from technical work to sales after several years as a systems engineer and moved after passing sales school. Obviously as I was new in sales it contained its fair share (or more) of hopeless accounts that no one else wanted. I rang the IT manager of one to introduce myself and ask to meet him. He said that he couldn't see me this month, but if I rang again in a month's time he would be able to. I thanked him politely and asked if he could tell me what was happening to make this month so busy. He said, "Well, I think we're going bust in two weeks' time, but if we don't I'm happy to meet you." [Anecdote from an ex-IBM employee]

Moral: Not sure but keeping abreast of company news in the financial sections of the press might be useful.

Mainframe instructions. During the 1970s, there was a sheet of paper appended to many IBM mainframes that purported to give operating instructions. At first glance, English speakers would say, "Damn, it's in German," until they actually examined it in detail. Nobody seems to know the origins of this notice but it has caused laughs around the world, particularly in Germany. A copy of the original is reproduced in Figure 6.1.

Moral: A little operations knowledge is dangerous. Keep your hands off if you don't know what you are doing.

The loop of ignorance: IBM had a habit of chasing various application types that obviously required equipment to run it and hence produce revenue. As various "flavor of the month" ideas came up, they would be assigned to someone in the branch to take on as a part-time task and be a contact point for that subject. These were normally nononerous tasks and the flavor often faded and was forgotten after a few weeks.

One day, a slim General Information Manual (GIM) dropped on my desk with instructions from on high to pick up the topic therein. The topic was *Personnel*

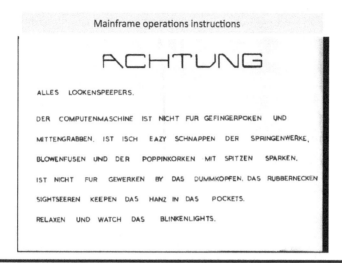

Mainframe operations instructions

ACHTUNG

ALLES LOOKENSPEEPERS.

DER COMPUTENMASCHINE IST NICHT FUR GEFINGERPOKEN UND

MITTENGRABBEN. IST ISCH EAZY SCHNAPPEN DER SPRINGENWERKE,

BLOWENFUSEN UND DER POPPINKORKEN MIT SPITZEN SPARKEN.

IST NICHT FUR GEWERKEN BY DAS DUMMKOPFEN. DAS RUBBERNECKEN

SIGHTSEEREN KEEPEN DAS HANZ IN DAS POCKETS.

RELAXEN UND WATCH DAS BLINKENLIGHTS.

Figure 6.1   Mainframe operating instructions (*Deutschprachig*).

*Information System** and I thought, given the slimness of the GIM that it would be an easy task. Not knowing anything about it and the GIM did not help much as it was written in IBM-speak, I telephoned around the company to see who knew enough to update me on it. After a day or two I was getting nowhere so I redoubled my efforts and set aside a half-day to thrash this one out via the telephone. Eventually, all the people I rang (and re-rang) gave the same advice: "Ring Terry Critchley. He seems to be the expert on this subject."

Moral: Don't pick up hot potatoes, especially half-baked ones, without gloves and ask the requestor what benefits this topic will bring to the customer and your company. If the answer is a loud silence, freeze it; senior management will understand if you are quizzed over it.

The invisible presentation. In 1979, IBM organized an internal storage workshop, held over several days, at the London Tower Bridge locations. The seminars took place in hotels where delegates were staying and also on boats on the River Thames. One presentation I attended was given by a German or Italian (I can't remember). He was putting his own transparencies on the projector and got through about six normal transparencies before displaying a completely blank transparency.

"Ah," he said. "Ze secretary must have forgotten to type zis one but I will carry on." He then proceeded to talk about what *should* have been on the foil, often referring to it. "So you see here, in bullet 3 [pointing to the projector screen], that the total storage ..." and carried on talking through the blank transparency! No one

---

* Human resources (HR) today.

said anything at the time but there was an explosion of laughter when he left the boat at the end.

Moral: If your material is prepared by someone else, check it out! If you are in such a situation, switch the projector off and carry on addressing the audience, offering to produce the transparency later and send it on.

Computer music. These incidents were not in my sphere of experience but are nonetheless amusing:

- An IBM colleague found that if you divided (I think) 91919191919 ... by 1 on a 1950s Marchant electric calculator, the resulting sound was a marvelous impression of a train going over a complicated set of points.
- There is a musical matrix printer in the following link and there are other binary musicians listed alongside this video: "Rocky's Printer—Eye of the Tiger on a Dot Matrix Printer," https://www.youtube.com/watch?v=u8I6qt_Z0Cg

Happy days!

Face to Face

Most IT people are smart enough to think on their feet, but some phrases can strike home with a customer or prospect and enhance your argument.

Useful Sayings

You can sink or swim in meetings by the use of phrases that embellish or reinforce your message. Here are some of the more effective ones:

- If you think education is expensive, try ignorance. This can be applied in other circumstances, for example, where people gripe at the cost of achieving good performance or high availability.
- Colleague dragging you into a deteriorating situation he has caused. Just say: "A lack of planning on your part does not constitute an emergency on mine."
- Customer/Prospect: "Well ... I'm not sure about your system."
     You: "Would you have it if it was free?" If he still hesitates, leave. He's not going to have your IT kit or whatever you are selling at any cost.
- Vaporware. The marketing of blue sky futures or unannounced products is around so learn to spot it. Of course, it is usually promoted by others, not your company.
- "Their products/your implementation are rubbish." They may be but don't explicitly call anyone's baby ugly. Use the term *suboptimal*, a word I've used in such circumstances and got away with it.

- To initiate some action in a sluggish project where talk is the main activity, you might perhaps use the Mark Twain expression: "Everybody is talking about the weather, nobody's doing anything about it."
- Another handy phrase, used in the appropriate circumstances is "There are people who make things happen, people who watch things happen and people who say 'what happened?'"
- In convincing people about your suggested course of action, try the following Sherlock Holmes quote, it may be appropriate: "When you have eliminated the impossible, what remains, however improbable, must be the truth."
- Often, people quote a single source for some fact or other, whereas my thesis is to take a *consensus* from people who know the topic in question. The Abraham Lincoln quote may be of use: "You can fool some of the people all of the time and all of the people some of the time but you can't fool all of the people all of the time."
- Sometimes you and your team may be doing something that may be apparently *invisible* to some managers who wonder why we need to employ people to do this when everything is working smoothly. Such invisible benefits could be high availability and consistent response times that are due to good design and management. If challenged to justify your and the team's existence, remember the following story, which bears repetition:

A man was walking round my hometown of Warrington, UK, scattering a green powder. A second man saw this and asked the first man, "Why are you scattering that powder?" to which the first man replied, "To keep the elephants away." The second man looked puzzled and said, "But there are no elephants in Warrington." "No," said the first man, "this powder is very effective isn't it?"

Banal Sayings

I was introduced to the world of daft phrases and ideas by a colleague when we were in a meeting with a customer. We were all discussing something when this guy piped up and said: "Yes … it is just like throwing a pebble in a pond, where the ripples travel outward to the edges." The rest of the group stared at each other in bafflement, waiting for an explanation from the speaker but none was forthcoming. He must have assumed we all knew exactly what he meant. I must ring him one day to try to solve the mystery of the ripples. Here are some other gold-plated inane sayings:

- "Run it up the flagpole and see who salutes it." Inane and meaningless except to the dead brain. This was used by a manager in IBM who I did not like and he did not like me. Therefore that phrase is *verboten*.

- "Going forward …" Meaningless. Use "In the future" or "If things pan out as we plan." If there is no tangible future or explainable plan, shut up.
- "One stop shopping through the blue channel. Buy only from us." These days, if you try to limit a customer's options, you will soon be out on the street.
- "Does what it says on the tin." Is that your technical or business explanation? Using phrases like that just irritates intelligent customers and others.
- "X needs careful planning and staffing." Mouth music. We all know that, stupid—give examples, a list, a reference. Better still, sit down with them and help.
- "I've got a warm feeling about it [a sales situation]." The normal response from IBM management was "That's what happens when you wet yourself."
- "Flexible, modular and easy to use." But then so is a garden hose. That tells nobody anything but is used in nearly every flyer or data sheet I get my hands on—software as well as hardware.
- Silly bloated verbiage.*
  - Using the words "air movement device" for "fan," used in an BM announcement flyer.
  - The system "offers a higher level segment overview." This meant "you can see over it," as it was not as tall as the previous generation (part of a 1980s processor announcement).
  - A "confluence of concerned personnel" is a meeting, believe it or not.

Such "prose" buys you nothing and puts you in the up-and-coming wally class.

How to Treat People

Aside from being offered good products and super technical expertise, customers like people who are friendly and genuinely considerate.

- *With customer.* "I believe it's your birthday today? How old? 50. No, you are kidding me." Works wonders. However, be careful how personal you get in your schmoozing. A man from New Zealand was asked by his customer why he left there and he replied, "Everybody there is either a rugby player or a prostitute." Customer (indignantly), "My wife comes from New Zealand!" Man, "Really? Which team did she play for?"
- *Customer aggression.* Don't respond to customer aggression with aggression. There are ways to defuse situations by humoring them or approaching your differences as the Zulus and Bob do (we met Bob and the Zulu technique in Chapter 1).

---

* These are true; I came across them personally in my career. The United Kingdom, thankfully, is not prone to this ailment.

■ *Customer foibles.* I had a biscuit manufacturer as a customer at one time and visited a certain IT man quite regularly. He was a competent man but had a habit of drifting into a dreamy state (reverie) in midsentence. He would remain in this state for about 15 seconds (a long time when you are sitting staring at him wondering what to do) and then recover. He would then say something 100 km away from the conversation in progress, something like "Do you play golf?" You would answer and then business would proceed exactly where he left off, as if nothing had happened. This happened on average twice each meeting.

Moral: In the interests of peace, it is best to ride with the punches in these situations and accept them as the norm.

■ *Treatment of minions.* Sometimes we have a tendency to look at people who are not in the upper echelons of a customer or your own business as being of no importance to your aims and ambitions. This is not always the case; witness my experience with an IT man at an insurance customer. Before almost any IT decisions on equipment was made, he had to examine it in detail and make a go/no-go recommendation to higher management.

We learned to deal with him with a lot of respect once we recognized the scope of his influence. The lesson here is to treat everyone you come across as an important cog in the customer's machinery. Sometimes, a chart similar to Table 6.1 (a sample) can be useful when completed. A table like this is a very useful way of seeing who is who in an organization (including your own), but don't let the people in it see your judgments of them. That would be career limiting.

■ *Learning from competitors.* We sometimes treat competitors (even in your own organization) with some disdain. This is not always a beneficial attitude since you can probably learn something from them. In such situations, I try to work on the 4 Es principle: examine, evaluate, emulate, exceed. This means looking at their strengths, evaluating their usefulness to your environment, emulating the good, and exceeding their performance in it. Don't fall prey to *binaryism* in these or any other matters.

Table 6.1 Sample Power versus Influence Table

Name	Position	Power	Influence	Other Facts
J. Smith	Chairman	High	Low in IT	Likes golf
A.N. Other	IT CIO	High	Medium	IT knowledge low
...	...	...	...	...
I.M. Meek	IT Ops	Low	High	Must be consulted

Binaryism: A Modern Disease

Binaryism is my own term for people who place the world in polarized categories. Let me illustrate this with an example from a TV program that aired in the United Kingdom in October 2015. It was an experiment where Chinese teachers took classes in English schools and applied their own methods, with startling results. We all know how hard the Chinese work in school and, as a result, gain top world rankings in math and English.

English opponents of change pointed out that the Chinese system was too demanding and exhausting and therefore should not be adapted in England.

Probably true in the binaryist world, but could not the best elements in that system be adopted and melded into the current system (my 4 Es system)? A similar argument rages over communism and capitalism, where the conclusion is that capitalism is superior to communism (which is true), so let's go 100% capitalist. There are big holes in capitalism that might well be plugged by adopting suitable methods and mantras from communism.

Binaryism is the sworn enemy of lateral (out-of-the-box) thinking.

Hints for Managers

Much of the material in this book applies to all people in IT, but there are a few things that are managers' initiatives. Some of the more useful ones are in education and training of staff. IBM, in the period I was there, mandated 22 days a year education for technical staff (systems engineers) and 15 for salesmen over and above basic training to qualify. I suspect very few companies do this amount of on-the-job training in these times. Here are a few suggestions:

■ *Mobile education.* I wrote earlier about my radio-less period in the car and its beneficial effects on my performance, but there is possibly a case for some kind of "noise." If you imagine an employee doing 20K miles/year at an average of 40 mph, this equates to 500 hours a year driving doing nothing useful and learning nothing. This is about 62 man days if you call a working day 8 hours. That is a lot of time essentially wasted. For 1000 employees at this mileage (or more or less), this is nearly 180 years of wasted time. There is a case for producing educational CDs for use by employees in cars on topics that do not require visuals to get a message across. It may be possible to produce such material that carry a message over verbally but the message enhanced and fixed in the person's mind.

Figure 6.2 Teamwork and responsibilities.

- *Support your people.* Some people will get into difficulties and will need support rather than castigation (Figure 6.2). Give them the support they need, then straighten them out on the points that got them into the mess. Remember the message in the phrase, "I'll support you Jim, but I won't carry you."
- *Lunchtime briefings.* I introduced these when at IBM with the help of several people who could present well for 15 to 20 minutes on a current topic of which they were *au fait* with. It can be a shortcut to understanding certain things you were afraid to ask about.
- *Trade events.* Visits to relevant IT trade events can be useful for learning about products and methods plus what your competitors are doing if you are employed by an IT vendor.
- *Industry knowledge.* If your IT activities are attached to an industry (even your own organization's if you are internal) in some way, try to learn something about it. My IBM education was rounded off with a 1-week course on the industry you were assigned to in your branch.
- There are probably other examples of time being used without purpose, which might be reclaimed to benefit both the individual and company.

This chapter has hopefully given the readers some amusement and light relief. The messages and morals in it are, however, deadly serious. Avoiding the gaffes and nonsense talk outlined above will add enormously to your credibility and place you in the category of trusted advisor, the highest accolade in IT.

Final Thoughts

I hope that you have found this tale of my troubles and triumphs informative in your current role as an IT person or a potential IT recruit. What I have attempted to do is show the evolutionary progress of IT technology, the permanence of the IT management disciplines, and the current status of IT. Remember the acronym FUMPAS:

Application success factors	
F	Does it do what the end user wants it to do?
U	Does it have an absolutely clear and logical user interface?
M	Can its host system(s) be managed properly?
P	Does it deliver the required (SLA) performance?
A	Is it designed and implemented to have the appropriate availability and recovery features?
S	Does it/the system have appropriate security?

Certain other things you should also carry away with you:

- Technology will advance, but choices will often need to be made because of the plethora of products and endless configuration possibilities.
- Technology is not the be-all and end-all of IT.
- Technology is subservient to business requirements and the processes generated by them.
- These processes lead on to an architecture and the architecture implemented and maintained by technology.
- IT can be rewarding and it can also be fun. If it isn't, make it fun.
- Your progress in an IT career depends on
  - Using the disciplines
  - Understanding the technology

- Using personal skills in the many areas covered in this book*
- Being proactive
- Always seeking to improve
- Continuing to learn
- Understanding the importance of a business sponsor for any major IT project or working system

■ Your advancement also depends on your ability to keep abreast of IT developments and continue to learn. People who already know it all don't survive for long in IT, except in backwaters.

■ Have a basic familiarity with cloud and virtualization, which is essential, as is the recognition of the factors for success in any IT endeavor: FUMPAS.† Screw one of them up and the risk of failure rises considerably.

■ Be prepared (Boy Scouts motto).

■ For every plan you have, think of a plan B should it fail.‡

■ Think (old IBM mantra).

■ Talk to yourself about your aims and ambitions before choosing an employer or line of business. The shortage of IT skills in Europe (at least) means you will always be in demand, but if you are job-hopping, successive employers will take a dim view of it.

■ Remember:
  - There are people who make things happen.
  - There are people who watch things happen.
  - There are people who say "What happened?"

The Ten Commandments of IT

1. Thou shalt not put technology before requirements.
2. Thou shalt manage thy resources wisely and squander them not.
3. Thou shalt not be moved by the siren sounds of vendors or geeks who seek to ensnare thee and move thee from the paths of righteousness and standards.
4. Thou shalt learn the disciplines of righteousness.
5. Thou shalt tend thy customer flock and lead them into the pastures of eternal secure, performant uptime.
6. Thou shalt love thy customers as thyself for IT's sake.
7. Thou shalt not pulleth any wool over thy customer's eyes to hide thy SLA sins.

---

* I know people who have mastered this aspect and cruised through many years without knowing too much about the other aspects of IT.

† Functionality, usability, manageability, performance, availability, and security.

‡ I sometimes go to places such as restaurants where their Wi-Fi credit card machine sometimes doesn't work. None of them has a plan B, which is the old-fashioned slide machine, which takes an imprint of your card details on a multipart slip and you sign it. Elementary.

8. Thou shalt deliver documentation at all times according to the IT scriptures.
9. Thou shalt constantly instruct thyself and thy IT flock in the ways of computing.
10. Thou shalt love IT for its own sake and forsaketh it not for the lures of mammon.

In this, thou wilt be deemed worthy of the name *Master of Information Technology.*

Go forth and enjoy a man's (or woman's) life in information technology!

APPENDICES

These sections are meant to convey knowledge about certain disciplines that apply across most professions and organizations. They are the means of *employing* and *controlling* technology and not the other way around.

Technology is the slave and management the master in IT situations and is dictated by end user requirements and not its "gee-whiz" rating. Using technology alone as a tool is like slapping top-class paint on a canvas and expecting to produce a Mona Lisa painting; it needs thought, skill, and an objective.

The techniques and methods in these appendices transcend time and are technology independent, which alone makes them of value. In the increasingly complex IT world, these methods will repay handsomely any investment of time in learning and using them.

The purpose of spelling out these disciplines is not for the reader to pick them up immediately but to serve as a reference and, more important, to show there is more to IT success than technology.

Appendix A: Assessments, SWOTs, and Follow-Up

One thing you need when moving into unknown territory is to get your bearings, which, in real parlance, means understanding your customers be they external or internal. You also need to understand the worlds they inhabit and how your world integrates with it; this exercise is commonly called an *assessment*. Its form is issues, best practice in solution, and what the vendor/IT can do or suggest in this area.

IT Assessments

In war, good generals always made a point of studying their opponents' leaders to understand how they thought and operated in battle. This is based on the notion that you cannot engage the enemy without some knowledge of them and this applies in IT just as much but in the context of a customer; this might be a customer of a vendor or your internal business users who rely on IT for their work. This is where step 1, the assessment, comes in any IT/business engagement.

Sample IT Assessment

There are a number of areas and a lot of questions that could be asked to assess the quality of an IT service. Talking to the customer in an open manner may persuade him to unburden himself and spell out his issues and areas of concern. Once you know what you are talking about you should be able to put together a plan for remedying the faults.

This is a straightforward task if you are a vendor and have customers, but what if you are internal IT and your customers are the businesspeople? In that case you need to winkle out of the business representative where the IT service needs improvement or even redesign.

The internal IT assessment is then a SWOT (strengths, weaknesses, opportunities, and threats) exercise with the business, who give IT its thoughts in these four areas of IT support. It is still an assessment, however.

Assessment Template

A typical template for an assessment is shown in Table A.1. It was developed a few years ago. The heading will change in today's environment but the principles do not alter significantly. Remember, unless you can identify and define a problem (root cause, not just the symptoms) you have little chance of solving it.

Sample Output

The output in Table A.1 is fictitious but represents the sort of language and items that might appear in any assessment.

Assessment Areas

In Table A.1, the types of disciplines might be

- Preproduction activities; starting an IT project
- Business continuity (see the next section for an example of this)
- Malware
- Availability management
- Performance management
- Security management
- Event/problem management
- Change management

Table A.1 Issues and Best Practice Assessment

Discipline: <name here>	
Issues	*Best Practice*
Lack of business sponsor	Identify suitable manager as sponsor
No tangible objectives	Develop via a service level agreement
Inadequate help desk	See URL ... for good practices
Poor inter-party communications	Review/revise using best of breed info
...	...

Note: Capability Level: 1 to 5 (low to high). Plan for increasing it.

- Operations management
- Staff skills (and retention)
- Procurement strategy
- Web environment
- Others pertinent to the environment in question

The basis of all this is to establish

- What needs to be done to manage our environment
- How well it is being done
- How it can be improved (best practice)
- A prioritized remedial action plan
- Skills (internal and external) available from us to help

In essence, it is navel-gazing. It is a lot of work but will pay dividends in developing the best of breed solutions for the business or customer. As an IT representative, the business or company will judge you on the success of this.

Business Continuity Assessment

1. Issues

- Unsuitable support contracts for 24/7 systems
- Single points of failure in system, network configurations, or power supply
- Poor chip and server design from the vendor
- Lack of staff skills and experience
- Loss of staff
- Inadequate help desk, systems management, and operations procedures
- Sabotage or malicious damage
- Lack of knowledge of the impact of system failures
- No hot swap facilities to avoid downtime

2. Best Practice

- Match support contracts to the required availability for all elements that support the applications
- Employ redundancy, clustering, mirroring, etc.
- Choose a vendor with reliable hardware and software
- Develop staff skills with a top training organization

- Develop a staff career and retention plan
- Implement solid service management disciplines, using vendor skills and suitable software skills
  - Preproduction activities
  - Service-level agreements (SLAs)
  - Business continuity
  - Problem management
  - Resource management
  - Security and audit management
  - Change/configuration management
  - Operations management
  - Other areas identified as key
- Physical security of IT sites
- Perform a business impact analysis (BIA) on key business applications

3. Our Vendor Offerings*

- Our business continuity service
- Backup/recovery software (BakItUp product)

This type of business continuity assessment and remediation plan exercise can be carried out in the areas key to the business' success.

SWOT Exercise

A SWOT analysis is a useful technique for understanding the *strengths* and *weaknesses* of an organization or other body, and for identifying both the *opportunities* open to it and the *threats* it faces. It can be used in a personal context to help you develop your career in a way that takes best advantage of your talents, abilities, and opportunities. It is the technology equivalent of navel-gazing.

It can be used in many situations as a sort of *health check* on

- Yourself in your personal life or job; this is a useful exercise if you are honest with your answers. It is even more valuable if someone who knows you well also does the same exercise with you as the target for the SWOT analysis.
- A company or part of one, for example, the IT department. Again, this can be done by an insider or someone who uses that department, like a businessperson who knows IT.

---

* This means you as the vendor or you as the internal IT total support function.

■ A football or other sports team or individual, a salutary exercise when the coach can't quite pinpoint why the team/person is not successful. Results can flow from this exercise when done by members of the team in isolation, for example, via Delphi and also by an impartial spectator or two.

Strengths	*Weaknesses*
Technology	Sell technology instead of solution
Innovator/visionary	Technology only view of sale
Java	Java as the solution to all ills
Customer satisfaction/loyalty	Business acumen
People/employees	High-performance computing (HPC) visibility and credibility
Product line	Credibility in the data center
Services	Sales "box" mentality
No conflicting hardware architectures	Account management/control
	Communications—Internal/external

Opportunities	*Threats*
Old "iron" (migration) (to us)	Quarter on quarter targets (mentality)
HPC—Needs beefing up though	Thinking equality with others in data center
Green field sites and applications	Field attitude to solutions; slowly changing
HPC consolidation	Senior management attitude to solutions
"Me too" but with delivery capability	"Me too" without having the full solution
Slow down NT enterprise growth	NT; when it gets its act together
Services revenue	HP solution center
	Underselling to meet target

The true value of a SWOT analysis is in the *action plan* that should follow it. It is pointless doing the analysis, documenting it, and then going back to sleep or to the golf course.

The process is best illustrated with the preceding example. This is the real outcome of an exercise carried out on a well-known IT vendor company some years ago, together with some follow-up activities and suggestions, shown next. Although it is quite old, you can take this as a template in this important area.

Steps to Address Weaknesses and Opportunities

Education
- What is enterprise computing—the vision not the boxes?
- How do customers use "big" computers and for what reason?
- How we can help them justify their purchase/usage?
- Credibility in what we say/deliver

New opportunities
- Expanding the installed base territory
- Replacing existing/legacy (see later)
- Bid templates to support/lead sales

Migrations from the competition
- DEC VMS/UNIX generic migration plan(s)
- ICL VME 80% of opportunities; third-party help available
- IBM MVS/VSE services implementation delivery capability

Consolidation
- Server consolidation difficult to sell
- Applications/license rationalization, Rev of products easier
- Reduction of management/effort, O/S numbers key
- Consolidation is easier in scientific environments

HPC
- Applications? Without them how do we grow in this area?
- Mind-set: Need people to sell the applications, not the Hokey Cokey 2000 processor alone
- How about a "Molecular Modeling" day rather than a "H-K 2000 Speeds" day to show the HK 2000 in useful action

Reference: http://articles.bplans.com/the-ultimate-guide-to-creating-a-swot-analysis-free-ebook/.

Summary: This example hopefully shows the purpose, the execution, and the proposed follow-up actions of a SWOT analysis, which is why it is run. Don't be hidebound by my interpretation; use whatever suits your purposes within the boundaries of a SWOT analysis.

Service-Level Agreements (SLAs)

In legal terms, an agreement here is a contract, but applied to IT deliverables to a business via a service. These represent the quality of service (QoS) baselines for managing the service.

SLAs: The Dawn of Realism

If you want to buy a Ferrari or Maserati and walk into a car showroom dressed like Detective Columbo, the salesman will immediately think "Can this guy afford one?" The same sort of question is often asked when the business user states his business service requirements to the IT people as "responses of 0.02 seconds (or less) and 100% availability (or greater) until judgment day (and beyond, if required)." The IT department will dutifully go away and do total cost of ownership (TCO) calculations for such a system/service and present it to business user management, to the nearest £10 million ($15 million), and ongoing, operational and depreciation costs, and so forth, in round millions.

The businesspeople, having seen the estimate, will then retire crushed.* Over a coffee or a Jack Daniels and some financial reflection, they will modify their demands and settle for something the enterprise can afford, and then the serious business of planning, designing, and delivering the service can begin. I know, because I saw a scenario similar to this played out at a well-known aerospace company in the United Kingdom where the users were setting impossible service-level targets for IT.

When the dust settles, the parties involved will need to draw up an agreed set of deliverables, requirements, constraints, charges for a service, and penalties for nonfulfillment. This set is called a *service-level agreement* or *SLA*. Notice the word *service* as opposed to *system*.

What Is a Service-Level Agreement?

A service-level agreement (SLA) is a contract between a service provider, internal to a company or an outsourcing agency, and a customer that specifies, usually in measurable terms, what services the network service provider will furnish, when and for how long, without interruption. Many Internet service providers provide their customers with an SLA.

More recently, IT departments in major enterprises have adopted the idea of writing a service-level agreement so that services for their customers (users in other departments within the enterprise) can be measured, justified, and perhaps compared with those of outsourcing network providers.

---

* A wonderful expression for retreat, paraphrased here from the G. K. Chesterton's Father Brown story called *The Queer Feet*.

To be able to offer a quantifiable service or set of applications, the provider will need some IT disciplines to support and measure the components of the service. This set of disciplines is commonly known as system management (service management is a broader topic involving SLAs, operations, user liaison, service/help desk, and a host of other things).

Why Is an SLA Important?

This basic contract, and it is a contract, supplies a *raison d'etre* for all the tools used and effort expended in IT for measuring everything that varies or moves. If the end users don't care about response times, availability, hours of service, and so on, SLAs don't matter. But users do care about these things so they do matter and the SLA is the referee between the two parties involved: IT and business.

I think that says all I wanted to say here about SLAs and their importance. They are key for end users, providing different perspectives on IT life.

Also covered in this appendix are the benefits of SLAs to both "demander" and "provider," an aspect often forgotten in some literature dealing with the topic.

Aside: SLAs are about targets or objectives. Remember our Intensive Planning discussion in Chapter 2 under "Problem Solving." An answer given by the "inventor" of IBM intensive planning meetings, after allowing his colleagues about an hour to think about it, was "something which stops you achieving an objective." Illuminating and difficult to argue with.

Again, we have already seen the corollary of this is "if you don't have an objective, you can't have a problem." SLAs are about objectives, their measurement, their management, and safe delivery. The UK elite forces motto can be paraphrased here in an SLA context as "Who cares, wins."

For more detailed examples of SLAs, see the very good papers in the following two references:

"Cisco (Network):" http://www.cisco.com/en/US/tech/tk869/tk769/technologies
_white_paper09186a008011e783.shtml#step4
"RL Consulting:" http://www.itsm.info/Sample%20SLA%20Templates.pdf

There are also SLAs for *cloud-based systems* but that is another story and adds a level of complexity via tiered SLAs.

Delphi Technique*

One process used to *facilitate* any exploratory meeting is called the *Delphi technique*. Its name comes from the all-knowing Oracle at Delphi and the actual

---

* For the knowledge geek, http://is.njit.edu/pubs/delphibook/delphibook.pdf is a 618-page document on Delphi and, for all I know, the Freudian and Jungian implications of the method.

method was developed during the Cold War to forecast the impact of technology on warfare. This technique was further refined and developed by the RAND Corporation for the U.S. Department of Defense in the 1950s. Although originally intended for use as a psychological weapon during the Cold War, it has since been adapted for use in business and other areas of endeavor. Before going into the technique itself, here is a little tale about the surprising outcome of a Delphi-like session involving an IBM facilitator and senior executives from a large chemical company:

> The facilitator asked them to work alone and produce a list of the six most pressing issues in the business then present them briefly to the rest of the executives. The outcome was an eye opener. They disagreed totally on what the major issues were and expressed surprise at some of the issues raised by their peers in their own sector of the business. "I didn't know that stock levels were a serious issue," said the finance director. "I could have helped you there." The same scenario was repeated among them for other important issues, each new to someone in the team. Even though their expectation was one of immediate consensus on what the issues were, they found the exercise very useful in bringing these thoughts to the surface.

This is one of the beneficial effects of the Delphi technique used properly. Although the executives were unaware of the technique, they were actually partaking in a diluted, short-term version of it.

Note: In general, the Delphi method is useful in answering one, specific, single-dimension question. There is less support in the field for its use to determine complex forecasts involving multiple factors. Such complex model building is more appropriate for other, more esoteric models, perhaps with Delphi results serving as inputs. This makes it useful for single IT issues in the right circumstances and with today's communication methods and networks the traditional snail-mail and days/weeks time frames can be short-circuited. This is what I have called the *turbo-Delphi technique*,* an exercise tailored to fit the necessary decision timescale for an IT issue.

Look at the simplified flowchart of the technique in Figure A.1 with the steps explained.

---

* Traditional Delphis might take days or weeks when involving people in different locations or even countries using traditional communications methods, like snail mail. This shouldn't present a problem in an IT department with modern communications techniques.

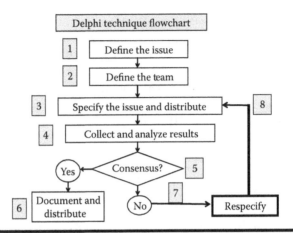

Figure A.1   Delphi technique flowchart.

Delphi: The Steps

The essence of the Delphi technique is as follows (refer to Figure A.1):

1. A *facilitator* is chosen, probably for the whole project or , who will lead the issue definition task. It should be someone familiar with the project and having some leadership and analysis skills. If this is part of a major project, it should already have a *sponsor*. He or she should initiate any documentation on the project.
2. A *panel of experts* is chosen. This is more than likely the IT team involved in the subject involved together with a business contact. An *expert* can be defined as an individual with relevant knowledge and experience of a particular topic.
3. Define the *problem* that needs to be understood and input given on.
4. Set out the *questions* that require input from the experts. The answers should be correlated for commonality of views. A second set of questions based on the input should then be issued. In a "turbo" version of Delphi, the whole thing might be done in conference mode around a table with "think" breaks to gain independent input from the team. Collect the results.
5. *Analyze* the input and findings and put an *action* plan together for the issue in question. If the facilitator finds broad agreement, the "solution" is documented and distributed. If not, the variations of opinion are documented and distributed, and a second round of opinions is sought and the analysis repeated.
6. When some form of consensus is reached, *initiate* the project, make a recommendation, and so forth.

There are other design and evaluation methods, one of which is discussed next. They sometimes overlap and it is up to the account which elements of which method it uses. The common sense method should be applied here, as elsewhere.

IT Project Cycle Revisited

The design and assessment phase's objective is to identify and define the sequence of operational solutions to be implemented (i.e., the Solution Roadmap), to verify in theory that the required benefits can be delivered, and to understand the costs and risks involved so that the feasibility of the whole exercise may be assessed at the end of the exercise.

The inputs to the phase are the A Point system itself and its relevant documentation, the statement of quantified business benefits to be achieved by the eventual B Point system, and the IT strategy/policy of the organization involved. The phase's activities are described in more detail next (refer to Chapter 1, Figure 1.6).

1. A Point Assessment

The A Point represents the IT environment today. There are two main tasks in the assessment:

1. The technical assessment of the A Point IT systems under investigation is to understand exactly what is to be migrated. This is a detailed study of the operational, data, and architectural aspects of the A Point and forms a necessary input to the definition of the B Point. It also specifies the business environment it supports and what the relevant company IT policies are in the whole exercise.
1a. The assessment of the costs associated with the A point if this is required.

Here, we are stating our starting point before moving on to specify our destination, and hence our route to get there. If you don't know where you are or where you are going, there is little chance you will get there in one piece or even arrive at all.

2. IT Options Definition

The options available are in theory very large but when tempered by current systems investment and skills, new business requirements (on IT) plus the organization's IT policy, the options will shrink. It may be as simple as "distributed or centralized?" but SLAs will have a part to play.

3. Solution Roadmap Definition

The Solution Roadmap is defined using the A Point technical assessment, IT Policy, and required business benefits as input. Although any one stage is aimed at implementing the next stage of the whole migration, all the B points need to be identified upfront so that the decisions made in the first stage are suitable for all. Issues to be considered in deciding B points include:

- Network topology
- Client/server versus nonintelligent terminals
- Physical data placement
- Hardware and operating system software
- Application software
- Service-level definitions
- Predictive costs based on inflation, price/performance enhancements, and so on
- Constraints dictated by business, legal and other requirements
- Security and audit requirements
- The viability of employing emerging technologies
- Resilience requirements (RAID, clustering, replication, etc.)
- Coexistence requirements

These considerations should include the possibility of using traditional technology, if this option has not been precluded previously.

4. B Point Definition

The B points are the intermediate and ultimate target environments to be delivered by the migration. As implied by Figure 1.6 (Chapter 1), the initial activity is one of iteratively refining the Solution Roadmap and B Point functional specifications with reference to the IT options.

5. Technical Architecture Definition

This identifies the application and data architectures and the hardware, software, and network infrastructures. It addresses the next intended B Point primarily but takes into account the future B Points also so as to avoid unexpected problems in evolving to them.

It is likely in all but small migrations that there will need to be connections between the old world and the new to fulfill various coexistence requirements. A simple example is the migration of a payroll system to a new UNIX environment. However, the application that calculates hours worked, bonuses, and so forth remains, for the time being, on the legacy system. When running the payroll, information from the legacy time recording system will need to be accessed before pay can be calculated.

Coexistence requirements are unique to the organization performing the migration from A to B, and they need a tailored solution. There are a number of standard ways of connecting applications on different systems and these can be employed in setting up and implementing the coexistence *architecture*:

■ Physical tape transfer of files
■ File transfer across a physical connection using file transfer software
■ Database transfer functions
■ Use of other middleware required
■ Use of third-party middleware
■ Program-to-program communication if used
■ Other organization IT aspects

6. B Point Functional Requirements Definition

The major functional attributes (specifications) of the B Point must be specified. This includes such attributes as

■ Service-level requirements
■ Geographic availability
■ User functions
■ Transaction volumes
■ Other factors

If the project is large and hence multistaged, there could be several B Points, one at the end of each phase or step so as not to lose focus; Phase 1 to B1, Phase 2 to B2, and so on. Also note that where necessary there may be *pilots* (small-scale trials) in a multistage project.

7. B Point Sizing

The sizing exercise can take several forms, depending on whether basic (A Point) data about the transactions, scripts, batch jobs, and so on are known. These can then be applied to assess CPU (processor), disk, RAM, cache, and network requirements for the new system. If such base data is unavailable, then other techniques can be used by relating the anticipated workload to certain, appropriate, benchmarks, and measurements and extrapolating.

Theoretical techniques such as these are not as accurate as actually running the anticipated workload but are useful in identifying a suitable machine range. As long as the range chosen has scalability, any inaccuracies in the method will not have disastrous long-term consequences on performance.*

---

* Which it did in the old days when processor increments were very expensive.

8. B Point Cost Analysis

The cost analysis considers the total costs associated with the target environment, not just hardware and software. It is important to note that hardware costs are only a fraction, typically one-third and decreasing, of the total cost of system ownership. The distinction between capital costs and true cost of ownership needs to be borne in mind. Of course, this cost analysis will have to be reassessed, as the realization of the solution is refined, especially when a packaged application is selected.

9. Solution Appraisal—Feasibility Phase Exit

The final activity of the feasibility phase is a review to assess whether to proceed. Does the proposed solution achieve the required business benefits at acceptable cost and risk? This is not an IT-only exercise and the business should be represented in some way. In fact, a business representative should be present at many IT deliberations or, at the very least, informed of the outcomes of them.

Remember the saying "A camel is a horse designed by a committee." If the business wants a horse, make sure IT gives them a horse.

10. Risk Analysis

Risk analysis identifies the risks involved and discusses their management. Risk management is covered later in this appendix. This placing in the flow does not mean this is exactly where the risk exercise fits, as it should be a constant factor in any designs or plans, preferably using a devil's advocate.*

Note: This plan, as with all suggested flows and sequences in this book, are open to modification for your organization's or customers' needs but the principle of following an orderly sequence of activity is important. Choosing the right people to be involved is also key as is the support of a *sponsor* in the business. The sponsor is a senior manager who has great interest in the success of this project and is also senior enough to remove nontechnical obstacles to progress or completion.

Project Definition Workshop (PDW)

A short conversation from Lewis Carroll's *Alice in Wonderland* will outline the need for and indicate the direction of a PDW:

Alice: Would you tell me, please, which way I ought to go from here?
Cheshire Cat: That depends a good deal on where you want to get to.

---

* A person who tries to find possible holes in any plans, based on Murphy's law: If anything can go wrong, it will.

Alice: I don't much care where.
Cheshire Cat: Then it doesn't matter which way you go.
Alice: So long as I get SOMEWHERE.
Cheshire Cat: Oh, you're sure to do that, if you only walk long enough.*

This conversation illustrates to a T my take on project definition workshops, a simple principle that you can expand to implement in several ways. Today, a PDW is a common vehicle for setting up projects and was common fare in IBM in the 1970s and 1980s, and still exists today but under a different name. It is not a project management and control technique but a way of defining the content of a project as unambiguously as possible. It does not replace project management tools and technologies and is usually independent of them, although such tools can be used in carrying out the actions and work items coming out of the PDW.

The bare bones of the process are as follows:

■ Define the A Point, which is where you are now
■ Define the B Point, which is where you want to get to
■ Develop and refine the activities needed for the transition state A to state B
■ Classify them under disciplines, that is, operations, development, systems management, security, and so on
■ Develop an action plan against these items and assign to people
■ Document in a project initiation document (see later) and get on with it
■ Seek a peer review by someone not involved directly

The beauty of the PDW is that it works, assuming it is done properly!

Outline of the PDW

The purpose of the project definition workshop is to allow an organization to reach a common understanding of the business requirements and operational parameters for the delivery of an identified project, for example, a high availability (HA) design and implementation. This information will allow the development of a solution to meet the users' requirements, and to manage the integration of the proposed project approach into the users' business with maximum chance of success and minimum disruption.

A *project definition workshop* can be used at several stages of the project. Outputs from the workshop enable the top-level deliverables, project acceptance, and signoff criteria to be agreed. The key skills and resources are identified and the project pricing expectations are set.

---

* I have lived in Cheshire (UK) all my life and very close to Lewis Carroll's (Charles Lutwidge Dodgson) original home at Daresbury. However, I still have no idea what a Cheshire Cat is or how it differs from other cats.

Input. To aid the PDW process, a *project brief* should be prepared that will describe the requirements and environment for the project, and will normally include:

- Background—Where it came from and who it is for and the sponsoring manager
- Outline business case and drivers—Cost and business impact of downtime
- Project definition—Explaining what the project needs to achieve, and including
  - Project goals
  - Project scope—Setting boundaries to change and technology
  - Outline project deliverables or desired outcomes
  - Critical success factors (CSFs) (not cost, as that is a constraint not a CSF)
  - Exclusions, constraints, assumptions, and interfaces
- Success and acceptance criteria; IT and user
- Risks involved; these are to be addressed in the PDW
- Project organization (overall responsibilities only)—Detailed roles and responsibilities come out of the PDW actions

Output. The output of a PDW will be a draft project initiation document (PID), covering many of the same topics, but eventually in more detail and with more certainty.

PDW Method Overview

The normal way of running a PDW is via a facilitator, internal or external. That person will direct operations but an overview of a typical PDW is presented here. It is assumed that the A Point and B Point are defined in some way or other, perhaps via a Delphi session or a predefined business requirements document.

It is then necessary for the team and facilitator to extract all the actions needed for the journey A to B. A typical rough output of such a session is a series of activities across a number of charts or black-/whiteboards. It is then necessary to decide what area each activity comes under (operations, security, application development, database, OLTP, etc.) and a manager assigned to that area; in Figure A.2 they are the responsibilities of Jim, Fred, and Sue.

The progress in these areas should be subject to frequent meetings, both within the discipline and cross-discipline, and hence be subject to the organization's *change management* methodology. All this is driven by, and feeds into the PID.

The PID is the project start-up *blueprint*.

Project Initiation Document (PID)

The PID is a core document for the project and its format and content is pretty consistent across vendors, consultants, and the like. I have worked on several of these

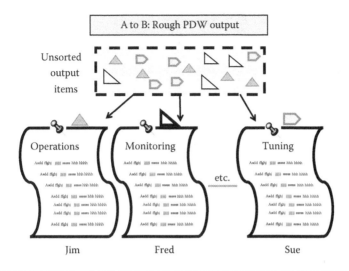

Figure A.2   PDW: Session output categorized and assigned.

documents in a big UK bank, not all initiated by me, but maintained, updated, and used as input to various reviews.

The documents were a very useful inheritance for me at contract start and for people who took over from me at contract end. We'll examine a typical structure and content headings and discuss its creation, maintenance, and use. Of course, if your organization has its own mandatory document standards, it shouldn't be difficult to fit a PID around the appropriate ones.

There are two basic ways of developing a high availability solution:

1. *Ab initio*, that is, from nothing through to a working solution
2. A *delta* increment across the whole of an existing configuration

The output of the PDW will obviously be different in both cases. In my view, the second scenario will be the messiest to handle, partly because nearly everything done will be a change. A third possible route is specific *delta* work on a few components of an existing system which are proving the most vulnerable to, for example, outages in the case of an HA project. The route chosen will depend on user requirements, costs, and available skills.

PID Purpose and Structure

The PID is the document that will answer the questions why, what, when, and who, which covers management information and approval, what it entails, progress via milestones, and who is doing what to ensure that progress. Whatever project management method is used, it can fit in with a PID, even if it mandates its own documentation. PIDs are recognized by PRINCE (projects in a controlled environment) and so cooperation is not a big issue. A major thing to remember is that the PID should be a living document nurtured by progress and any changes rendered necessary by circumstances.

The PID should include the working flipcharts and notes generated at the PDW plus the events and documentation leading up to the PDW, including previous attempts or experience from similar projects. This is important if remedial reworks or backtracking prove necessary.

PRINCE documentation suggests the following table of contents for a PID but they are not carved in stone, and I have seen variations used to cater for an organization's own needs, often using their own documentation standards:

- Purpose of the document, what is this project all about? Relate to the business aspects (remember this is what IT is for)
- Background to the need for it (new business initiative, new regulatory laws. etc.)
- Project definition, I would hammer the A Point to B Point and viewpoint ways of looking at things
- Method of approach, probably devised and communicated by the facilitator but along the lines outlined in this appendix
- Business case, including losses if we don't do it
- Project organization, possibly with virtual teams
- Communications plan for all stakeholders
- Project quality plan criteria
- Initial project plan from the PID
- Project controls and checkpoints
- Initial risk and issues log, these pages will get red hot I can assure you; the document should chart actions and progress against these issues and risks
- Financial management, this could be a totally different document; this log needs frequent review and follow-up
- Contingency plans
- Project filing structure, that is, where can I find things out regarding this project

PID Notes

1. The beginning of the document can contain the usual features of your organization: who has copies, contact names, revisions, and dates, and so on.
2. A PID need not be a single monolithic document but an outline and holding document that points to other, separately maintained documents.
3. The document will obviously state what is in the project plan but equally important is an understanding of what is not in the plan, in other words, *exclusions*. This has been found necessary to avoid situations where certain

things have been *assumed* as implicit in the plan when they have not been requested or designed explicitly.

4. The reader will be aware by now of my discomfort at blindly following prescriptive activities. The key here is to use common sense, decide on who the document is written for, and ask yourself if everyone involved disappeared, would the PID be enough for a new team to take up the reins and drive on.

There are several sample PIDs to be found on the Internet. Searching for "PID, sample document" will yield a number of PIDs from various sources to give a feel for them.

Multistage PDW

Where a project is large or requires phasing, it is convenient to have several A Points and B Points, where the B Point of phase 1 is the A Point of phase 2, and so on. Each one then requires a mini-PDW, handled exactly the same as before while ensuring continuity from one phase to succeeding phases. It may be advisable to have a multistage PID unless you wish to produce a single PID, resembling *War and Peace* in size and scope.

Root Cause Analysis (RCA)

In the context of I.T., Whack-A-Mole is a slang term that refers to the process of continually trying to fix a recurring problem that appears to be fixed, but keeps reappearing.

How-To Geek Newsletter

Root cause analysis (RCA) is a method of problem solving that tries to identify the root causes of faults or problems. RCA practice tries to solve problems by attempting to identify and correct the root causes of events, as opposed to simply addressing their symptoms. By focusing correction on root causes, problem recurrence can be prevented.

An example of root cause versus symptom is a failing electrical component. This may be replaced but recurs in the same component or a similar one. The root cause may well turn out to be the power supplies blowing the components and these are the *root cause* of the problems, not the components.

Root cause analysis is a four-step process after the recognition of the problem and involves the following:

1. Data collection; relating to the problem.
2. Causal factor charting; a rather grand title for how did we get to the crunch point of the problem. Generic discussions of this step have imposing flowcharts, but in all my time in IT I've never seen one applied to RCA.

Table A.2 RCA Post-Problem Record

Problem	Related Events/Issues	Resolution
NIC failure	Power, component	New NIC, plan power supply review by 12/12/15
…	…	…

3. Root cause identification, not the symptoms. This is the difficult part and is very installation-specific.
4. What do we do about it (in short)? This will depend on the amount of disruption caused by any suggested solutions.

There are activities around this technique since RCA is not a remote island of activity:

- Notification of the problem from the first recognition to those responsible for its analysis and correction. This is a communication factor that is in itself important and needs specification.
- Documentation and classification of the resolved problem for reference and the recognition of similar or identical problems in the future.
- Postfix notification of people who have been affected by the problem.

The reference given has a post-problem reporting step that is a bit elaborate for most IT purposes. I would recommend as an aid to documentation and a simple classification table (see Table A.2) along the same lines but IT-oriented.

There are any number of articles and books on this topic but the following references provide readable coverage of the topic. The key to accessing and using other material is to extract and translate what is relevant to you organization: IT, acute, and chronic problems. Don't overelaborate and use a sledgehammer to crack a very small nut.

- http://asq.org/learn-about-quality/root-cause-analysis/overview/overview.html
- http://asq.org/quality-progress/2004/07/quality-tools/root-cause-analysis-for -beginners.html

Component Failure Impact Analysis (CFIA)

Component failure impact analysis (CFIA) is a proactive method to determine the potential impact on service delivery in the event that a particular component (or configuration item) should fail.* It can be used in the *design* and *operational* phases

---

* Definition from http://itsm.certification.info/cfia.html.

of development and implementation. In the operational phase, failure to deliver to expectations (SLAs) can be looked at from different angles for causes:

- Incorrect design? Back to the drawing board.
- Incorrect build? Rework? Is our documentation good enough to do this?
- Incorrect installation? Reinstall?
- Incorrect operation? Review procedures and implement revised versions.
- Incorrectly maintained? Review procedures and implement revised versions.
- Bad external influences (malware, malice) or hostile environment? Review and improve if possible.
- Deliberate damage or interference? Interview personnel, as a large proportion of malicious damage is carried out by internal staff.

CFIA is a useful tool as it can create a visual tabular view of services and their required component items and, if used, a searchable information base for analyzing future problems.

The CFIA as part of the availability management process, as our example, will involve technical specialists who understand the way that the infrastructure is arranged and organized. A basic CFIA will target a specific section of the infrastructure: just looking at simple binary choices (e.g., if we lose component X, will a service degrade or simply stop working). This what-if method can be applied across other project topics.

CFIA Development: A Walkthrough and Risk Analysis

A risk analysis identifies important functions and assets that are critical to a firm's operations, then subsequently establishes the probability of a disruption to those functions and assets. Once the risk is established, objectives and strategies to eliminate avoidable risks and minimize impacts of unavoidable risks can be set. A list of critical business functions and assets should first be compiled and prioritized.

Following this, determine the probability of specific threats to business functions and assets. For example, a certain type of failure may occur once in 10 years. What is the impact when it does happen? Are we prepared for it?

From a risk analysis, a set of objectives and strategies to prevent, mitigate, and recover from disruptive threats should be developed. Structured walkthroughs are familiar things in program development. It is possible, even desirable, to perform a similar exercise on a system/service to develop the CFIA list discussed earlier, otherwise there is a lot of guesswork involved.

How do we do this? It is a question of getting a group of peers together to walk-through the delivery process of a service* through a system, usually via a facilitator

---

* Obviously, this exercise is applied to services that are critical to the business—high S value.

and a blackboard to plot the flow of work. We will continue with our high availability example.

At each stage of this journey, the things to be done and the questions to be asked are*

- ◼ Determine the function of the system/service components.
- ◼ Create functional and reliability block diagrams.
- ◼ Document the above and the objectives/requirements of the system/service.
- ◼ What happens if this component fails (failure effect)?
- ◼ Can we prevent the failure upfront (buy the best, keep it cooler, etc.)?
- ◼ How easy and practical is it to fix without undue business impact? To hand or will someone have to mail it to us.
- ◼ Can we cover for the failure in some way if it is permanent (redundancy, hot plug, alternate route, etc.) but not a disaster recovery (DR) situation?
- ◼ What other functions or services are affected if it fails?
- ◼ What is the total business impact of each failure identified? Failure mode effects analysis (FMEA) suggests ranking the failures for criticality but, as I implied earlier, this is optional.
- ◼ Rank the exposed failures in terms of impact and recovery effort/time and weigh against available resources.
- ◼ Which failures constitute DR invocation situations? If this cannot be decided here, suggest some criteria for making the decision when a major failure occurs.
- ◼ Develop follow-up and corrective actions (we are going to document all this aren't we!).
- ◼ And so on. A *businessperson* and an appropriate *technical expert* should help.

The analysis should be used to create a CFIA table, a schematic is shown in Table A.3. In real life, it will be much more detailed and organization-specific.

CFIA Table: Schematic

The exercise could be carried out on an existing system or on the design and architecture of a proposed system and documents what-if scenarios and their impact. Table A.3 is extracted from a real-life impact and single point of failure (SPoF) analysis of a single service of a large bank. It ran to five pages and involved several stakeholders in a review of the outcome. Knowledge of the application is vital to assessing the impact of any failure.

---

* Some of these are failure mode effects analysis (FMEA) recommendations.

Table A.3 CFIA Activity Table Schematic

Failure Point	Impact	Recovery Action	Notes/Owner
Data Center Firewall	All remote services would stop	Switch IP address to "warm" standby within 4 hours (SLA)	Migrate to BT Firewall Svc? / Alan V.; Proc 23
Application 1 DB	Data is RAID so loss can be catered for	None needed initially	Harry S. to schedule recovery Proc 26
Image Scanner	Other scanners will take over	Recover failing component and reinstate; check RCA/document	Remaining scanners must support peak load / Joe S.; Proc 33
Fax Server	Other fax servers would continue but impact felt at peak period	Recover server using Runbook Section 3.1	Install another fax server as warm standby? / Dave D.; Proc 43B
System Console	Temporary "blip"	Configure multiple console support	Done already? / Alan V.; If not done Proc 7
Loss of Data Center	Total loss of service	Invoke DR and reroute traffic to; London DR site	Team/Review DR plan afterward; Procs DR1 - 16

Note: "Proc" refers to procedures to be followed.

A CFIA table should generate documents that highlight SPoFs, recovery options and their recovery times, and what action is recommended to reduce similar incidents.

More advanced CFIAs can be expanded to include a number of variables, such as likelihood of failure, recovery time, and cost of failure. Remember, the seriousness (S) of an outage situation is

S = (Business) Impact × Probability (likelihood) of occurrence

Some installations may make an assessment of the probability of any particular failure based on either experience or vendor data.

Have you ever wondered whether the operator or other vital support personnel are SPoFs? If one of your DBAs is on vacation/strike and the only other one has just walked under the number 12 bus, what do you do? Have a backup support agreement with a consultancy or vendor on a pay-if-we-use-you basis? (See Appendix C.) If you think this is far-fetched, look at the following true incident of a personnel SPoF:

> Then a serious disruption occurred. On a Saturday, with all 750 Anytown branches open in 17 states, most storage area network (SAN) connectivity was lost, forcing branches to conduct limited business offline for six hours. "Essentially, one of the existing solutions blew up," says Jim. "Joe [Bloggs] was away celebrating a wedding anniversary and Harry [Lime] was on vacation."*

Quantitative CFIA

My experience of CFIA in IBM was quantitative as well as qualitative where the configuration was communicated to IBM Customer Engineering for analysis. They had figures of estimates for the reliability of various IBM components, which were used to provide an estimate of the reliability of a configuration as specified. Such output was obviously vendor-specific but could be done for other vendors, given that the reliability figures for the components of the system were available. However, not all vendors publish such figures, even if they are known. You can attempt this yourself if you have some failure statistics and understand Lusser's law.†

CFIA: Other Factors

It may escape notice, but there may be other services that depend on the service in question when carrying out a CFIA, for example:

- Were there files and other data sets being created that are used elsewhere and left open after the failure?
- Is there a job waiting for output from the failing system and what is the impact if it cannot run on time?
- Is there a mechanism for informing all stakeholders of the failure?

In essence, using our high analysis scenario, I am asking if there might be knock-on effects on other services and systems from the failure of the service we are dealing with. No application is an island.

---

* Bank incident in 2011 from a banking IT magazine, with names changed to protect the guilty.
† Hint: This is covered in my book *High Availability IT Services*, https://www.crcpress.com/High-Availability-IT-Services/Critchley/9781482255904.

Risk Management

A wise man once said to a doubter of the value of his intense devotion to risk possibilities and their elimination or minimization: "You know son, the more risks I find, the luckier I get."

> Risk is a measure of the extent to which an entity is threatened by a potential circumstance or event, and typically a function of: (i) the adverse impacts that would arise if the circumstance or event occurs: and (ii) the likelihood of occurrence.
>
> Information system-related security risks are those risks that arise from the loss of confidentiality, integrity, or availability of information or information systems and reflect the potential adverse impacts to organizational operations (including mission, functions, image, or reputation), organizational assets, individuals, other organizations, and possibly the Nation.*

You will see by the last phrase of the previous statement that you carry an enormous responsibility on your shoulders. Don't let your country down by not factoring *risk* into the HA/DR deliberations.

Who Are the Risk Stakeholders?

There are several categories of people who should be involved in any risk analysis and action plan:

- Executives, managers and, above all, the sponsor. They are the decision makers and removers of nontechnical hurdles.
- Project leader and team who are doing the design, implementation, operations, and subsequent review plans.
- Clients who can indicate their level of risk tolerance and expectations (SLAs).
- Vendors and other third parties involved who can highlight any risks and considerations associated with their products and services.

Risk management is, or should be, a hot topic in today's IT environment.

Risk management is not a one-off exercise but an ongoing task throughout the project and afterward.

---

* NIST 800-30.

Where Are the Risks?

There are two broad areas you need to consider as posing risk:

1. The *project* itself. If it fails to deliver a "fit for purpose" system then its game over.
2. The *deliverables* themselves. There is the possibility that even though they (the system) are designed and implemented well, they can still be at risk of failure due to some outside force or agency. This includes the risks to the security and integrity of the system from outside influences.

> In all these areas there needs to be a *risk assessment* and a *risk management* plan of action to handle the identified risks.

How Is Risk Managed?

Apart from ignoring any risk, there are at least four things you can do about them once they are identified and assessed for impact:

Mitigation—This as a common solution to risk where the flaw, when it occurs, is fixed or sidestepped in some way to reduce the likelihood and impact of it. A good example of mitigation is a software fix (patch).

Transference—Transference is the act of getting another party to accept risk on your behalf. We do this with car and other insurance deals.

Acceptance—This mode simply allows the system to function as planned with a known (identified) risk and take a chance.

Avoidance—This is the practice of removing the vulnerable aspect of the system via an alternative design or perhaps using redundancy.

There are numerous checklists for assessing risk, which vary depending on the type of project or undertaking. For example, you wouldn't use the risk checklist for a submarine in assessing risk for an IT project. The risks are items that can jeopardize the successful completion of a project/undertaking or degrade the quality of the deliverables.

A checklist will normally contain a list of questions that a project/undertaking team asks itself and takes appropriate action to reduce or eliminate such risks. However, some risks are more easily mitigated than others and some methods put a value of the mitigation possible for a particular activity:

Level 1—Total mitigation possible
Level 2—Some risk

Table A.4 Sample Risk Check/Action List

Item	*Risks*	*Level*	*Likelihood*	*Action*	*Other Info*
Tire	Flat	1	Rare	Reinflate	Check for damage
Wheel	Losing	4	Very rare	Change	Report it
...	...	...	...	...	...

Level 3—Manageable risk
Level 4—Partially manageable risk
Level 5—Mitigation possibilities uncertain

There is also an important parameter of *likelihood* of a certain risk occurring.
A decent way of classify and acting upon risk is to have a table (see Table A.4).

References

"Managing Investment Risk by Parsing Uncertainties:" http://www.cxoadvisory
.com/61/big-ideas/managing-investment-risk-by-parsing-uncertainties/
"Creating a Risk Management Checklist:" http://www.brighthubpm.com/risk
-management/55271-creating-a-risk-management-checklist/
"Risk Management Best Practices" by Anixster: http://www.datacenterdynamics
.com/research/risk-management-best-practices/94001.fullarticle. *The link above
from DCD-intelligence covers IT-related risk factors, among other areas.*

A search on the Internet for "risk management checklist" or "risk management
best practices" should produce other links to documents that may be suitable or
adaptable for your purposes.

Note: Even if your organization does not have a full-time risk manager, the topic
should be an add-on to someone's job specification or any IT person's reading list.

Data Center/Enterprise Proposals

Note: This section assumes it is written by ACME Co., an IT product and services
vendor. The invitation to tender (ITT) or request for information (RFI) could
be written in a form that mandates this response structure. A similar, tailored
structure might be applied to any bid for business products or services, internal
or external.

Proposal Examples

I use the term *proposal* here as a generic term covering the following scenarios:

- A proposal bid from a vendor to a potential customer for hardware, software and services
- An internal document to business users' IT representative for a new system to support stated business requirements
- An outline of products and services on offer from you as a vendor or an IT supporting the business

The customer is anyone you are addressing with your document.

The following sample has an IT slant but that does not exclude the use of the structure in other situations, modified to suit.

The Document

The document should be a joint effort of vendor/IT people, and should emphasize the fit of the proposed solution to the customer requirements and what role you will play in the installation and management of the resulting system. A suggested breakdown of a proposal is shown next, and you should make sure you understand the *viewpoint** of the various people expected to read each section:

1. Management summary (this is the management eye-catcher since they won't read much of the rest of the document)
2. Statement of customer requirements
3. Proposed system architecture to meet requirements
4. Implementation plan
5. Service management and support plan†
   - Account team
   - Professional services
   - Enterprise services
6. Technical Information supporting items 2 and 3 (the correct place for feeds and speeds, not upfront) and answering the eternal so-what question
7. Costs, and terms and conditions
8. Appendices on support, services, and similar
9. You should be prepared to give a presentation to the customer on your bid

---

* That is, will he understand what you have written?

† The service management element covers help desks, operations, and the systems management disciplines, and these need to be covered in any data center proposal. If the customer is moving from an established legacy environment, he will insist on these. You will vary the format if it is an internal document but in general, it is a proposal for, say, an SLA or an idea for progress or change.

This structure allows senior customer personnel (internal or external) to understand what is being proposed at a higher level than feeds and speeds. If such a person reads some proposals I have seen, he will switch off at the first picture of a processor server range or disk drive, particularly front and views, as if they were selling women's dresses.

I have been involved in several proposal evaluations when at Oracle. Some proposals had been mentally rejected by page 4 since they were spouting technology and patently the writer(s) did not understand, or care about, the customer requirements. The ones that followed the preceding outline were always in the hunt until the death.

Important: There should be no surprises in either presentation or proposal for the prospect; they should merely be formalities. There should be a check-and-balance with customers. Things like "We understand your main business issues are x, y, z and your preferred technical strategy is c/s/Java/3 Tier, and so on. Is that correct?" This allows the customer in effect to unwittingly help you in writing the proposal and when he sees it, he has almost total empathy with it because it is partly his baby.

Vendor bids. If the potential customer is one of those who gives answers to your questions to the others in the bid, then ask some daft questions that don't give away your architecture or strategy. I have always thought the practice a little unfair since the questions might relate to some advantageous and novel solution being bid and this is passed on to the competition.

Better still, lead the competition up a blind alley by implying solutions you have no intention of bidding. In the proposal, you then explain why you didn't go along that line. It's called an *Aunt Sally*, dealt with elsewhere in the body of this book. In addition, if you know the competition is bidding solution type X, then say that we'd thought of it as an option and then destroy it—you're not knocking the competition then. Simple examples would be a distributed solution versus centralized and multiple boxes versus a big server.

It is also very effective to tailor any proposal to the industry anyone is bidding for business in, even when using boilerplate material, to demonstrate some industry knowledge of the customer. Proposals need not be the size of *War and Peace*. Items 1 to 3 can be 2 to 10 pages; the rest will vary according to the situation. It is key to keep sections at the level of the intended audience and not drop a level or two into feeds and speeds and other nitty-gritty matters and then going up a level. The audience will switch off. Always remember the viewpoint way of structuring proposals and other documents.

When talking about technology it should be relevant and related to customer needs. "Gee-whiz" selling will not work on most business or IT veterans and the so-what test applied to technology elements of the proposal.*

---

* Bob, who we have met before, when confronted with gee-whiz speak, would counter with "What does it mean to the end user?" This normally sinks the speaker without trace.

Internal Proposals

Not all proposals are aimed at potential customers and persuading them to buy something. An internal proposal might be suggesting new systems or configurations, an idea for a service-level agreement, and so on. The main rules outlined earlier apply:

- Cater to viewpoints of possible readers (speak their language).
- Sell a process or methodology, not technology.
- If the proposal is pure technology, be prepared to answer the likely questions so what or what does it buy us.
- Outline the costs, where possible, and the ensuing benefits. If there aren't any benefits, the proposal will be canned.
- Spell out extra skills and other resources that will be needed.
- If possible, spell out the critical success factors (CSFs), including any risks.

Tailored Customer Documents

It would be a nice touch if you included the company/department logo in the document you present but without overdoing it. In addition, using the same font style that that company/department uses will generate empathy with what you write.

Viewpoints

Viewpoints is a useful concept to grasp in the IT world.* It is a representation of something connected with IT that is tailored to the audience it addresses and excludes detail of no interest to that audience. In presenting an IT topic, for example, a development proposal, the proposer might need to construct several viewpoints for the various stakeholders involved.

Consider a proposal to develop a high availability system for an organization to run a new key application. The *CEO* will be interested in the flow of the work and where the benefits lie, for example, faster production of invoices or better stock control. The *operations manager* will be interested in the configuration, volumes, feeds and speeds, monitoring and maintenance, and so on. The *software manager* will be concerned with the various layers of software, skill gaps to support it, and possibly development requirements. *Users* will want yet another view of the system and its functions and so on.

This will probably necessitate different diagrams with different descriptions aimed at different people, that is, multiple viewpoints. The example in Table A.5 is

---

* It also applies outside IT. Erin Meyer's *Harvard Business Review* paper "Tailor Your Presentation to Fit the Culture," talks about formulating your message to suit the culture (country) you are dealing with: https://hbr.org/2014/10/tailor-your-presentation-to-fit-different-cultures.

Table A.5   Data Conversions to Usable Metrics

Raw Data	Operational Metrics% Utilization	User/SLA Metrics
01110100110	Disk A access time (ms)	Average response time
00111000110	Wait time disk A	90th percentile response time
00110000110	Response time disk A	Throughput (transactions/sec)
00111100110	CPU utilization%	Throughput (queries/minute)
10110110110	CPU wait time%, etc.	Etc.
...	...	...

measurements made on an application system to report on a SLA negotiated between users and IT. It shows a breakdown of who is interested in what, operations versus user, from all the performance measurements routinely carried out in such systems.

The case in Table A.5 shows performance metrics as an example of catering for different viewpoints of the same type of data. The idea of viewpoints is also important in delivery of information to people in written, presentation, or any other media.

Data versus Information

Table A.5 brings up another important point, which is the difference between data and information. In essence, information is data "cooked" to a recipe to suit the consumer. It should have a value, in operations or postoperations, otherwise it shouldn't be collected.

Masses of data is normally useless in finding trends, spotting anomalies and generally assessing what all this data tells us. In other words, What does it all mean? The list of the heights of every man in the United Kingdom when printed out or seen on screen tells us very little. However, the calculation of the average height and comparing that figure with the same figure from 50 years previously has a value to some people. The same data might be analyzed in another way (recipe) for other purposes and, to take a trivial example, for builders to decide on future standard height for doors.* In short, data alone tells us little; analyzed data can provide people with different viewpoints with the information they need in different formats. This sort of operations data is being used more often in predictive mode using the past data as the lever.

---

* U.S. visitors usually smack their heads when entering old buildings in the United Kingdom as part of their tours. The heights of doorways built hundreds of years ago are often very low, prompting many to put up a sign saying, "Duck or grouse."

Summary

If you understand the following simple edicts of IT and nothing else, you are 50% on the way to being an IT Passport holder. Believe me, I know; I've seen too many technology foul-ups and embarrassing situations created by very clever people who nevertheless are unaware of these rules of thumb.

A clever person is not necessarily a wise person.

---

1. Don't genuflect at the altar of technology nor worship at its shrine.
2. Technology is a tool to help implement solutions, not the be-all and end-all. Similar considerations apply to detailed queuing theory and simulation tools.
3. A badly designed solution is not helped by technology, it only serves to reach the disaster quicker.
4. Similarly, super gee-whiz project management tools are useless if the project design or the process is flawed. It is just made open to view by graphs, radar charts, and other fancy output showing it going down the drain faster than it would otherwise.
5. Any IT project—application development, complex installations, modernization, migrations and so on—consists of steps, each of which is part of a chain from initiation to operation.
6. Any step in this mainly linear chain is a possible point of failure that can jeopardize the whole project. Lusser's law* holds here and it shows that the chain is even weaker than it weakest link.
7. Each step must be self-contained but interface with the overall plan elements before it and after it. Isolated development of component steps is the slippery slope to disaster.
8. Do a walkthrough of any complex undertakings, including, if possible, with a competent person outside the project boundaries. They will spot things you won't.
9. Document what you are doing, for audit and back covering purposes if it comes to a finger-pointing conclusion.
10. Above all, *think*, and don't just work blindly from checklists prepared by someone else.

---

* Explained in my book *High Availability IT Services,* http://www.crcpress.com/product/isbn /9781482255904.

Appendix B: IT Projects

Application Development Process

The schematic in Figure B.1 shows the flow of the steps in a typical application implementation plan. This was the format used when I was employed by Sun Microsystems as a generic plan for almost any application installation. The format is *activity* and *time* before the live date (production date, PD) that the particular activity should take place or start. Thus (PD − 14) means this activity starts 14 weeks before the live (or production) date. These factors will vary in size depending on the magnitude and complexity of the application, and what is presented here is a typical (real-life) one.

These points are usually known as *milestones* in a project.

Benefits

The key benefits from using this plan can be summarized as follows:

- A faster implementation of the business applications, gaining the business benefits of the system earlier
- The minimization of risk in the planning and implementation phases
- A comprehensive plan developed early in the cycle, avoiding retrofitting features overlooked in the first place
- A robust, stable applications platform offering reliable service and the ability to cope with change and growth through a service management plan
- More satisfied and productive end users of the system: internal, external, or the general public in the case of a website

It is well known that the *cost of correction* rises dramatically as the project progresses, hence the need for getting it right first time. Under each heading, shown here just for the first activity, are subheadings that scope that activity.

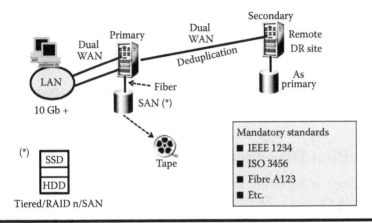

Figure B.1 An IT architecture: Performance example.

The Steps

- Review of Current Status (PD – 17 weeks)
  - Scope of this step
  - Effort required (estimate) in man days
  - Resources needed and available to do this step
  - Deliverables at the conclusion of this step

These headings are repeated where applicable in all the following steps:

- Service-Level Agreement (SLA) Workshop (PD – 15 weeks)
- User Workload and Geography Specification (PD – 15 weeks)
- IT Support Requirements Workshop (PD – 14 weeks)
- Network and System Sizing (PD – 14 weeks)
- Technical Architecture Specification (PD – 13 weeks)
- Risk Analysis
- Detailed System Specifications (PD – 12 weeks)
- System Review and Walkthrough
- Installation Plan (PD – 12 weeks to PD – 11 weeks)
- Project Management (PD – 11 weeks to PD + 3 weeks)
- Service Management (PD – 10 weeks [planning] PD onward [operations])

These may be capable of working in parallel, subject to manpower and interstep dependences.

Service Architectures

I have stated numerous times in this book that technology is not the first port of call in developing an IT system to support applications, business or scientific. The flow of such developments should follow at least the following:

1. User requirements
2. Architecture selection to meet 1
3. Sizing, walkthrough, and feasibility and management
4. Technology selection to implement 1, 2, and 3 (sizing)
5. Implementation

In particular, note the order of these activities. Start with 3 and your chances of success are minimal for a new environment. It will probably be all right for speeding up an existing environment.

Architecture versus String and Sealing Wax

I did some basic work on architectures and the flow of their development, and the following is a summary of my deliberations and research. It is essentially a checklist, which I think will provide a different perspective to the development of IT systems.

System Architectures

What Is an Architecture?

A difficult concept to pin down or explain, as *architecture* means different things to different people, particularly in an IT context. For our purposes, I would like to define an IT architecture as a set of standards and components, which can preferably be represented diagrammatically, which form the basis of systems aimed at maximizing performance of work running on it.

Such an architecture might comprise other architectures, for example x86, relational database, I/O attachment architecture and a network specification. It is impossible for me as the author to lay down an architecture for everyone to follow but I can simply illustrate the principles of an architecture aimed at performance as an example.

The architecture documentation should explain the reasons its components and their relationship with the workload they are designed to optimize; this is the difficult bit. Costs and return on investment (ROI) will also be an issue when proposing an architecture.

A customer of mine once proposed a new data center to the board of his company without a cost/benefit analysis that he had been advised by a data center guru to prepare. He was dispatched by the board with a flea in his ear and told to prepare such a case. He promptly put the onus on me, representing IBM, to help him out but we managed it in the end! The solution, incidentally, was centered on people productivity and some consolidation of resources.

Sample Performance Architecture

Figure B.1 shows a sample (not necessarily perfect) of a performance architecture where you will note that specific products are not named. This sort of diagram can be produced for the other architectures discussed next. *Performance* is taken here as an example of an architecture versus a product specification list.

This architecture is vendor product neutral, although it does contain techniques and standards in its specification and this is normal in my experience. I have seen diagrams purporting to be architectures when in fact they were more like wiring diagrams for a nuclear missile. If an architecture is to have any longevity, it should ideally be

- As independent as possible of products specifics apart from some necessary ones like minimum speeds, which may dictate a particular component of a solution
- Simple to understand (remember the Lord Rutherford quote*)
- Be feasible, manageable, and implementable by human beings with existing technology
- Dovetail with other architectures where necessary; don't design one without reference to other parts of the IT environment it will live in
- Be documented so that it can be reused either in its entirety or "diluted" for less important use

The output of an architecture study should ideally be a product-independent architecture that can have one or more implementations. Indeed there may be cases where more than one architecture matches the customer requirements and may be amenable to several implementations. In essence, it is a level of *abstraction* above the hardware software and other operational entities.

It is vital that an IT architect understands the difference between an *architecture* and an *implementation*. An architecture is often independent of how it is implemented, for example, a drawing of a house architecture might be "implemented" in brick, stone, wood, or even paper if you live in Japan. Only by assessing the detailed needs of the occupant is it possible to guide the architecture to the most appropriate implementation. For example, if he or she lives at the foot of a volcano that spews hot ash out every other week, it would be inadvisable to implement the design in wood (or paper).

---

* Everything in physics should be capable of being explained to a barmaid.

One Architecture or Several?

If the business units (BUs) within an enterprise use separate systems, then it is possible to have a different architecture of the same category for each strategic business unit (SBU), for example, two different availability architectures (see Table B.1). If they use the same system, this is more difficult. Once an architecture has been defined, it can probably be reused in a *diluted form* as an architecture for another system. Sun Microsystems had a Reusable Enterprise Architecture Library (REAL) containing this sort of information. I am not sure if it currently exists, but the idea is perfectly good and valuable.

For example, a backup/recovery architecture can be reduced in availability features and size for a system whose requirements are not as stringent. This would mean reducing the hardware redundancy employed, and possibly the amount of software, to reduce the cost to match the benefit. This is known as *architecture reuse*, a very cost-effective and time-saving way of doing things.

Table B.1   Architectures in an IT System

Architecture	Definition
Information architecture	This architecture defines the business questions that IT will address, including the major information repositories in the business, the information flow between them, and the access methodology.
Storage architecture	This architecture defines the storage strategy for the business. It is also a subarchitecture to many of the other architectures, such as the availability, application, coexistence, and management architectures.
Application architecture	The application architecture defines the major applications, their interaction, and their delivery. For example, client/server, thin client, web-based, and n-tier.
Coexistence architecture	This architecture defines the integration of the major systems supporting the information architecture. It will include the definition of the interfaces between major systems, for example, provision of services for both homogeneous and heterogeneous environments.
Security architecture	This architecture defines the security requirements for the information architecture. This will probably be a requirement for multilevel security. For example, the demands of an Internet installation will typically be more stringent than those of an extranet. Bring your own device (BYOD) makes this architecture key to data and application security, and, hence, to business continuity.

(Continued)

Table B.1 (Continued)   Architectures in an IT System

Architecture	Definition
Availability architecture	This architecture defines how the availability criteria that are required for each major component of the information architecture will be met. It would include subarchitectures such as backup and recovery strategy, archive strategy, and disaster recovery planning. There should be major input from the business, for example, business impact analysis (BIA).
Management architecture	This architecture defines the support strategy for the services that maintain the information architecture, including systems, storage, networks, and applications.
Development architecture	This architecture defines the development environment, test and quality assurance processes, and deployment strategy. It should include function and load testing of the application(s) and an estimate of software maturity enabling it to be issued.
Production architecture	This architecture defines the production schema for applications and day-to-day operations, such as backup and housekeeping.
Data architecture	This architecture defines the characteristics of the data that flows through the information architecture. It would typically provide data volumes, storage technologies (RDBMS, text files), availability and security requirements, volatility, and importance.
Web/ e-commerce architecture	This architecture defines the web/e-commerce infrastructure, the delivery targets and mechanisms, and how the security and availability requirements are addressed. This will involve several of the other architectures in this table, for example, availability and security.
Enterprise printing architecture	This describes the framework for supporting the printing needs of the organization or SBU. Factors include security, priorities, color, and synchronous and asynchronous printing.
Cloud and virtualization architecture	This is new on the architecture scenarios pioneered by Zachman, TOGAF, and others, and is outlined here for completeness in handling entities new to high availability. However, I would advise against overelaborate architectures, which is possible if you take everything these seminal architecture methods set out.

Warnings

1. It is crucial to design successful architectures that avoid solutions to which there is no known problem.
2. A wiring diagram is not an architecture.
3. Neither is a beautiful diagram of what you have already (self-fulfilling prophecy).
4. An architecture should be amenable to different implementations.
5. It should be capable of being explained to a barmaid (Lord Rutherford).

Don't worry. Such architectures need not be of the complexity of the Empire State building or St. Paul's Cathedral but they should be thought out, designed top-down, open to more than one implementation, and capable of being explained to a barmaid in 5 minutes or less.

In addition, you don't need to complete them all before implementing a system; just the one for the core of the system, for example, a large database application.

Enterprise Architectures: My View of Categories

Where is your network architecture, I hear you cry? Network architecture is not covered in Table B.1 as a separate item since it really underpins the other architectures and, as such, depends on the physical requirements of the supported architectures. In other words, it cannot be designed in isolation of the other architectures listed, in fact, even they will have mutual dependencies.

Appendix C: IT Modernization

Why Modernize?

Modernize is a much used term meaning changing from one IT state to another; no more, no less, and hence project definition workshop (PDW)-able. However, there is the implication that the move is to a more *modern* platform, meaning hardware and software. Terms like *agility*, *hybrid*, *digital revolution*, and *cloud* abound, but the basic reason for doing it has to be a business reason.

The change to a more modern, and hence cheaper, platform may have benefits, but at a risk to the business applications if they are left out of the equation. For example, "We are moving from state A to state B for the following reasons:

- Improve our business processing and customer service, and so forth
- Take advantage of newer technology where it assists this goal
- Save on ongoing expenditures as a result and provide a platform capable of growth and modification to meet the needs of the business"

If the first reason is not present, you may be going down a blind, one-way alley.

Migration, Rationalization, and Consolidation

Some wiseacre once said "Two things are certain in this life; death and taxes." I would add an extra certainty related to IT: *Technology will continue to advance at pace, but if it is not managed and employed correctly, it is like having a tiger by the tail. Uncontrolled technology is like a raging fire. Properly managed technology is a boon; unmanaged technology thrown at a problem is likely to be a disaster.*

IT Yesterday and Today*

The IT world today is far more complex than it was 20 or more years ago when the Internet, data warehousing, and knowledge engineering were relatively rare. The mainframe, under centralized control, still ruled the roost although UNIX, and latterly Linux, was being considered for new applications that may have been on a 2-year backlog in the mainframe environment. In addition, there was a surge in the availability of application packages, a thing unknown on the mainframe, where nearly all applications were bespoke, very organization-specific, and probably written in Assembler or COBOL.

Many of these still exist today as core business applications, often because they do the required job and that there is a massive investment in those applications. However, the skills needed to maintain or enhance these programs[†] are becoming scarce as their owners retire. Some programs running today were written nearly half a century ago.

As IT moved out of finance into other areas of businesses, business managers decided to cut the wait for applications by purchasing peripheral IT systems, often employing business application packages. DEC was probably the first vendor to allow managers to break out of the mainframe prison with the new inexpensive (by the standards of the day) VAX machines and a third-party software catalog to die for at the time.

UNIX soon got in on the act and Windows New Technology (NT) duly followed. UNIX was a prime target for independent software vendors (ISVs) because of its apparent "openness," creating a wider market for their software products. In theory, the idea was "write for one flavor of UNIX, run on any." In fact when Sun Microsystems was looking for an operating system (OS) to drive its groundbreaking workstations, UNIX seemed the answer.[‡] Developing one's own OS is not an enviable task. UNIX then morphed into Linux, Linux runs on IBM mainframes and the rest is history.

The Transition Era

There followed a period of organizations buying applications and systems for "best business fit," resulting in a proliferation of different systems, each needing their own support structure. The central control mold of the mainframe had been broken, although mainframes continued to do the bulk of the core business processing.

---

* Or "How did we get into this fine mess?" (attributed to Oliver Hardy).
† Often written in Assembler or COBOL.
‡ It became SunOS, evolving into Solaris.

The issue then became the need for rapid and convenient access to core business data, held on the mainframe, by distributed systems, for example, call centers, the Internet, data warehouses, and nonmainframe applications. Systems integration and data transfer became necessities, but the management and control of many disparate systems ("server sprawl") was still an issue.

Resource utilizations also presented problems, for example, a call center system was perhaps used from 8 a.m. to 8 p.m. but unused overnight. Ideally, the processing power of that system could be immensely useful in, for example, overnight batch work in helping reduce the batch window for processing an increasing amount of work. There is obviously some sense in trying to rationalize this scenario in some way. But how?

Some Terminology in This Area

We will look at activities know as rationalization (R), consolidation (C), and migration (M). They are not exclusive terms and any situation could involve all three, though hopefully not at the same time.

Rationalization

The word *rationalization* in general refers to the reorganization and simplification of functions and the supporting environments. A non-IT example is the reduction of many chemical plants to a few (or even one) and the reduction in the number of chemicals sold as a cost-saving exercise.

In the context of IT, I mean for rationalization to cover the reduction in the number and types of software and possibly hardware for cost, manageability, and support reasons, among others. This process might take place *in situ*, meaning at the existing IT site or at a new site.

Some installations had more than one system of a particular type but with different operating systems. For example, an IBM site might well have MVS and DOS and possibly other systems like 8100 distributed systems, running the DPPX, or possibly DPCX for word processing, operating systems—what we call in Britain a dog's breakfast.

This sort of environment presented many problems of cost, support (technical and help desk), maintenance, and complexity, particularly in connectivity. As installations grew, so did the needs to simplify this morass of tin, wire, and software, but this was not always easy as there could be a bewildering number of options involving workflows, applications, and systems (hardware and OS).

The process and functional consolidations are covered in the Wilkerson document referenced later and I shall concentrate on hardware and software (application and system).

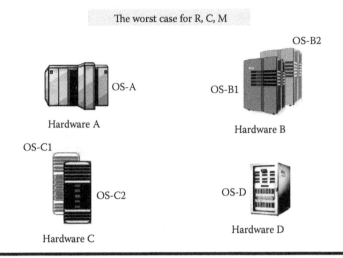

Figure C.1 Pre-rationalization IT scenario. OS, operating system; -A, -B1, -C1, and so on, are types of operating systems.

The pre-rationalization (pre-everything) scenario is illustrated in Figure C.1, which was a typical environment in the 1970s–1980s.

Benefits of Rationalization

There are many benefits to a properly planned and executed *rationalization* or *consolidation* and some could apply to a pure *migration*:

■ Reducing hardware inventory and hardware maintenance costs
■ Moving to a more modern platform
■ Reducing software license costs
■ The possibility of using new software not available on the old platforms
■ Less staff needed to support and manage fewer systems
■ Improving reliability by reducing proliferation of systems and networks
■ Improving centralization of control, backup, etc.
■ Optimizing cost/performance of mature and legacy systems if they are the subjects of the exercise
■ Assist a changing business organization
■ Other advantages you can list for your particular scenarios

Consolidation

Consolidation is a subset of rationalization since it can be done without rationalizing hardware and software, just compressing everything into fewer systems.

There are essentially two types of consolidation:

1. *Homogeneous consolidation* where similar systems are consolidated within the same architectures (hardware and software). They might be consolidated onto a different set of architectures, but the source systems are the same (homogeneous). An example might be the consolidation of several UNIX systems onto one UNIX system or perhaps an IBM MVS system.
2. *Heterogeneous consolidation* where disparate systems are consolidated to one of the source architectures of even a different one. One real situation I came across was a bank that used
   a. An IBM mainframe
   b. A Tandem system
   c. An IBM AS/400 (now -iSeries)
   d. A DEC VAX system
   e. A Bull DPS8 system

Can you imagine the costs and diversity involved in developing and supporting this collection of systems? As you can imagine, there are any number of permutations of possibilities in rationalization and consolidation and it isn't possible to generalize here.

Consolidation Background

In about 1990, with the advent of credible UNIX solutions to problems normally the preserve of the mainframe, people began to take applications off the mainframe, or replace them, on UNIX systems that were touted as much cheaper solutions. This led to the "distributed" systems phenomena where several UNIX systems might perform the job of a single mainframe.* This often culminated in the philosophy of "one system for every application or application set" and resulted in support anarchy, often with little or no central control or support. The increasing need to share, manage, and control data made the distributed model difficult and expensive to manage and control. Indeed, Kathleen D. Smith of IBM said in 1998: "Every week there's another baby on the doorstep" of the data center. Babies need looking after as everyone knows.

This dilemma was summarized succinctly many years ago in a presentation from Champion Computer Corporation, an IBM Business Partner at the time, with the 10 top reasons for consolidation of resources:

1. You have more systems administrators than you have users.
2. You spend more money on server upkeep than the U.S. government owes.
3. Physical security could only be accomplished by *Star Trek*-like shields rather than locking the door to a single room.

---

* Often called "downsizing" or "rightsizing" in the 1990s.

4. Utilization rates for more than half your servers are in single digits.
5. Department managers routinely purchase and install their own hardware (but leave management to you).
6. Capacity planning is a synonym for buying more servers and disks.
7. You don't know if you are in compliance with all your software licenses.
8. You're running 15 different operating systems.
9. Your hardware is having seizures over scalability.
10. You start losing track of your servers.

Although these reasons appear trite as they are written, any old stager in IT will tell you they have a solid basis in truth in many installations.

Another problem with this tangled environment was *resource sharing*. It was quite possible for one distributed system to have spare processor and disk capacity, whereas another system was desperately short of one or the other, or even both. In general, the spare resources could not be temporarily assigned to systems short of those same resources, to be returned later when they were needed by the "donor" system.

A survey by InfoWeek covering the centralization/decentralization market showed that in 1990, some 55% of organizations planned more decentralization versus about 26% planning more centralization. For 1998, the projection was reversed, with about 18% planning decentralization and some 58% planning centralization. The modern term for these activities is *modernization*.

What Is Consolidation?

Consolidation is a bringing together of entities of some kind to achieve some goals of importance to the consolidator(s). In IT terms, it generally means moving the work on a number of servers to fewer servers, and possibly rationalizing the hardware and supporting software at the same time.

Gartner has identified three basic approaches to IT consolidations:

Logical consolidation—The systems remain distributed but support and other procedures are standardized across the enterprise. This can be achieved today by tools that can monitor and manage heterogeneous systems across an enterprise, but the return on investment (ROI) of such a consolidation is probably the least of the three options.

Physical consolidation—The IT systems are moved to a single site but, like logical consolidation, does not reduce the number of servers. Benefits include staff synergy on the same site, easier housekeeping, better physical security, and asset management and control. In both these cases, most of the reasons for consolidation still apply.

Rational consolidation—A combined logical and physical approach to distributed applications; databases and services are combined on fewer, bigger servers.

However you define what you are doing, certain immutable facts take over, mainly in the area of cost–benefit.

Scope of Consolidation

Consolidation is normally associated with servers, whereby several systems are consolidated on one or two systems to (hopefully) achieve economies of scale. There are, however, other forms of consolidation, storage, print, and backup, for example.

Storage Consolidation

In general, the storage associated with consolidated servers will have to move to (or be replaced at) the consolidation site(s). This is not true for storage consolidation since the data still belongs to the applications on the consolidated servers. Today, storage consolidation is the goal of storage area networks (SANs) or, in some cases, network attached storage (NAS). There may be consolidations involving both these architectures.

In a SAN, storage is available across servers and applications via a switch of some sort, although it is not a free-for-all. There has to be management software controlling what goes on across the SAN. In a NAS environment, the storage is attached to a local area network (LAN), for example, switched Ethernet, via a suitable adapter and can be shared by users on the LAN. The "before" situation is a set of servers, each with its application storage and with access to several files servers, either directly attached or via a LAN. The "after" is a consolidated network of storage.*

Print Consolidation

In the consolidation of servers and applications, a decision has to be taken about whether printing facilities are consolidated as well. Bulk printing not immediately needed could be moved to the consolidation site(s) but often, users need low volume printing available locally at short notice. What can be "consolidated" is the control of the print streams using print management software, available from several sources—vendors and ISVs.† This replaces the individual print management facilities previously on the distributed systems before consolidation.

---

* "Storage Area Network Overview," http://www.computerweekly.com/feature/Storage-area
-network-overview.
† It is important to check that any such software can operate in a heterogeneous environment, if
that is a requirement. Not all print management packages do.

Network Consolidation

Physical consolidation. The factor often forgotten in consolidation and migration exercises is the rationalization of the network (LANs, WANs, routers, etc.) to accommodate the changes. It is difficult to be prescriptive about this aspect since it depends on how the consolidation is designed and implemented. This is a major design issue and may eat into any savings accruing from the consolidation in whatever areas are chosen.

Logical consolidation is essentially the software-defined networks (SDNs) scenario, dealt with in Chapter 4. It can exist with current networks or be superimposed on a physical consolidation of a network.

Migration

In the strict sense of the words, consolidation and rationalization could be classed as *migrations*, but in the old sense of 25 or so years ago it meant moving an application from one hardware and software platform to another, possibly changing the application language in transit, say, from IBM Basic Assembler Language (BAL) to COBOL or COBOL to C and other variations of this transition.

The world of *open systems* ushered in applications that were inherently portable and the relatively large number of special vendors migrating code X to code Y, possibly on a different platform reduced. I used to know them all but the only one I can call to mind today is Sector 7, a DEC to several other platform migration companies. They are skilled at migrations in general and can offer assistance and services in this area.

If the migration is code to code in the same environment, it still needs management, but if it is code going to a different environment then there are several other considerations. These are outlined in Figure C.2.

Why All These Different Terms?

Simply, because you will come across them in various documents and on websites. In essence, they are examples of *environment change* and can be interpreted to mean roughly the same thing. The point I am making is that this change involves two environments:

- Where we are today, which is the *A Point*
- Where we want to be tomorrow, which is the *B Point*

Sound familiar?

Like any journey, we need a route map to move from A to B and this route map comes from, for example, a *project definition workshop* (PDW), described in Appendix A.

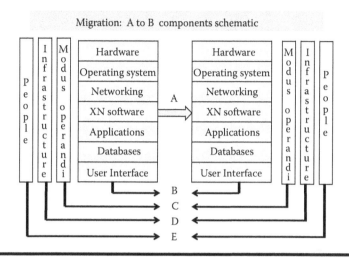

Figure C.2 **Migrating environments A to B.** *Legend*: **The unnecessary A Point baggage goes in the rubbish container (not shown in this figure).**

What Is Involved?

A lot more than you think is the short answer. You are not just changing some hardware and software for some other hardware and software, you are changing environments, as illustrated in Figure C.2.

There will be functions in this transition, and possibly hardware and software not being replaced, that will need to be carried over in one form or another to the new environment. There will also be excess baggage that should be left behind since it is pointless migrating something you don't really need any more. These items should come out in any decent planning exercise.

Someone once said "Those who fail to plan, plan to fail."

The rules for migrating from A to B are the same as those for designing and implementing A: FUMPAS—functionality, usability, manageability, performance, availability, and security. Lose one and in certain circumstances you will lose the project outcome.

Transitions A to E will involve, among lots of other things:

Transition A (overall move)
  - PDW (many things will drop out of this process)
  - Pilot scheme
Transition B
  - B Point requirements
  - System sizing
  - Database design
  - Web setup
  - Benchmarks

Transition C
- Operations
- Documentation

Transition D
- Service and systems management aspects
- Service-level agreements (SLAs) renegotiated

Transition E
- Training
- Vendor/third-party support
- Workflow

Many of the papers I see on this topic leave half of these items out, either because the author has forgotten them or is unsure of his or her ground.

The Modern World

Modernization is a current buzzword that may mean different things to different people. When my wife tells me to *modernize* my wardrobe of clothes, she means "get with it" and buy the latest trendy fashions. In such circumstances, the word *modernization* to me means buying new versions of the same clothes, assuming this is possible.* Modernization normally takes on the former meaning, which is a bigger task than just updating current ways of doing things: websites, big data, mobile devices, and so on. In terms of the preceding discussions, this leads to the pseudoequation

$$M = f(R, C, M, N)$$

that is, a function of all three activities above plus N(ew) environments; not an easy task despite what the avid modernizers (digital revolutionaries) say and write.

References

"IT Rationalization—Essential Building Blocks for Modernization Strategies and Operational Efficiency," http://www.thompsontalent.com/articles/it-rational ization-essential-building-blocks-for-modernization-strategies-and-operational -efficiency/

---

* There aren't many shops that sell top hats and powdered wigs anymore.

Phil Wilkerson (independent consultant and Thompson Technologies contributor) classifies the IT equivalent of the "Seven Ages of Man," in this useful, no, excellent paper on the subject at hand. I have adapted this to show where rationalizations, migrations, and consolidations fit.

High Availability

In consolidating multiple servers into fewer servers, there is always the danger that outages will disrupt many or all the applications on those servers. A key element in the design of the consolidated platform will therefore be that of ensuring high availability of the platform. In a distributed environment, an outage often affects only one or two applications.

Service Levels

In such a radically changed environment, the question of service levels and service-level agreements (SLAs) will arise. It is almost certain they will have to be revised and their requirements taken into account when designing the consolidated platform(s).

Systems/Service Management

Again, it will be "all change" in this area with new skills, tools, and techniques needed to operate and support the new environment if different from the old environment.

People Aspects

There will in general be a sea of change in the involvement of people in changes of the nature we have been discussing, including skills and other training, operations, documentation, interaction with the business, and with third parties.

Costs of Modernization

Obviously, there is a cost to any move from IT state A to state B with the expectation that over time, the net cost will be negative, that is, a profit. This is not necessarily the case unless you add business benefit in alongside any hardware and software savings from rationalization, consolidation, and other economies. The simple cost equations are

Cost = New HW/SW + Effort + Write-off of old equipment + Other costs

Benefit = Measureable business benefit + HW/SW savings + Ongoing operations costs

Net benefit = Benefit − Costs

For this to be financially viable, Benefit > Costs.

Can you see the danger of not having a measureable business benefit? There are two possible outcomes of such an exercise:

1. The transition is financially *exothermic*, that is, it gives out money or has a positive benefit.
2. It may be *endothermic*, that is, consumes money and is a negative benefit. This may be justified if the outcome has some other, desirable benefit.

In my experience and in my reading, I often see a blind rush into a *digital revolution* using the latest technology and so forth without considering the business benefits, if any exist.

One thing is certain: the executives in the company in question will not be pleased if the exercise turns out to be endothermic. According to research from Gartner, more than 50% of data center migrations exceed budget, exceed the migration window, and/or result in unexpected business disruption. You have been warned.

Designing a Data Center

What has gone earlier is key information about dragging your IT (and your business) into modern times, but where do you operate this brave new world? Probably in a data center, either your own or someone else's with clouds very visible overhead or on the horizon.

The IT "Big Bang"

Years ago, there was a move to distribute processing, having systems, suitably configured, dedicated to applications or business areas. The monolithic data center was dead—long live distributed processing! This has now gone into reverse and the data center concept, often implemented as a cloud, is *de rigueur*.* It is rather like the notion that after the big bang, the universe originated at a point and will expand for a few billions of years then contract to the point from whence it came, then explode and repeat the whole cycle forever.

Beware

You will be bombarded by vendors touting *modernization* as the way to go and showing you the benefits when you reach your destination, glossing over the journey

---

* Meaning everyone is doing it!

You too can have a body like mine!

Figure C.3   In no time at all!

and its difficulties.* You also need to be aware of any limitations at your destination that might preclude doing what you did at home. If this is the case, you either change destinations or cull the baggage you planned to take with you.

Charles Atlas (Angelo Siciliano; see Figure C.3) had great success in the 1940s and 1950s with his Dynamic Tension exercise regime but never implied it was easy as some other gurus do today: "Just 3 minutes a day and get a great body." The Bard of Avon had something to say about this kind of trickery: "O wicked wit and gifts, that have the power so to seduce!" (*Hamlet*, William Shakespeare).

I was involved in a data center design in 1986–87—a different proposition from today's complex and volatile environment. There are other factors to consider: sustainability, modularity, ease of upgrade, and the modern word *agility*. If the old data center was a strong but lumbering heavyweight, the modern data center, in whatever form it takes, needs power, nimbleness, and adaptability.

What does remain from the old days are the basic rules: business requirements first, architecture next, technology afterward. Costs are also important but often overlooked in the frenzied dash for the latest technology

I'm sure you'll get the drift of this argument.

---

* Remember the wagon trains of the Old West. "Go west young man and grow with the country" (Horace Greely), meaning for many go to California. Great except for the small migration issues of the Rockies, native Americans, bandits, thirst, heat, and other hazards.

Appendix D: IT Service Management

The management of any IT service supporting the business of an organization is essential for several reasons, not least the fact that there will probably be a service-level agreement in force or some other agreement regarding quality of service (QoS). These agreements specify user requirements in a number of areas, which, in turn, impose objectives, often numeric, on the IT department. To meet these numbers, the IT department must monitor, analyze, and act upon these numbers if they are out of line with agreements. This activity, along with related tasks, is known as service management.

The bulk of this Appendix comprises checklist items that can be scanned at a first-pass reading to appreciate how much is involved in service management but considered in detail in service management implementations. There are no shortcuts in this area.

Service Management Disciplines

Several of these disciplines will be linked, and some will cover several areas, such as security across data, access, application, and system. This list is not 100% comprehensive and has few details, but it will serve to lead to factors that need to be covered in managing business systems. Whatever is measured and controlled will be assigned importance via a service-level agreement (SLA).

- Help/service desk and other support
- Application (response times and throughput)
- Availability (architecture, measurement)
- Recovery (reactive, proactive)
- Audit
- Security
- Problem
- Change
- Performance
- Capacity

241

- Network
- Data
- Software
- Configuration/asset
- Operations (batch, online, housekeeping)
- Print
- Off-site data storage
- Disaster recovery plan
- Other SLA-specified factors

Availability Management

Availability management is a complex and many-faceted discipline aimed at essentially keeping the show on the road. There are many factors and tasks involved but suffice it to say here the key elements are

- Business requirements for high availability; it isn't free so you cannot in general overengineer everything for every application
- From this develops a business continuity plan
- Design for high availability of the service, not just the hardware and software
- Monitor and report on availability
- Use tools and methods for component failure impact analysis (CFIA) and root cause analysis (RCA)
- Plan for recovery, both *normal* after failure and *disaster recovery* after the whole system location is taken out
- Ensure security of the applications as a compromised system or application may have to be taken down for a while

More details can be found in the following references, one is my own work, which contains checklists and other design hints and tips (after much research):

- "ITIL: Availability Management:" https://en.wikipedia.org/wiki/ITIL#Availability_management
- "ITIL-Checklists: Availability Management:" http://wiki.en.it-processmaps.com/index.php/ITIL-Checklists#Availability_Management
- "High Availability IT Services:" https://www.crcpress.com/High-Availability-IT-Services/Critchley/9781482255904

Disaster Recovery Plan

- Business continuity (recovery) planning (BCP), a big topic and important exercise
- IT security planning
- Availability of data and systems

■ Integrity of data
■ Confidentiality of data
■ Disaster recovery service
   – Backup/recovery plan recovery time objectives (RTOs) and recovery point objectives (RPOs)
   – Hardware provision
   – Technical skills and support

Problem/Fault Management

■ Specify major points of failure (disks, hardware, software, etc.)
■ Specify contact/support points for each, both internal and external (e.g., the vendor)
■ Specify predefined bypass/recovery procedures
■ Define escalation procedures and timescales
■ Use a war room and review schedule
■ Define procedures for handling "soft" errors
■ Uncover the problem
■ Log and report problem details
■ Determine the nature and impact of the problem
■ Initiate action to resolve the problem
■ Progress and log corrective actions
■ Log the solution
■ Classify the problem: human error, hardware, software, environment; analyze by vendor so that action can be taken
■ Root cause analysis
■ Amend operations and recovery procedures if necessary

Performance Management

■ Understand key metrics (utilization, percentiles, etc.)
■ Identify key measurements/metrics
■ Identify measurement tools
■ Set up thresholds/"danger levels"
■ Identify ensuing corrective actions
■ Install tools and scripts
■ Analyze data for deviations (exception reporting)
■ Take necessary corrective action, possibly tuning
■ Report uncorrectable situations to problem management
■ Feed relevant data to capacity management
■ Produce SLA reports for IT and users
■ Log the data
■ Revise current procedures if necessary

Capacity Management

- Define user activity profile by subsystem
- Estimate peak processor load
  - Via graph of CPU utilization versus time
  - Via peak utilization method; cater for peak usage
- Produce load forecast
- Compare to existing capacity and upgradeability
- If necessary, benchmark projected workloads
- Document capacity requirements
- Plan any purchases necessary to meet shortfalls
- Real-time monitoring and analytics (IT operations analytics [ITOA]), the latest trend

Change Control/Management

- Identify change "team" (may be whole or part person)
- Identify relevant tools and processes
- Record change request and circulate
- Prioritize changes by business benefit if possible
- Schedule changes if no clashes apparent
- Monitor installation of change and propagate
- Back out changes if unsuccessful
- Report back and log

Network Management

- Operations
  - Start-up
  - Monitor
- Performance/tuning (see performance management list)
- Assess the relevance of network "sniffers"
- Consider backup/alternate routes
- Availability considerations

Software/Asset Management

- Receive/verify software changes
- Apply changes to master machine and verify
- Schedule changes for other machines
- Apply changes
- Log successful changes
- Back out/recover unsuccessful changes

Data Management

- Logical
- Physical
- Backup
- Deduplication
- Recovery
- Fragmentation
- Reorganization
- Adding space
- Error detection (e.g., database crash, space limited)
- And so on

Security and Audit Management*

Security

- Identify security requirements (password change dates, data access, etc.), plus physical security
- Identify relevant tools and processes
- Set up security environment
- Decide on violation/status reporting
- Monitor/administer system

Audit

- Identify audit requirements
- Identify relevant tools
- Set up audit environment
- Decide on audit reporting requirements
- Monitor/administer audit log(s)

Operations Management

Manual

- Start-up/shutdown procedures
- Tape handling procedures
- Central print management and procedures
- Housekeeping procedures (daily, weekly, monthly, yearly, etc.)
- Emergency procedures (recovery, damage limitation, etc.)
- Operations log and shift handover "will"
- Message suppression for message overload; limit display to important ones

---

* This is a rapidly changing environment that requires constant attention as threats continue to evolve and increase in number and sophistication. It's not a "we will do it when we get time" activity.

Automated

- Use of *cron* (timing of activities)
- Timer events
- Data fragmentation recording and reporting
- Data occupancy (%) recording and reporting
- Collection of performance data
- Monitoring of other system data
- Commercial scheduling tools
- Service recovery plan

Print Management

- Local versus central
- Distribution of printout to users
- Print anywhere facilities needed?
- Confidentiality of output
- Alphanumeric, graphics, and image requirements
- Local responsibilities (paper, consumables, etc.)
- Consider scheduling to avoid clash with interactive work

Service Desk/Help Desk

The service desk is a vital part of the systems management infrastructure. Its purpose is to provide a single point of contact for both users and IT staff about systems management issues and queries. The ITIL approach considers the service desk to be the central point of contact between service providers and users and customers on a day-to-day basis.

It is also a focal point for reporting *incidents* (disruptions or potential disruptions in service availability or quality) and for users making *service requests* (routine requests for services). The function may be separated into more than one function, each having a function within the concept of end use or customer help. In the rugged mainframe days, the help desk might have been situated above the machine hall, like the bridge of a ship and was often called the "bridge."

The main point to remember is that there must direct and constant contact between operations and the desk receiving the calls for help. It is a two-way active process (full duplex) where

- Operations forewarns the help desk of pending problems, for example, a potential slowdown due to a change that is being made
- The help desk informs operations immediately of issues raised by end users or customers of a service*

---

* "Help Desk," https://en.wikipedia.org/wiki/Help_desk.

Glossary

This glossary is not meant to be totally comprehensive, but attempts to highlight terms and areas in IT that you will come across often, whether you understand them or not. Other important state-of-the art concepts are also introduced in the body of this book, mainly in Chapter 4, your make-or-break chapter.

For other definitions and references to defined topics, see

- "Internet Terms," TechTerms: http://techterms.com/category/internet
- "Technology Dictionary," Techopedia: https://www.techopedia.com/dictionary

abstraction (IT): In computer science, abstraction is a technique for managing complexity of computer systems. It works by establishing a level of complexity on which a person interacts with the system, suppressing the more complex details below the current level. The programmer works with an idealized interface and can add additional levels of functionality that would otherwise be too complex to handle.

A simple example of abstraction is the plug and socket on your wall that represents your access to power. It is simple and you can soon learn to switch it on and off and maybe even change a fuse in the plug. At the back of this, theoretically invisible to you, is a power line, transformers, and a power station that might be altered in many ways but (hopefully) transparent to you, the user.

analytics: Analytics is the discovery and communication of meaningful patterns in data. Especially valuable in areas rich with recorded information, analytics relies on the simultaneous application of statistics, computer programming, and operations research to quantify performance. Analytics often favors data visualization to communicate insight (key actionable information to the British).

There is a movement to use real-time analysis of operational data for minute-to-minute information and to use the accumulated data to make predictions for the resources monitored.

APM: Application performance measurement is the monitoring and management of performance and availability of software applications. It also includes an element of the detection, diagnosis, and fixing of performance issues, mainly to fulfill the obligation to the service-level agreement (SLA).

autonomic computing: This name refers to the self-managing characteristics of distributed computing resources, adapting to unpredictable changes while hiding intrinsic complexity from operators and users. Started by IBM in 2001, this initiative ultimately aims to develop computer systems capable of self-management, to overcome the rapidly growing complexity of computing systems management, and to reduce the barrier that complexity poses to further growth in IT services.

An autonomic system makes decisions on its own, using high-level policies, and will constantly check and optimize its status and automatically adapt itself to changing conditions.

benchmark: Software run on a computer system to measure its performance under specific operating conditions. The word is also used to describe the act of running a benchmark or speed test. There are many benchmarks, some accepted by the industry as standards, other are developed by individuals or companies for very specific circumstances. The latter are often available, free of charge, to the world in general.

big data: A term applied to data that has characteristics far from those the IT industry has been used to over many years. The paper referenced below says "we apply the term big data to any data set that breaks the boundaries and conventional capabilities of IT designed to support day to day operations."

complexity: A long way from simple alphanumeric stuff of the old days.

high transaction volumes: These may be so high that traditional data storage hits queuing bottlenecks in I/O.

size of data: This may cause bandwidth bottlenecks for records and objects (BLOBS, etc.) that are encountered these days.

variety: All types are now being captured (structured, semistructured, unstructured).

velocity: How fast the data is coming in.

volume of content: This may be so high that it exceeds the capacity thresholds of traditional storage and would need hundreds or thousands of disks to satisfy demand.

Big data technologies describe a new generation of technologies and architectures, designed to economically extract value from very large volumes of a wide variety of data, by enabling high-velocity capture, discovery, and/or analysis, according to the IDC.

See http://www.panasas.com/sites/default/files/uploads/docs /SSN-Hybrid-Array-Snapshot-Report.pdf and http://www.odbms.org /free-downloads-and-links/big-data-and-analytical-data-platforms/.

cluster: According to *Wikipedia*, it generally refers to multiple servers (nodes) that are linked together in order to handle variable workloads or to provide highly available operation in the event of one or more node failures. Each computer is a multiprocessor system itself. For example, a cluster of four computers, each with 16 CPU cores, would enable 64 unique processing threads to take place simultaneously.

A cluster of servers provides fault tolerance and/or load balancing. If one server fails, one or more servers are still available. Load balancing software distributes the workload over multiple systems and "locking" software handles the concurrent access to shared data to avoid clashes and the "deadly embrace," well known to older IT people.

colocation: A colocation (colo) is a data center facility in which a business can rent space for servers and other computing hardware, according to TechTarget.

component failure impact analysis (CFIA): It was originally a process defined (but not necessarily invented) by IBM Customer Engineering in the 1980s to improve assessment and quantification of availability. It was a software-based process of analyzing a particular hardware/software configuration to determine the true impact of any individual failed component. Data was supplied by the requestor, usually field personnel.

computer performance: The amount of useful work accomplished by a computer system compared to the time and resources used. Depending on the context, good computer performance may involve one or more of the following:

- Short response time for a given piece of work
- High throughput (rate of processing work); this can include transactions, program compilations, HPC (see *HPC*) or commercial jobs and other work
- Low utilization of computing resource(s)
- High availability of the computing system or application

converged infrastructure: Converged infrastructure (CI) is an approach to data center management that seeks to minimize compatibility issues between servers, storage systems, and network devices, while also reducing costs for cabling, cooling, power, and floor space. A converged infrastructure can be implemented with a CI reference architecture, with standalone appliances, or with a software driven hyperconverged approach, according to TechTarget.

CPU: Abbreviation of central processing unit. One or more CPUs give a computer the ability to execute software such as operating systems and application programs. Modern systems may use several auxiliary processors to reduce the load on the CPU(s).

CPU bound: A system in which there is insufficient CPU power to keep the number of runnable processes on the run queue low. This results in poor interactive response by applications.

deduplication: This is a method of copying data from one place to another but avoiding the transfer of duplicate blocks or records. This reduces the storage needed for copies or even source data, and minimizes the bandwidth needed to carry the transferred data across a network. These and other reductions will also reduce costs. Once a deduplicated "file" has been transferred, only changes to the primary file need to be transferred subsequently to keep the secondary file up to date.

disaster recovery: This is the process or procedure related to preparing for the continued operation of computing resources after a disaster or failure. This, as we say elsewhere, is the IT part of a business continuity plan (BCP) for an enterprise.

flash storage: This is a semiconductor medium that came to the fore in 2014–15 and which some gurus say should replace SSD and HDD. They have forgotten that IT likes evolution more than revolution. Flash storage describes any device or system that uses flash memory. It's a broad term that can describe anything from a simple USB flash drive to a complex enterprise system that uses flash memory (flash RAM) as part of the storage system (see *storage tiering*).

Flash storage evolved from the EEPROM chip flash, which was invented by Toshiba in the mid-1980s and named after its ability to erase a block of a data in a flash.

See "Flash Memory," http://www.pcmag.com/encyclopedia/term /43272/flash-memory.

FLOPs: Floating point operations per second, used in high-performance computing (HPC) as a basis for specifying the speed of computation of a computer. In modern times, the FLOP is too small a unit and multiples of FLOPs are used: kilo-, mega-, giga-, tera-, peta-, and so on to measure and compare HPC results.

forward error correction (FEC): In telecommunication, information theory, and coding theory, forward error correction (FEC) is a technique used for controlling errors in data transmission over unreliable or noisy communication channels. The method is for the sender to encode the message in a redundant way by using an error-correcting code (ECC). R. Hamming pioneered this field in the 1940s, and invented the first error-correcting code in 1950: the Hamming code.

The redundancy allows the receiver to detect a limited number of errors that may occur anywhere in the message, and often to correct these errors without retransmission. There are two basic types of FEC codes: block codes and convolution codes.

FEC information is usually added to storage devices to enable recovery of corrupted data, hence its inclusion here.

hard disk drive (HDD): This is what it says on the tin, a normal hard disk drive. The current contenders for the storage championship of the worlds are HDD, SSD, and flash storage (see *storage tiering*).

hardware scalability: The number of physical processors (N) is incremented in the hardware configuration while keeping the user load per processor fixed. In this case, the number of users executing per processor (e.g., 100 users per processor) is assumed to remain the same for every added processor. For example, on a 32 processor platform you would apply a load of $N = 3200$ users to the test platform.

high availability: Refers to a system or component that is continuously operational. When a high availability solution is implemented, computing systems can continue to perform the tasks they were designed to perform with minimal downtime.

HPC: High-performance computing, a term normally applied to intensive scientific computation where many numeric operations need to be carried out as fast as possible. Given sufficient speed, it is possible to use more sophisticated models to simulate the real world. An example of this is weather forecasting where a number of simultaneous equations describing the atmosphere can be increased to produce a more accurate forecast. Another is the simulation of cosmic events to explain and predict the behavior of the universe.

hyperconvergence: A type of infrastructure system with a software-centric architecture that tightly integrates compute, storage, networking and virtualization resources and other technologies from scratch in a commodity hardware box supported by a single vendor, according to TechTarget.

hypervisor: A hypervisor, also called a virtual machine manager, is a program that allows multiple operating systems to share a single hardware host. Each operating system appears to have the host's processor, memory, and other resources all to itself. However, the hypervisor is actually controlling the host processor and resources, allocating what is needed to each operating system in turn and ensuring that the guest operating systems (called virtual machines) cannot disrupt each other.

    Early examples of hypervisors are IBM's Virtual Machine/370 (VM/370) and Amdahl's Multiple Domain Facility (MDF), both Type 1 hypervisors. Also known as a native or bare metal hypervisor, a Type 1 hypervisor runs directly on the host computer's hardware. Also known as a hosted hypervisor, a Type 2 hypervisor runs under an operating system environment (OSE).

instruction cycle: The time period during which one instruction is fetched from memory and executed when a computer is given an instruction in machine language.

ITIL: IT Infrastructure Library (ITIL) is a mature approach to IT service management (ITSM) and provides a cohesive set of best practice, drawn from the public and private sectors internationally. ITSM derives enormous benefits from a best practice approach. Because ITSM is driven both by technology and the huge range of organizational environments in which it operates, it is in a state of constant evolution.

Expert advice and input from ITIL users is both current and practical, and combines to generate these IT best practices for the discipline. See http://www.itil-officialsite.com/.

malware: The word "malware" is short for "malicious software," often used synonymously with "virus," but a virus is actually just a specific type of malware. The word "malware" encompasses all harmful software, including all the ones listed next. Most malware these days is produced for profit, and ransomware is a good example of this. Ransomware doesn't want to crash a system and delete your files, just to cause you trouble. It wants to take something hostage and get a quick payment from you. Some of these examples of malware are limited to personal computers used by individuals but that may not remain the case forever. The perpetrators of these activities may well conclude that extracting money from an organization is easier and more lucrative than attacking an individual.

The era of personal devices being used for business system access is here (BYOD, bring your own device) and therein lie potential end-point security problems.

measurements of data:

Bit = one binary digit (1 or 0); "bit" is derived from the contraction of "binary digit" where 8 bits = 1 byte

KB = kilobyte (1024 bytes)

Kb = kilobit

MB = megabyte

Mb = megabit

MB/s = megabytes per second

Mb/s = megabits per second

Kb/s = kilobits per second

bps = bits per second

MIPs: Millions of instructions per second, a very old, now mainly discredited, measure of computer power. It is the rough equivalent of FLOPs, the scientific power unit. It once ruled the roost, but today, workloads are so complex that a more general metric is required. There are, however, benchmarks specific to types of work, such as graphics or transaction processing, web access, and so on, where generic benchmark metrics will mean little across these work types.

mobile security: Mobile security is the term normally applied to access security when services are accessed from mobile devices, such as tablets and handheld devices. This can be from anywhere in the world and often from a person's own device. Simple password protection is not thought to be stringent enough to prevent unauthorized access and possible fraud in such environments.

Two-factor authentication is a security process in which the user has to provide two means of identification: one of which is typically a physical token, such as a card, and the other of which is typically something memorized, such as a security code. A common example of two-factor authentication is a bank card: the card itself is the physical item and the personal identification number (PIN) is the data that goes with it. This sort of access needs some modification in the physical aspects for mobile devices.

monitor: Software that monitors the progress of activities within a computer system, particularly resources providing a service. This can be architected as a standalone system monitoring another system(s) or a standalone system cooperating with software (agent) on the monitored system. In theory, a system can monitor itself, but if the monitor is measuring availability then it goes down with the system.

OLTP: Online transaction processing, an interactive way of working, normally via a workstation or terminal, and involving a remote server and database. They are in essence short pieces of work that have a beginning and an end, whereby the state of a database is altered permanently. It is also used for queries where no permanent state change occurs (read-only).

Typically, OLTP systems are used for order entry, financial transactions, billing, and retail sales. Such systems have a large number of users who conduct short pieces of work (transactions). Database queries are usually simple, require subsecond response times, and return relatively few records.

operating system: The software that manages access to a computer system's hardware resources. It also hosts specific software such as databases, transaction processing, Internet software, and other, utility-style applications.

paravirtualization: Paravirtualization (PV) is an efficient and lightweight form of virtualization introduced by Xen and later adopted by other virtualization solution suppliers. Paravirtualization does not require virtualization extensions from the host CPU and thus enables virtualization on hardware architectures that do not support hardware-assisted virtualization. However, PV guests and control domains require kernel support and drivers that in the past required special kernel builds, but are now part of the Linux kernel as well as other operating systems. These live alongside the standard VMs on a system.

Full virtualization can mimic PV by adding modifications to the operating system (OS) or making the OS completely PV-aware.

percentile: In terms of transaction response times, imagine a curve or bar chart showing the number of transaction (vertical axis) against the response time of those transactions (horizontal axis).

A percentile measure gives the percentage of transactions with a response time of a certain number or less. For example, an SLA might state that 90% of transactions of type 1 must have a response time of 1.7 seconds or less, representing a vertical line drawn 90% across the area of the total curve or bar chart.

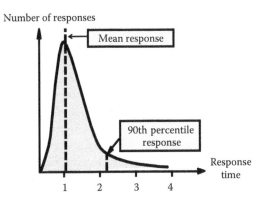

This figure shows, somewhat exaggeratedly for effect, the difference between a mean and a percentile response measurement. In this chart, the 50th percentile would lie somewhere between the mean and 90th percentile responses.

See the passionate discussion in the following article on the differences between averages and percentile measurements: "Why Averages Suck and Percentiles Are Great," http://apmblog.dynatrace.com/2012/11/14/why-averages-suck-and-percentiles-are-great/.

RAID: RAID is short for redundant arrays of independent (or inexpensive, in the original definition and original *raison d'etre*) disks. It is a category of disk drives that employ two or more drives in combination for fault tolerance and performance. RAID allows the storage of the same data redundantly in a balanced way to improve overall storage performance. There are numerous implementations of RAID, some proprietary, but in practice only about three or four find widespread use. RAID implementations can be effected by hardware (disk controllers and microcode) or software. Both have their plusses and minuses.

resource: An IT entity that can be divided into software and hardware resources. Software resources may be specific to applications, or they may be kernel data structures such as the process table, open file, and in-core inode tables, buffer and certain caches, multiphysical buffers, and character lists. Hardware resources are a computer's physical subsystems. The three main subsystems are CPU, memory, and I/O. The memory subsystem can be divided into two resources: physical memory (or main memory and caches) and swap space (or secondary memory). The I/O subsystem comprises one or more resources of similar or different types: hard and floppy disk drives, tape drives, CD-ROMs, graphics displays, network devices and unit record devices (printers, optical character readers [OCRs], card readers, etc.).

response time: See *computer performance.*

root cause analysis (RCA): A method of problem solving that tries to identify the root causes of faults or problems. RCA practice tries to solve problems by attempting to identify and correct the root causes of events, as opposed to simply addressing their symptoms. By focusing correction on root causes, problem recurrence can be prevented. Root cause failure analysis (RCFA) recognizes that complete prevention of recurrence by one corrective action is not always possible.

For example, an outage may well manifest itself as a power failure, but that failure itself may have a deeper, possibly "invisible" cause, such as moisture, external overload, and road works cable severance. Working on the power supply itself might not prevent a repeat occurrence of the outage. Thus, the words "root cause" are significant.

service (IT): Services, as used in this book, "refers to the application of business and technical expertise to enable organizations in the creation, management and optimization of or access to information and business processes. The IT services market can be segmented by the type of skills that are employed to deliver the service (design, build, run). There are also different categories of service: business process services, application services and infrastructure services. If these services are outsourced, they are referred to as business process outsourcing (BPO), applications outsourcing (AO) and infrastructure outsourcing" (from Gartner, "IT Glossary").

This is what IT is all about; the alpha and the omega of it. Period.

service-level agreement (SLA): An agreement between an IT service provider and a customer. A service-level agreement describes the IT service, documents service level targets, and specifies the responsibilities of the IT service provider and the customer. A single agreement may cover multiple IT services or multiple customers (from ITIL Continual Service Improvement, ITIL Service Design definition).

SSD: A solid-state drive (often incorrectly referred to as a "solid-state disk" or "electronic disk") is a data storage device that uses integrated circuit assemblies as memory to store data persistently. SSD technology uses electronic interfaces compatible with traditional block input/output (I/O) hard disk drives. SSDs do not employ any moving mechanical components, which distinguishes them from traditional magnetic disks such as hard disk drives (HDDs) or floppy disks, which are electromechanical devices containing spinning disks and movable read/write heads, according to *Wikipedia.*

storage tiering: A data storage system made up of two or more types of storage based on their access speed. For example, magnetic disk and solid-state disk or magnetic disk and optical disc are used in a tiered storage system. An early example of this was Hierarchical Storage Manager (HSM), which organized and placed data onto a tier of storage devices of different access times and data rates.

This allowed the use of slower (and hence cheaper) devices to be used for applications where rapid response times were not needed. These tiers or storage layers were not visible to the programmer and hence were a form of abstraction. Data in a tiered configuration stays where it is initially placed, but with dynamic data tiering, data that become more active or less frequently accessed can be migrated to a different level in the storage hierarchy.

The following reference is somewhat product-oriented but covers the principles of storage tiering quite well and in generic fashion. The second reference is less product focused. See "IBM Easy Tier Automated Storage Tiering," http://www.slideshare.net/IBMIndiaSS/tsl03080-usen and "Five Tier Storage Model," http://wikibon.org/wiki/v/Five_Tier_Storage_Model.

time: A fundamental property of the universe that ensures everything doesn't happen at once. It is also useful as the horizontal axis, symbol t or T, in many of the graphs in this and other books. It has no substitute and is not a renewable or repairable resource. It is also the stuff of which life is made so try not to waste it. Time on a computer is measured by a clock and various time intervals, for example, instruction execution time, are measured in clock cycles. Clocks with dates can falter, for example, as they did at Y2K. The next blip will occur in January 2038 when the UNIX and similar clocks overflow.

unified communications: Unified Communications (UC) is a marketing term describing the integration of real-time, enterprise, communication services, such as instant messaging (chat), presence information, voice (including IP telephony), mobility features (including extension mobility and single number reach), audio, web and video conferencing, fixed-mobile convergence (FMC), desktop sharing, data sharing (including web-connected electronic interactive whiteboards), call control, and speech recognition with non-real-time communication services such as unified messaging (integrated voice mail, e-mail, SMS, and fax). UC is not necessarily a single product, but a set of products that provides a consistent unified user interface and user experience across multiple devices and media types, according to *Wikipedia*.

virtual disk: A disk composed of pieces of several physical disks.

virtual server: A server, usually a web server, that shares computer resources with other virtual servers. In this context, the virtual part simply means that it is not a dedicated server; that is, the entire computer is not dedicated to running the server software, according to Webopedia. This is an example of abstraction where the possibly intricate partitioning of various resources is hidden from the "user" who visualizes a single server of his own.

virtualization: A variety of technologies for managing computer resources by providing a software interface, known as an "abstraction layer," between the software (operating system and applications) and the hardware. Virtualization turns physical RAM and storage into logical resources. See "Virtualization," http://www.pcmag.com/encyclopedia/term/53961 /virtualization.

wire data: The access for monitoring purposes of all data passing along paths through a network. According to *Wikipedia*, "Wire data is the observed behavior and communication between networked elements which is an important source of information used by IT operations staff to trouble-shoot performance issues, create activity baselines, detect anomalous activity, investigate security incidents, and discover IT assets and their dependencies. According to Gartner, wire data is one of five types of data that will need to be handled by emerging IT Operations Analytics plat-forms. Gartner defines wire data as 'the data contained in the headers and payloads of packets and their associated flow data as traffic moves from one node to another across a distributed IT system.'"

"Wire data is all L2-L7 communications between all systems. This source of data has traditionally included including deep packet inspection and header sampling but recent advancements allow for far deeper, real-time wire data analysis," according to ExtraHop (http://www.extrahop.com).

With wire data, it is possible to assess what every component and server is doing in the application delivery chain. It is also possible with such data to spot emerging performance variances in behavior and predict potential larger variations. In addition, real-time views of application data can be inferred from L7 data, that is, application data and not just network traffic volumes.

Wire data for OSI model levels 2–7 can be collected at various points in a system to provide a complete data and control the data transmission picture.

Index

Page numbers with f, n, and t refer to figures, notes, and tables, respectively.